SOCIAL CARE IN THE UK'S FOUR NATIONS

Sustainable Care

Series Editors: **Sue Yeandle**, University of Sheffield, **Jon Glasby**, University of Birmingham, **Jill Manthorpe**, King's College London and **Kate Hamblin**, University of Sheffield

---

Arising from research in the *ESRC Sustainable Care: connecting people and systems* programme, this series provides novel, interdisciplinary and internationally informed contributions to understanding care systems, care work and care relationships. Contributions are based on studies conducted in the UK, with international partners studying linked topics in their own countries.

The series focuses on 'sustainable care', a concept which contributors theorise in new and distinctive ways. It makes an innovative and distinctive contribution to understandings of future care challenges and how care arrangements could be made more sustainable in the future.

Forthcoming in the Series

Care Technologies for Ageing Societies

An International Comparison

Edited by **Kate Hamblin** and **Matthew Lariviere**

Combining Work and Care

Carer Leave and Related Employment Policies in an International Context

Edited by **Janet Fast**, **Kate Hamblin** and **Jason Heyes**

Find out more

policy.bristoluniversitypress.co.uk/
sustainable-care

SOCIAL CARE IN THE UK'S FOUR NATIONS
Between Two Paradigms

Catherine Needham and Patrick Hall

First published in Great Britain in 2024 by

Policy Press, an imprint of
Bristol University Press
University of Bristol
1-9 Old Park Hill
Bristol
BS2 8BB
UK
t: +44 (0)117 374 6645
e: bup-info@bristol.ac.uk

Details of international sales and distribution partners are available at
policy.bristoluniversitypress.co.uk

British Library Cataloguing in Publication Data
A catalogue record for this book is available from the British Library

ISBN 978-1-4473-6464-1 hardcover
ISBN 978-1-4473-6465-8 paperback
ISBN 978-1-4473-6466-5 ePub
ISBN 978-1-4473-6467-2 ePdf

Cover design: Robin Hawes
Front cover image: iStock/Andrey Danilovich

Contents

Series editors' preface

Sue Yeandle (University of Sheffield)
Jon Glasby (University of Birmingham)
Jill Manthorpe (King's College London)
Kate Hamblin (University of Sheffield)

This book series arises from the *Sustainable Care: connecting people and systems* research programme delivered by a multidisciplinary partnership of 35 scholars in eight universities, funded by a UK Economic and Social Research Council Large Grant. It offers novel, internationally-informed interdisciplinary contributions based on work by linked research teams studying care systems, care work and care relationships.

The focus of the book series is timely and important. We hope it will inform and inspire scholars, policymakers, employers, practitioners and citizens interested in care. Books in the series offer new empirical, conceptual and methodological writing, in scholarly but accessible form, and aim to make an innovative and distinctive contribution to understandings of care challenges and how these can be addressed.

The books bring together data, practices, systems, structures, narratives and actions relevant to social care. Some relate specifically to the UK's unique policy, demographic, cultural and socio-economic circumstances, but all have clear global relevance. Similar concerns are salient around the world, especially in other advanced welfare states, where population ageing is profoundly changing age structures; developments in technology and healthcare mean more people who are ill or have long-term conditions need support at home; and 'traditional' gendered sources of daily caring labour are dwindling, as levels of female labour force participation rise, and family networks become more dispersed. The Covid-19 pandemic has amplified all these challenges.

Subject areas, disciplines and themes

The series critically engages with crucial contemporary debates about care infrastructure; divisions of caring labour and the political economy of care; care ethics, rights, recognition and values; care technologies and human-technological interactions; and care relations in intergenerational, emotional, community and familial context. Within its overarching concept, sustainable care, its subject areas span social and welfare policy and systems; family and social gerontology; ageing and disability studies; employment and workforce organisation; diversity (including gender and ethnicity); social work and human resources; migration and mobility; and technology studies.

The new multi-disciplinary work on care we offer embraces progress in global scholarship on diversity, culture and the uses of technology, and engages with issues of inequality, political economy and the division of labour. These distinctive features of the Sustainable Care programme are highlighted and developed in the book series. We are grateful to all who contributed as researchers, programme administrators and research participants, to our funders, our advisory group, and to members of the public who have engaged with our studies so far. Our work continues in new developments, including the ESRC Centre for Care and IMPACT, the UK's new adult social care evidence implementation centre. We hope books in this new series reflect the quality of our colleagues' contributions, and thank each book's editors, authors and Policy Press for their commitment to sharing new ideas, knowledge and experiences about care.

List of figures, tables and boxes

Figures

Tables

Boxes

About the authors

Catherine Needham is Professor of Public Policy and Public Management at the Health Services Management Centre, University of Birmingham. Her research focuses on social care, including personalisation, co-production, personal budgets and care markets. She has published a wide range of articles, chapters and books for academic and practitioner audiences. Catherine led the Care in the Four Nations work package within the ESRC (Economic and Social Research Council) Sustainable Care team. She is now leading research on care systems as part of the ESRC Centre for Care and is also a member of IMPACT, the UK centre for evidence implementation in adult social care. She tweets as @DrCNeedham.

Patrick Hall is a social care policy researcher, currently undertaking an ESRC-funded PhD at the University of Birmingham on care commissioning. He was the main researcher on the Care in the Four Nations work package within the ESRC Sustainable Care team. Prior to that he contributed to the European Commission's 2018 peer review of Germany's latest long-term care reforms. Patrick is a former Fellow of the King's Fund, where he co-authored two key publications on social care for older people. Before the King's Fund, he worked with the Department of Health and Social Care, local authorities and NHS organisations on the implementation of the Care Act 2014.

Acknowledgements

The research that underpins this book was funded by the Economic and Social Research Council (ESRC) as part of the Sustainable Care: Connecting People and Systems programme grant (ES/P009255/1, 2017–21). The Sustainable Care programme was led by Professor Sue Yeandle, and we would particularly like to thank Sue for her support for the four nations research. Sue, along with Kate Hamblin and Jill Manthorpe, also gave very insightful comments on drafts of this manuscript and we are very grateful for their input. The broader Sustainable Care programme team helped shape our thinking on care in the four nations and more generally were a great group of colleagues who we hope to continue working with in the future.

Jennie Knight gave invaluable research assistance with some of the care data used in the book. We are also grateful to Natasha Curry and Camille Oung at the Nuffield Trust, along with Graeme Atkins, Grant Dalton, Andrew Phillips and Alex Stojanovic from the Institute for Government, who let us use their four nations care data in the book, and whose own comparative work has been a really helpful guide to our own.

We are really grateful to the people we interviewed who gave up their time, despite the many pressures of their work. The COVID-19 pandemic began part-way through the research and writing of this book, with its devastating consequences for many people linked to social care. It stopped all of us in our tracks, and reminded us why better social care is so vital.

Sustaining the momentum to write a book is a collaborative effort at home as well as at work. Catherine would like to thank Blake, Ray and Jean for the cups of tea and pep talks. Patrick would like to thank Radha for her support and Roshan and Arun for arriving during this project!

Comparing adult social care systems in the UK

Introduction: from slow collapse to urgent crisis

In writing a book on adult social care policy in the four nations of the UK, we were researching systems that observers said were 'in crisis' (Dahl, 2021), at a 'tipping point' (O'Dowd, 2016) and 'approaching collapse' (Dayan and Heenan, 2019). Over the 25 years since different care systems developed in England, Scotland, Wales and Northern Ireland, they came to be seen as first, under strain and then, in crisis. This was a gradual collapse – a sense that things couldn't continue as they were – although somehow (through the heroic efforts of many people), they did. A government-commissioned care report in Northern Ireland – *Power to people* – used the language of 'a system collapsing in slow-motion' (Kelly and Kennedy, 2017: 66).

Then, in 2020, the COVID-19 outbreak happened, plunging the social care sector from slow decay into a rapid and deadly crisis. The pandemic highlighted the weakness of these care systems and the poor understanding of their complex organisation (Daly, 2020). Many deaths occurred in care homes, and the dire state of the formal system of home care delivery was brought to the nation's attention. Staffing shortages, intensified by Brexit (the UK's departure from the European Union), went from chronic to acute. Yet the pandemic also raised the profile of the care sector. The realities of providing unpaid care for family and neighbours became more prevalent in the national consciousness. Community support initiatives increased the visibility of people requiring care and support. As the perception of crisis in adult social care systems intensified, there was renewed interest in finding ways to 'fix' social care.

Content analysis around the phrase 'care crisis' reaps plentiful results (Dayrell et al, 2020). The use of the phrase has increased in recent years, due to a perceived lacuna in the quality of care and caring relationships for modern societies' older people and disabled citizens (Keating et al, 2021). The framing of the care crisis as a once-in-a-generation challenge can be seen in New Labour's *Building the National Care Service* White Paper from 2010:

> We face a challenge no other generation has had to confront: an ageing population rightfully demanding greater dignity, self-respect and

support in old age and increasing numbers of people with disability, rightly demanding care and support which enables them to learn, work and contribute to society. The current care and support system is no longer sufficient. It cannot meet our needs, nor match our aspirations. If left unchanged, it would not cope with the extra demand in years to come. (HM Government, 2010: 22)

Over 10 years on from this assessment, its analysis of the issues and the call for urgent action remains little changed. Indeed, if anything, a decade of austerity has intensified the strain (IFS, 2017). Although social care expenditure has been more protected than other areas of local government expenditure (for example, libraries, roads and youth centres), additional demographic pressures as well as the implementation of the National Living Wage have contributed to unprecedented strain on publicly funded social care services. The British Social Attitudes Survey from 2021 found public satisfaction with social care to be sitting at 15 per cent, around half the level of satisfaction with the National Health Service (NHS) (at 36 per cent) (Curtice et al, 2022). Chaney's analysis of party manifestoes across the UK shows that at each election in the last 20 years the salience of social care has increased: 'this indicates political parties' attempts to address the prevailing popular discourse over a crisis in social care provision' (2: 162).

Given that the UK is now made up of four different social care systems, we were keen to explore how the challenges of recent decades have been experienced in England, Scotland, Wales and Northern Ireland. We wanted to look beneath the broad-brush concept of 'crisis' to understand how different policies and populations in the four nations were affecting care and support for older people and disabled citizens. Through analysing policy documents, talking to policy makers and synthesising data, we studied what policy makers considered the goal of adult social care to be, what policies they were putting in place to achieve that, and how well the policies were working. It was clear that many of the demographic challenges faced by the four nations were very similar, but that there were important differences between them. For example, in relation to public service cuts in the deepest period of austerity (2011–16), there was a UK-wide cut in spending of 9 per cent. However, by disaggregating this into the four nations (see Table 1.1), we can see the extent to which most of this was born by England (which also starts from the lowest base), with spending going *up* in Scotland and Northern Ireland and only falling slightly in Wales.

In capturing the ways in which the four nations have faced different challenges and developed different care systems, our approach was informed by realism (Gorski, 2013). We were interested in the real and material conditions of social care systems, but also in the framings and interpretations

Table 1.1: Social care spending per head in England, Scotland, Northern Ireland, Wales and the UK: real spending (2018/19 prices) and percentage change between 2011/12 and 2015/16

	Real per capita adult social care spending (2018/19) (£)		
	2011/12	2015/16	% change (2011/12 and 2015/16)
England	398	365	−8.2
Scotland	492	530	7.7
Wales	495	486	−1.8
Northern Ireland	482	555	15.1
UK	456	415	−9.1

Source: Lee and Stoye (2018: 15). Data: Population data from ONS mid-year population estimates, 2009 and 2015, accessed through NOMIS on 23 March 2018. Nominal health spending from HM Treasury Public Expenditure Statistical Analyses 2017.

made by policy actors. We analysed documents and undertook interviews to understand how those with policy responsibilities were framing key issues. We drew on the structure and resources of realist evaluation to trace the relationships between context, mechanisms and outcomes. The context is the broad set of care arrangements (the existing configuration of family, state, market and community support in the four nations relative to levels of demand). The mechanisms are the strategies and policies that are used to shape adult social care, which may be new laws, such as extending rights for carers, or the indirect effects of changes to, for example, benefit entitlements or inheritance tax. Outcomes may be formal measurements – for example, England's Adult Social Care Outcomes Framework (ASCOF) – but also relate to qualitative assessments of how far the mechanisms achieved their aims. In undertaking comparison we used Pollitt's (2002) framework to differentiate discursive, decisional, practice and results convergence. In assessing outcomes, we drew on McConnell's (2010) work on policy success to consider whether policies such as Scotland's free personal care allocation have been successful.

The book considers the context (Chapters 2 to 3), mechanisms (Chapter 4) and outcomes (Chapter 5) in care systems in the four nations, and then explains the patterns of convergence and divergence that we found. We look at the 'territorial policy communities' in London, Edinburgh, Cardiff and Belfast (Chapter 6), drawing attention to differences in the mechanisms of policy scale, style and scope that have had an impact on care policy design and implementation. We then, in Chapter 7, shift attention to the implementation of long-term care reform, discussing the challenges of both transformational and incremental approaches to change. We also discuss the 'policy mix', highlighting the tensions between some of the reform mechanisms, which can inhibit effective implementation.

The subtitle of this book is *Between two paradigms*, and we set these out in Chapter 7. Our findings pointed us to two rival care paradigms – the informal/differentiated and the formal/standardised – which we see as a fault line in care policy within all four nations. We argue that care policy gets stuck because policy makers in the four nations fail to acknowledge the tensions of calling for fluidity, differentiation, informality and co-production while also arguing for standardisation, regulation, formality and risk avoidance. Scotland's proposed National Care Service exemplifies these tensions, although versions of the same issues are evident in all four nations. Correcting decades of 'drift' in social care policy (Needham and Hall, 2022) requires an appreciation of how to manage the tensions between these two paradigms rather than blithely hoping for the best of both worlds.

In this introductory chapter we begin by defining key terms such as 'care', and 'adult social care' in particular, and comparative approaches to care systems. We set out the key policy changes in the 25 years since the devolution settlements occurred in Scotland, Wales and Northern Ireland in 1998. We describe our methodological approach to comparing the care systems, their composition, policy trajectories and outcomes. We also set out our approach to analysis and to exploring policy success, and give more detail on the structure of the chapters that follow.

What is 'care'?

The term and concept 'care' forms the basis for a whole field of moral philosophy: care ethics. Here, we take as our starting point Rummery and Fine's (2012) summary of the scholarship on care, updating Fine's exploration of the concept in his seminal book *A caring society?* (2007). Rummery and Fine highlight the elusiveness and ambiguity of the term 'care' in normal usage, and note two approaches to its definition: first, there is a 'confining' of the meaning to a specific set of tasks by a specific category of people (such as carers) in order to record and measure caring activity (Folbre, 2006); and second, there are attempts to 'delimit' the concept as a universal 'species activity' (Tronto, 1993). Rummery and Fine (2012) note that much theoretical conflict emerges from a tension between definitions. They offer a summary definition that takes in three elements: emotion and orientation; activity and labour; and relationship. Care is understood widely as an *emotion and orientation*, as a concern for others and their wellbeing, particularly children, disabled adults and frail older people. This emotion and orientation, they note, is culturally situated and also (often) implies *responsibility* to act. Care is also understood as *work*: activities that respond to the recognition of *need* in others in a competent fashion (they note that incompetent labour cannot be caring). Finally, to further differentiate caring labour from other work, Rummery and Fine (2012) define it as a *relationship*, taking in familial, voluntary and professional relationships of care involving complex dynamics of dependency and power, but never simple domination of the care recipient by the carer (Kittay, 2013).

Care is, then, an inherently 'social' concept according to this definition: caring about, caring for and caring with others. The use of the term 'social care' is not a reaffirmation of this so much as a way of locating our research in the contemporary arrangements for care in the UK. 'Social care' is the current UK term for what has in the past been called 'personal social services' and in other countries is often called 'long-term care'. These terms are concerned with the organisation of modern welfare states to respond to social and economic shifts associated with 'late modern' (Giddens, 1990; Giddens and Pierson, 1998; Archer, 2012) and 'post-industrial' (Bell, 1973) societies and their impact on the nature of care as orientation, labour and relationship. These shifts include changes in family structure, working life (including increasing female workforce participation), a fall in fertility rates and the extension of mortality – itself associated with related developments in age-related disability and disease requiring care (Tinker, 2002). These factors also imply the increasing isolation of older adults and a related impact on wellbeing (Courtin and Knapp, 2017). As populations have aged and families changed throughout the 20th century (Allan et al, 2001), care has come to be recognised as a *social* policy problem that spans the private and public spheres.

In their influential article 'The concept of social care', Daly and Lewis (2000) suggest the use of the term as a categorical tool able to capture the interpersonal dimensions of care and their embeddedness in social arrangements. They define social care as constituted by the activities and relations involved in meeting the physical and emotional requirements of dependent adults and children, and the normative, economic and social frameworks within which these are assigned and carried out (Daly and Lewis, 2000).

This definition, like much of the international literature on care, encompasses dependent children as well as adults. Drawing a distinction between them can be seen as artificial and a product of formal care structures rather than the reality of how care is done in families and communities. However, owing to the distinct normative and demographic challenges, our focus in this book is on *adult* social care, that is, relating to the care of older people and working-age adults with a disability or mental health condition. We argue that while these descriptors are themselves problematic and open to challenge, they do helpfully limit the scope of enquiry into the distinct ethical and policy considerations of support for adults rather than children.

Consistent with legal definitions, we use the term 'carer' to refer to someone who provides unpaid support (for example, a family member, friend or neighbour) and the term 'care worker' for someone providing paid support. While these categories can be blurred (for example, in some circumstances, friends and family can be paid for the support they provide), this distinction is the one commonly used in the UK care literature and policy.

Comparing care systems

Finding the edges of a care system can be difficult, even with children excluded from scope. To aid comparative analysis, some of the comparative literature has utilised the concept of a 'care regime', which is wider than the formal care system, and aims to encompass a range of caring relationships. Care regime analysis emerged from attempts to study the new social risks associated with an increasing demand for care (Morel, 2007), and increasing difficulty of the private sphere (and subsequently the rest of society) to supply it. Social recognition of the 'problem' of care, and welfare states' attempts to navigate it (Simonazzi, 2009), has prompted an interest in constructing typologies of national care regimes. These enable the composition and coverage of care systems to be compared, and make it easier for state and non-state actors involved in these regimes to learn from one another (Simonazzi, 2009; Theobald and Luppi, 2018). The typologies have attempted, in various ways, to describe the relationships between the family, the state and the market in the provision of care, as well as the assumptions and norms that underpin them.

Such typologies initially responded to the seminal work by Gøsta Esping-Andersen in *The three worlds of welfare capitalism* (1990). Esping-Andersen introduced the term 'regime' to refer to the organisation of welfare states as well as the cultural and social norms that underpin them. A central part of his analysis is that regimes differ in their degree of 'de-commodification', that is, the extent to which certain services can become 'rights' (hence removing them from market logic) and reduce market dependence among their consumers. The care regimes literature is partly a feminist critique of his work and an attempt to correct for what has been perceived as gender and care 'blindness'. It constructs alternative and complimentary models that incorporate care into an understanding of welfare states (Lewis, 1992; Orloff, 1993; Knijn and Ungerson, 1997), and is primarily focused on who provides care, taking a national lens. Ontologically, it often treats 'care' as a set of activities – what Rummery and Fine (2012) call 'care as work' – in keeping with the tradition of feminist and Marxist theories of social reproduction (Laslett and Brenner, 1989). Regime analyses operationalise this concept of care labour in a number of ways, using quantitative data to describe this labour in terms of intensity (number of hours); the identity of the carer (age and gender); work-care provisions; monetary benefits; and formal care services.

The concept of a care regime is ambiguous and contested, and has been particularly critiqued for focusing too much on the nation-state (Bertin and Carradore, 2016). It is important to acknowledge that contemporary societies are characterised by shifts in the scale and nature of governance, driven by both 'globalisation' and 'de-centralisation' (Rodríguez-Pose and Gill, 2003). Both these phenomena pose a challenge to typologies of care that characterise regimes according to nationally defined data. There has been a focus on the increased global mobility of caring labour, and on the salience of local and regional factors in shaping the nature of care regimes. In much of the world, migrants make a growing contribution (in both the formal, regulated care workforce and in the unregulated 'grey' market for care). Care migration is usually from poorer to richer countries (Yeates, 2009); it has been theorised in an extensive literature on 'global care chains', in which women from poorer countries leave their home countries to undertake work caring for children and older people in wealthier countries (Hochschild, 2015). In the UK, the globalisation of care has most visibly affected the composition of the formal workforce: 16 per cent of care workers are non-British (with about half coming from inside Europe and half outside) (Holmes, 2021). Reliance on migrant care workers is especially pronounced in some UK cities; in 2015 three in every five of London's care workers were born outside the UK (mostly outside the EU) (Independent Age, 2015). This reliance on immigration has added to the perception of crisis in care systems across the 'developed' world as part of a wider backlash against globalisation and in the UK, since the 'Brexit' vote to leave the EU.

The local level is also important in considering changing care regimes. Hanssen et al (2001) use the language of 'welfare municipalities' in discussing the formation of the welfare state in Norway, highlighting the importance of the local level in establishing social security programmes. In the UK it is the central state that has tended to take responsibility for health and social security, but in relation to social care there has always been an important role for what we can call (following Hanssen et al) 'care municipalities'. Kröger (2011), also writing about Norway, notes the way in which the role of the local state waxes and wanes in social care as the principles of local democracy and autonomy run up against the centralising forces of universalism and standardisation. We return to the importance of local diversity versus centralisation in Chapters 6 and 7 of the book.

In undertaking our analysis of social care in the four nations, we utilise the regime assumption that care is a broad set of arrangements that fall well outside the confines of the welfare state. However, we do not construct a formal taxonomy of the four nations in the way that is common to the regime literature. We find this limiting because of its focus on care as labour, rather than also including the relational and affective elements (Rummery and Fine, 2012). Instead, we use an alternative heuristic, the 'care diamond', to explore the balance between different elements of care – family, state, market and community (Razavi, 2011). We consider the ways that each of these is 'in crisis', and how policy responses in the four nations have sought to address this in different ways. This focus enables us to build up a comparative analysis of care in the four nations that goes beyond the quantitative analyses of regime taxonomies to consider also the framing and legitimacy of different approaches to care. It also enables us to bring in the importance of multi-level governance given that policy jurisdictions overlap between local government, the four nations and the UK state.

Twenty-five years of social care devolution

Studying social care in the UK's four nations requires an understanding of their shared and divergent histories. The social care system in the UK was created after the Second World War to address the social and economic risks facing people with long-term care needs (frail older people, working-age disabled people and people experiencing mental distress). It sat alongside the NHS in the Beveridge-inspired welfare state (Glasby et al, 2021). However unlike the NHS, it was a responsibility given to local government, with significant scope for local variation in the support provided. Prior to devolution in Scotland and Wales in 1998, there was no tier of government between the UK Government in Westminster and the local (city and county) authorities in England, Scotland or Wales. In these nations, local government continues to hold considerable discretion over social care; most funding for social care is allocated to local government through block grants, with some local revenue raising. Northern Ireland is distinctive. It had its own government until the introduction of 'direct rule' from Westminster in 1972, following which integrated Health and Social Care Trusts (HSCTs) were created, taking social care away from local government (Gray and Birrell, 2013). The five Trusts continued to manage health and social care after the reintroduction of self-government in Northern Ireland in 1998.

Unlike the NHS, formal social care is a means-tested service. People needing long-term care have their assets reviewed, and if they fall above the means test threshold they must pay some or all of their care costs. As a result, some people have to pay large amounts for care whereas others pay nothing – an inequity that does not occur for other welfare goods such as health and education, and which has become more keenly felt as more people are living longer with care needs. In 1999, a Royal Commission on Long Term Care for Older People (the Sutherland Commission) concluded: 'Long-term care is a risk that is best covered by some kind of risk pooling – to rely on income or savings, as most people effectively have to do now, is not efficient or fair due to the nature of the risk and the size of the sums required' (Sutherland, 1999). A series of reports and consultation papers in the 25 years since then have made the same point (see, for example, Wanless, 2006; Dilnot, 2011; Barker, 2014). However, the problems identified by the Sutherland Commission remain unresolved, and there is an enduring sense of unfinished business with regard to the state's role in social care funding.

These issues are a feature of all four parts of the UK, although they are experienced differently for reasons we discuss in the book. A key difference that shapes comparative analysis of England, Scotland, Wales and Northern Ireland is their relative sizes. England is by far the biggest in terms of population, with around 56.5 million people, as of 2022. Scotland is the next biggest, at 5.5 million. Wales has a population of 3.1 million and Northern Ireland of 1.9 million. These populations also differ from each other in relation to age profile (Wales has the oldest population) and affluence (England is the wealthiest per head). Population size is not proportionate to the size of the countries. England covers 130km^2 and Scotland is around half that, at 78km^2. Wales and Northern Ireland are both significantly smaller, with landmasses of 21km^2 and 14km^2 respectively. Scotland has the lowest population density. The size and population density of the nations are relevant to care systems, making a difference to the delivery of services and the way that different parts of each nation work together (Keating et al, 2009).

The four nations all have very different histories in relation to membership of the United Kingdom. The language of 'nation' itself may be contested, and we bracket off questions about nationhood, recognising, however, that 'nations' need not be coterminous with 'states' (Hastings, 1997). The similarity between England, Scotland, Wales and Northern Ireland prior to devolution in 1998 should not be overstated. Northern Ireland had elements of self-government in place for much of the last hundred years, interrupted by 'the Troubles' from the late 1960s, a period of violent conflict between Catholic and Protestant communities. Scotland and Wales had been governed from Westminster for all of recent history, although Scotland had a degree of administrative devolution, with separate education and judicial systems. The histories through which each of these territories came into union with England also has a bearing on the extent and tone of how devolution was designed and has developed.

Nonetheless, in the post-war era all four had care systems that derived from the National Assistance Act 1948 and (apart from Northern Ireland) had broadly similar structures for determining eligibility and providing care. The year 1997 marks an important break. In Westminster, Tony Blair's New Labour government swept to power on a manifesto promising to grant significant new powers to the people of Scotland, Wales and Northern Ireland. The government quickly published plans for referenda that year on the establishment of a Welsh Assembly and a Scottish Parliament, with the latter holding more significant powers. In September 1997, both nations voted to implement the proposals: Wales with a small majority, and Scotland with a resounding 70 per cent in favour. In 1998, the Good Friday Agreement proposed the establishment of a Northern Irish Assembly, which, too, was confirmed in referenda by a large majority. Since then, some key differences have emerged in the policy landscape in each of the four nations of the UK. We summarise the social care–relevant developments in Box 1.1.

As Box 1.1 indicates, there have been several key constitutional and policy developments affecting social care over this period. Scotland and Wales

---

Box 1.1: Social care-relevant policy developments in the four nations, 1997–2022

1997: Labour government elected in the UK on a manifesto promising devolution.

1998: Scotland Act, Government of Wales Act and Good Friday Agreement leads to creation of new governing institutions in Edinburgh, Cardiff and Belfast. Wales is given only administrative devolution and cannot make new laws.

1999: Sutherland Commission proposes free personal care – accepted in Scotland, but rejected elsewhere.

2000: Northern Ireland Assembly is suspended, the first of five suspensions over the period, including one of five years.

2002: Free personal care for over-65s begins in Scotland (extended to under-65s in 2019).

2006: Government of Wales Act creates an executive with some legislative powers, further extended in 2014 and 2017.

2007: SNP (Scottish National Party) becomes largest party in Scotland, and continues to hold power to the present day.

2010: UK General Election. Conservatives denounce Labour's plans for care funding as a 'death tax'. Conservative-Liberal Democrat coalition takes power.

2013: Self Directed Support Act in Scotland.

2014: Care Act in England; Social Services and Well-being (Wales) Act. Wales introduces a maximum weekly charge for home care and increases the means test threshold for residential care.

2015: UK election won by the Conservatives. English care funding reforms delayed and later abandoned.

2016: Scotland Act gives Scotland greater powers over income tax and social security.

2016: UK votes to leave the EU, creating uncertainty about care worker migration.

2017: Wales Act extends the jurisdiction of the Welsh Government to include all areas not reserved to Westminster.

2017: UK General Election campaign is dominated by Conservative proposals on care funding, dubbed a 'dementia tax' by opposition parties; Conservatives form a minority government.

2019: Conservatives win a majority at the UK General Election. Prime Minister Boris Johnson vows to fix social care 'within a year'.

2020: COVID-19 has a huge impact on the care sector, including high levels of care home deaths. Leads to further calls for reform of a 'broken' system.

2021: Scottish Government proposes a National Care Service. UK Government announces a health and care levy and a 'cap' on social care spending in England to limit personal liability for care costs.

2022: UK government announces that the levy will not go ahead and the care cap implementation will be delayed until 2025.

have developed distinctive approaches to policy, such as free personal care in Scotland and new approaches to charging for care in Wales. At the time of writing (2022), Scotland has announced plans to create a National Care Service, which, if introduced would radically reconfigure care commissioning (Scottish Government, 2021). The Welsh Government is considering whether to develop its own National Care Service (Welsh Government, 2021a). The UK Government proposed a new health and care tax (or 'levy') across the UK, and a 'cap' in England to limit how much individuals have to pay for care (HM Government, 2021). Both of these policies had been cancelled or postponed by the end of 2022. We discuss these, and other care policy developments, in the chapters that follow.

Box 1.1 also shows that the period of devolution has been marked by important changes in jurisdiction. Scotland and Wales have gained more powers over time; Northern Ireland has had several periods of direct rule from Westminster as the executive has been suspended. These are important factors in relation to how care policy has developed – it has been more difficult to pass new care legislation in Northern Ireland than elsewhere, for example. Change in England in this period has been more incremental. It has had no devolution settlement and no opportunity to develop its own policy community separate from that of the UK Government at Westminster. It is akin to an 'empty nester' who is left in the family home when other family members have moved out, and has to make sense of both continuity and loss. English regions have waxed and waned as policy-relevant units. The failed referendum on regional devolution in the North East in 2004 killed off hopes of English regional devolution to parallel the process in the other three nations. More recent 'city deals' have restarted a regional agenda within England, and raised the possibility of distinctive policy communities emerging, although this is at an early stage (Lowndes and Lemprière, 2018; Roberts, 2020). For most aspects of care policy, England remains the relevant unit rather than its city regions.

Although Scotland and Wales now have some discretion over taxation, most social care revenue comes to those nations through the Barnett formula, which allocates funding across the UK (Heald, 2020). The formula has been used for decades, but is controversial in allocating higher per head spending to the devolved nations than to England. The Institute for Government puts this differentiated spending per person as 125 per cent higher in Northern Ireland, 121 per cent higher in Scotland and 115 per cent higher in Wales in 2018/19 (Cheung, 2020). This differential is important when noting higher spending on social care in these nations compared to England, and the extent to which austerity has been felt more deeply in England.

Studying a care policy 'experiment': a realist approach

Our initial approach to comparing care in the four nations was to approach devolution as a 'natural experiment', such that, *all things being equal*, we could observe the impact of divergent policy and legislative environments on the outcomes for adults with social care needs. However, a number of factors get in the way of treating this as a natural experiment. The different histories and demographics of the four nations mean there was no common starting point in 1998. Care is not an intervention that can be linked to an outcome in a straightforward way. Care systems are open systems with blurred edges, in which attributing effects to policy changes is difficult. Understanding care systems requires appreciation of the normative claims and discursive framings as much as studying 'hard measures' such as levels of investment and methods of regulation. Nonetheless, care is also ontologically real: care and its absence has real-world consequences. These factors led us to an approach informed by critical realism and realist evaluation, through which we could explore the context, mechanisms and outcomes of care policy in the four nations.

Realism is both a philosophy of science and a research paradigm (Sayer, 1992). It is critical of positivism/empiricism as an approach to scientific enquiry, as well as having significant reservations about more extreme forms of social constructivism. It critiques both positivism and constructivism as committing the 'epistemic fallacy': assuming that the limits of our knowledge of reality constitute reality's limits (Danermark et al, 2019). Reality is neither limited by our observation of it (as positivism holds), nor the medium of that observation (as strong forms of interpretivism hold). Realism's assumption is that *there is a reality* that is (at least partly) independent of our knowledge of it. This reality is 'stratified': there are a number of 'layers' that compose the social and physical world that cannot be simply reduced to each other – the social world itself is 'emergent' from the physical, but has its own causal properties (Danermark et al, 2019).

Realism as a philosophy is distinct from what might be called 'naïve' or 'commonsense' realism in that it does not posit that the world (either social or physical) is straightforwardly comprehended by the senses. On the contrary, it holds that all knowledge of the world is partial and conceptually mediated: we cannot grasp it without theory. Importantly for us, realism holds that there are social mechanisms that cannot be straightforwardly apprehended by actors but might be observed and explained through social scientific approaches (Sayer, 1999). One of the key tenets of realism is the observation that the natural and social sciences have fundamentally different objects, and require different approaches to identify explanations for phenomenon. Social systems are largely 'open', that is, they are resistant to experimental closure whereby the relationship between cause and effect can be directly observed (Gorski, 2013). In comparing the four nations, the relationship between care policy and outcome cannot be closed. A number of external factors – economic, social, demographic, regional, historic – cannot be easily untangled in their contribution to outcomes. In this book we do not raise the banner of any one particular type of realist philosophy but pragmatically utilise the key aspects of realism to explore and explain convergence and divergence in adult social care in the four nations (Robson, 2016).

Key tools for comparison

To draw out different strands of care policy, we utilise Pollitt's (2002) comparative toolkit. In studying policy convergence between states, Pollitt (2002: 477–8) suggests that it is necessary to separate out four different elements:

- Discursive convergence: 'more and more people are talking and writing about the same concepts' (2002: 477), for example, in government documents and political speeches.
- Decisional convergence: states are adopting the same specific policies.
- Practice convergence, for example, professionals are working in more similar ways.
- Results convergence, that is, the outputs and outcomes of the activity are aligning.

As Pollitt points out, 'Clearly, convergence at one stage does not necessarily imply convergence at the next. … [O]rganizations routinely say one thing, decide another and do a third' (2002: 478). By separating them out, he suggests that researchers are better able to accommodate the apparent paradox where countries seem to be both converging and diverging at the same time.

We studied discursive convergence by looking at policy documents from the four nations, including White Papers (that is, government proposals), strategies and commissions. We assessed how the documents were framing social care, the problems it was facing and how these should be solved. We also interviewed policy stakeholders from the four nations. Combining document and interview data enabled us to assess decisional convergence, that is, the key policy decisions that had been made. This included, for example, the introduction of free personal care in Scotland and a maximum weekly charge for home care in Wales. We looked at practice convergence in terms of how far these policies were being implemented, using interviews, secondary data and other literature to understand aspects of implementation. For example, we looked at data showing the falling numbers of carers' assessments in England after the Care Act 2014 and the failure to introduce new carers' legislation in Northern Ireland. Nonetheless, we recognise that our study did not assess implementation at the front line, and therefore cannot capture all aspects of practice convergence.

Understanding what is meant by 'results convergence' – that is, outputs and outcomes – was a particularly central concern, and we used McConnell's (2010) work in relation to policy success. This included recognising that policy success has different dimensions that need to be unpicked. Comparative social policy research can imply a linear approach: placing nations in order, from success to failure, on a range of variables. But what constitutes success, or failure, in adult social care policy? How can we explain successful outcomes, and how far can they be attributed to policy makers? While the failure of the social care system seems to be widely implied in the 'crisis' narrative, what might success look like?

McConnell (2010), in his book *Understanding policy success*, adopts a 'pragmatic and realistic' definition of policy success (2010: 39), in line with our broader realist approach. He recognises the limitations of a foundationalist perspective that asserts objective standards for judging success, but also sees the limits of claims that success is only a matter of interpretation. He focuses on understanding 'success for whom?', recognising the plurality of perspectives in defining success, while retaining an assumption of some real basis for making judgements on policy success. His definition is:

> A policy is successful insofar as it achieves the goals that proponents set out to achieve. However, only those supportive of the original goals are liable to perceive, with satisfaction, an outcome of policy success. Opponents are likely to perceive failure, regardless of outcomes, because they did not support the original goals. (McConnell, 2010: 39)

Following this definition, we might say that social care policy is successful insofar as it achieves the goals explicitly set out in policy documentation. However, only those supportive of these goals will perceive their achievement as success. Opponents of these goals as a whole or in part are likely to perceive their achievement as failure, regardless of outcome. In addition, we need to recognise that there are ways to measure success beyond the opinions of policy makers. For instance, while civil servants and unpaid carers may differ in their perspective on the success of policy relating to carers, we can evaluate to some extent their respective claims against standards, although these standards are always incomplete and our judgement partial.

Research design

Our design drew on Robson's definition of a 'flexible' design (Robson, 2016). We derived data from document analysis, interviews and secondary quantitative data, supplemented by broader academic and policy literature. This allowed us to gather data that was both 'extensive' and 'intensive' (Sayer, 1992). We developed a 'context-sensitive' comparative framework in order to meaningfully theorise about the potential causal impact of social care policy in the four nations. An understanding of context required a statistical description of key characteristics in the four nations alongside an understanding of broad policy aspirations. The secondary quantitative data helped us to locate the respective care systems in relation to other types: what Sayer (1992) calls extensive research, that is, research concerned with a large number of observations, at an aggregated level. These data were drawn either directly from the Office for National Statistics (ONS), or from analysis developed by organisations such as the Nuffield Trust, the Institute for Government, the Institute for Fiscal Studies and the Health Foundation.

The documents further added to this extensive perspective. They were identified through asking interviewees to nominate key social care policy documents from the period since 1998. From the interviewee recommendations we developed a corpus of 32 documents (see Table 1.2), which were accessed from government websites and imported into NVivo 12 for analysis. Most of these were produced or commissioned by government. We also included two influential think tank reports that were mentioned by several interviewees: the 2006 Wanless Report and the 2014 Barker Report, both commissioned by the King's Fund. At a macro level in each nation the documents offer a description of key contextual factors, a diagnosis of the issues and a suggested way forward. We approached them as 'situated products' that 'represent and make things visible' and 'frame' issues in particular ways (Prior, 2003: 168). We used them to understand how key terms were defined, and what values were being articulated. We did not, of course, assume that the expressed policies had been implemented, even in cases where they had been passed into law. We used other data – interviews, secondary quantitative data, grey literature – to understand what had happened to the policy proposals and legislation set out in the documents.

The interviews then gave us an opportunity to look more *intensively* at the social mechanisms at play in the specific circumstances of national and local government. We conducted 65 semi-structured interviews with policy stakeholders in the four nations from 2019 to 2021. We worked with a third sector project partner in each nation of the UK to identify potential

Table 1.2: Social care-relevant policy documents in the four nations, 1997–2022

Title	Year	Country	Status
With respect to old age – Report of the Royal Commission on Long Term Care (Sutherland Report)	1999	UK	Royal Commission
Securing good care for older people (Wanless Report)	2006	England	King's Fund report (think tank)
Putting people first: A shared vision and commitment to the transformation of adult social care	2007	England	Concordat between UK Government and the social care sector lead organisations
Shaping the future of care together	2009	England	Green Paper
Building the National Care Service	2010	England	White Paper
A vision for adult social care: Capable communities and active citizens	2010	England	'Vision' document
Fairer care funding: The Report of the Commission on Funding of Care and Support (Dilnot Report)	2011	England	Government-commissioned review
Caring for our future: Reforming care and support	2012	England	White Paper
A new settlement for health and social care (Barker Report)	2014	England	King's Fund report (think tank)
Integration and innovation: Working together to improve health and social care for all	2021	England	White Paper
People at the heart of care: Adult social care reform	2021	England	White Paper
Fair care for older people	2001	Scotland	Proposals to inform legislation
Care 21: The future of unpaid care in Scotland	2006	Scotland	Report commissioned by the Scottish Executive
Changing lives: Report of the 21st Century Social Work Review	2006	Scotland	Government-commissioned report
Caring together: The carers strategy for Scotland 2010–2015	2010	Scotland	Government strategy document
Reshaping care for older people: A programme for change 2011–2021	2010	Scotland	Government strategy document
Self-directed support: A national strategy for Scotland	2010	Scotland	Government strategy document
Integration of adult health and social care in Scotland: Consultation on proposals	2012	Scotland	Government consultation paper
Adult social care reform for Scotland: A discussion paper	2018	Scotland	Government discussion paper
Independent review of adult social care in Scotland (Feeley Report)	2021	Scotland	Government-commissioned review

Table 1.2: Social care-relevant policy documents in the four nations, 1997–2022 (continued)

Title	Year	Country	Status
A National Care Service for Scotland – Consultation	2021	Scotland	Government consultation document
Review of health and social care in Wales	2003	Wales	Government-commissioned review
Beyond boundaries: Citizen centred local services for Wales (Beecham Review)	2006	Wales	Government-commissioned review
From vision to action: The report of the Independent Commission on Social Services in Wales	2010	Wales	Government-sponsored commission
Sustainable social services for Wales: A framework for action	2011	Wales	White Paper
Connected communities	2020	Wales	Government strategy
Rebalancing care and support	2021	Wales	White Paper
Transforming your care: A review of health and social care in Northern Ireland	2011	Northern Ireland	Government review
Prepared to care? Modernising adult social care in Northern Ireland	2015	Northern Ireland	Report from the Commissioner for Older People in Northern Ireland
A managed change: An agenda for creating a sustainable basis for domiciliary care in Northern Ireland	2015	Northern Ireland	Health and Social Care Board report
Systems not structures: Changing health and social care (Bengoa Report)	2016	Northern Ireland	Government-commissioned report
Power to people: Proposals to reboot adult social care and support in NI	2017	Northern Ireland	Government-commissioned report

interviewees. Interviewees were purposively selected to cover the key policy stakeholder interests across the nation and local care systems (politicians, civil servants, care providers, NHS, third sector, advocacy groups, regulatory and oversight bodies, Directors of Adult Social Services, commissioners, social workers). Interviewees spanned the national level (that is, policy actors focused on London, Edinburgh, Belfast or Cardiff) and also local policy stakeholders in each nation. Including the local policy perspective was a way to verify the claims made by national stakeholders and consider elements of implementation. Local government has statutory responsibility for social care in England, Wales and Scotland (although not in Northern Ireland where instead we focused on Health and Social Care Trusts).

We aimed for one local site in Scotland and Wales and two in England given its much larger population. We selected two contrasting sites in

England – a large urban authority and a rural county – narrowing down to specific sites by using an opportunistic approach through gatekeepers. In Wales and Scotland, our initial sites withdrew part-way through the project, reflecting the immense pressures facing local government social care teams. We were able to replace the Welsh site with another locality in Wales. In Scotland, several sites fell through. We were able to get one-off interviews from a number of local sites but were unable to get several interviewees from the same site. In Northern Ireland we focused on one of the five HSCTs that administer care services in the province (as local government does not have a social care role). Again, we were reliant on a local gatekeeper to broker access for us.

We aimed for 20 interviews per nation and recruited 22 interviewees in England, 17 in Wales, 13 in Scotland and 13 in Northern Ireland. Our interviews took place from 2019–21, and were substantially affected by the COVID-19 pandemic. From March 2020, potential interviewees were much harder to secure, as social care pressures, combined with lockdowns, home schooling and broader care responsibilities, affected their capacity to take part. This means that the fieldwork stage of the project lasted longer than originally intended and that we have interviews from before COVID-19, and from the first and second years of the pandemic. We recognise this as a potential limit of our data – it is not a snapshot of a common point in time. However we also appreciated the opportunity to listen to reflections on the impact of COVID-19 where possible.

The interviews were conducted by telephone by the authors, audio-recorded and professionally transcribed. They were imported into NVivo 12 for analysis. The University of Birmingham Research Ethics Committee provided ethical approval (ERN_18–1574). We agreed with interviewees that their contributions would be anonymised, and indicated only with a descriptor of the job role (for example, Wales, civil servant). Table 1.3 shows the interviews we undertook as part of the project. We have anonymised localities to avoid identification of interviewees. Our aim was to include people from each category in each country, but we were unable to fully meet this inclusion criteria in the COVID-19 context.

Our interviews were focused on policy makers or policy-influencing bodies in the four nations, in line with our inquiry's focus on policy comparison. We did not interview people who use social care services, unpaid carers or paid care workers. This was consistent with our focus on policy change at the level of the nation, but we recognise it to be a limit of our analysis, meaning that we are able only to have insights into what can be derived from policy stakeholders, documents and secondary data. Survey data is included in the secondary data but we do not have the voices of people using or providing care services to supplement the policy makers' perspectives.

Table 1.3: Interviewees

Role	England	Scotland	Wales	Northern Ireland	Total
Elected politician	2	1	2	–	5
Civil servant in care-relevant department (including one former civil servant)	2	1	1	2	6
Local government representative	1	1	1	N/A	3
NHS	2	1	2	1	6
Provider representative	2	3	1	1	7
Regulatory/oversight body (including Older People's Commissioner's Office in Northern Ireland and Wales)	1	1	2	1	5
Carers' organisation	2	2	2	2	8
Director of Adult Social Services	2	–	1	1	4
Care commissioner	2	1	1	1	5
Social worker	1	–	1	1	3
Care provider	5	2	3	3	13
Total	22	13	17	13	65

Analysis

We explored the data using the principles of abductive analysis. This is a qualitative data analysis approach aimed at theory construction. It relies on an iterative relationship between theory and data in order to produce speculative theory based on unexpected findings that are recontextualised in new theoretical frameworks (Bergene, 2007). We based our initial investigation, sampling and design of research instruments on understanding the care systems in the four nations, building up our understanding through note taking, memo writing, transcription and coding informed by the care diamond categories of family, state, market and community.

In analysing the documents and interviews, the first wave coding looked for content around the framing of social care:

- definition of social care;
- problems that needed to be solved;
- balance of responsibility between family, state, market and community;
- proposed policy reforms.

Codes were applied to whole sentences or paragraphs, relating to these points. We each separately coded a sample of documents and interview transcripts by hand, and then brought them together to compare similarities and differences through a consensus-coding approach (Cascio et al, 2019). We reflected critically on the passages and attributed a code, either confirming, challenging or amending the interpretation. From these discussions, we identified codes around key values (such as wellbeing, sustainability, fairness, rights and quality) and common policy objectives (for example, integration, personalisation and outcomes orientation) and applied these codes to our data. We then undertook second-phase coding of the data set based on emerging theories relating to key explanatory factors (for example, relating to features of the different territorial policy communities in the four nations, processes of policy change [such as drift versus layering] or different care paradigms [standardised versus differentiated]). We then coded the documents and interviews to these second-order codes.

In the chapters that follow we draw on illustrative quotes from the documents and the interviews that illuminate key aspects of the findings. Although we have aimed to bring in key stakeholder perspectives, we recognise that we are reliant on the interpretations given to us by interviewees, which are likely to be incomplete and rely on our interpretations of their meanings (Yanow, 2007). However, elite interviewing of key stakeholders is recognised as one of the only ways to understand how policy processes work, and why choices were made. By triangulating interview data with publicly available policy documents and secondary quantitative data, we offer a thorough understanding of the key issues, choices and framings that explain social care policy in the UK's four nations over the last 25 years.

The structure of the book

In Chapter 2 we consider how policy documents in each of the four nations define social care and what they set out as the goals of social care policy. We look at discursive convergence on what social care is for, highlighting the goals of wellbeing, fairness, rights and quality as the basis of a sustainable care system. In Chapter 3, we use the frame of crisis to explore issues of supply and demand for care in the four nations. We look at the extent to which demographic changes are increasing the demand for care and support. Using the care diamond framework, we then look at the respective contributions of the family, state, market and community to the 'quantum of care', and what it means to say that each of these are 'in crisis'.

In Chapter 4, we look at the decisions and practices around care in the four systems, in other words, the 'mechanisms' of care reform, setting out how they have been used in the UK nations. These are:

- Redistribute the costs of care
- Personalise support

- Support unpaid carers
- Invest in prevention
- Integrate with health
- Professionalise the workforce

In Chapter 5, we consider whether the UK's nations have achieved the outcomes that they aimed for in these six areas. We highlight that some of these policies are in tension, meaning that it is unlikely that they can all meet their desired outcomes at the same time. For example, the redistribution of costs through the introduction of free personal care may be in tension with the prevention agenda and with the move to greater personalisation. We also consider the question of 'success for whom?' (McConnell, 2010), noting that policies that work well for one set of interests (for example, paid care workers) may not necessarily do so for another (for example, direct payment recipients).

Having looked at convergence and divergence (Chapters 2 to 5), we then go on to use an explanatory lens to explain the patterns we have found. In Chapter 6, the focus is on the 'territorial policy communities' (Keating et al, 2009) in the four nations, which we use to explain some of the similarities and differences in their approaches to care. In particular, we draw attention to issues of scale, style and scope and how these play out differently in the policy communities around London, Edinburgh, Cardiff and Belfast.

In Chapter 7, we shift our explanatory lens to look at implementation issues facing reform of long-term care systems. We compare the challenges of transformational and incremental approaches to policy reform. We also discuss the 'policy mix' in the four nations, and suggest that tensions between the policies have been insufficiently acknowledged and explored. We frame these tensions around two rival care paradigms. The first emphasises formality and standardisation, while the second emphasises informality and diversity. We suggest that the fault line between these two approaches runs through care systems and reform endeavours in all four nations.

In Chapter 8 we summarise the findings of the book and consider how policy makers can more productively engage with the tensions between the two care paradigms in order to move towards a more sustainable care system. Otherwise care campaigners and policy makers will continue to be talking past each other in conversations about care.

2

What is social care policy for?

To assess and compare the four care systems of the four nations of the UK it is important to have a clear sense of what they are trying to achieve. In this chapter we focus on how policy documents in the four systems frame social care, and how care policy supports the aim of improving social care. This is what Pollitt (2002) calls the discursive aspect of convergence (or divergence). We look at what policy makers have set out in the documents as being their vision of sustainable care and a good life for people with care needs (in other words, the *ends* of care), and the ways in which this is reflective of their distinctive policy communities and identities. In later chapters we look at the *means* (or, in realist language, the mechanisms) through which to achieve these ends, which encompasses care funding, access, regulation and integration with health.

Solving the 'problem' of care

Care policy documents – White and Green Papers, legislation, formal policy commissions – provide an insight into the aims and aspirations of care policy. They identify the problems that need to be solved, the outcomes that are to be achieved and the mechanisms for achieving them. Of course, these documents do not all have the same status – some are embedded in legislation whereas others contain proposals that may never become formal policy. Together, as a body of documents, we see them as articulating what social care policy is designed to achieve in each of the four nations.

Almost all of the documents start with an account of the 'problem' of social care: the crisis that must be solved, the dysfunction that must be addressed. There is remarkable consensus across the four nations over more than two decades on what the problem is: the existing social care system cannot cope with the demographic changes that have led to rising demand and unmet need. Staff are insufficiently 'regarded, rewarded and supported' (Feeley, 2021), leading to high staff turnover and workforce shortages. The growing acuity and complexity in conditions of people using care services have further added to the strain, with a greater concentration of higher packages of care assigned to fewer people (Reed et al, 2021). The system has been put under additional pressure by funding cuts in England and Wales, which have only been partly mitigated by short-term cash fixes. A metaphor that recurs in policy documents from all four nations in relation to the problem of social care is the 'lottery'. This relates to the arbitrariness around who accesses care, where they live and how much they pay for it.

These pressures are considered to be temporally specific: 'We face a challenge no other generation has had to confront', as New Labour's 2010 White Paper puts it (HM Government, 2010: 2). The problems are seen as intensified by the changing expectations of current generations compared to previous ones (Wanless, 2006). Northern Ireland's *Power to people* report expresses a sense that social care has not kept up with social change:

> Why, if the population's needs, expectations and aspirations have changed so much, is the so-called 'market' for social care still offering the same services and doing much the same things? If the media was run in this way, we might still be watching the same three channels on a black and white analogue TV! (Kelly and Kennedy, 2017: 61–2)

And the challenge is urgent: reform is 'long overdue. We can wait no longer' (Dilnot, 2011: 80). This crisis framing is evident across the timespan of the documents, although it has been of limited efficacy in addressing policy drift (Crowther, 2018).

The most recent documents indicate that the COVID-19 pandemic has intensified the urgency, but also perhaps created an opportunity: 'This is a unique moment when we must continue to build on the audacious legacy that makes the NHS the very best of Britain. We must seize it. ... We must not go back to the old ways of working' (DHSC, 2021a). When setting up the Feeley inquiry to look into creating a National Care Service, First Minister Nicola Sturgeon told the Scottish Parliament:

> This is a moment to be bold and to build a service fit for the future. The National Health Service was born out of the tragedy of the Second World War. Let us resolve that we will build out of this COVID-19 crisis, the lasting and positive legacy of a high quality, National Care Service for all who need it. (Feeley, 2021: 38)

The unique and tragic context of the pandemic is considered to have created a new foundational moment, equivalent to the post-war reforms that established many of Britain's welfare state institutions.

Even before COVID-19, many of the documents were calling for an ambitious new social care settlement rather than tinkering around the edges. As England's *Caring for our future* White Paper puts it, 'It is clear that we cannot improve care and support by pouring ever more money into a system that does not work' (HM Government, 2012: 8). The Bengoa Report (2016: 9) calls for 'transformational change' in Northern Ireland. The *Power to people* report in Northern Ireland a year later makes the point, 'A mixture of incremental adjustments is no longer sufficient to keep an unsustainable system working … [and] a "pick and mix" approach to the proposals is not appropriate' (Kelly and Kennedy, 2017: 6).

Beyond this consensus about the need for urgent and systemic reform, there is a distinctive cast to some of the problems. Funding cuts have been much more extensive in England than elsewhere, and this is reflected in the way that the problems of care are framed. England also has many more self-funders than elsewhere (that is, people who pay privately for care), and their plight in having to deal with high care costs (such as selling their homes) is a more significant feature of the English documents than in the other nations. Northern Ireland has not had social care-specific legislation equivalent to that of the other three nations. There is recognition that the Northern Irish legislative framework is outdated, and lacks key elements that are in legislation elsewhere, such as rights for unpaid carers. A report from the Commissioner for Older People in Northern Ireland (COPNI) notes: 'Current legislation and policy guidance surrounding Adult Social Care is outdated, confusing and fragmented in Northern Ireland. Definitions and terminology used in the legislation need updating to fully reflect and meet the needs of modern society' (COPNI, 2015: 12).

There is therefore a clear understanding across the policy documents in all four nations that social care is failing in some way. Before we go on to look in more detail at what policy makers in the four nations want social care policy to achieve, we briefly consider how social care is defined in the documents.

What is social care?

Running through the policy documents are two accounts of social care: social care as a set of services and social care as a facilitating tool supporting people to flourish. This distinction can be summed up in the distinction between social care as something you go *into* versus something you use to move *up and beyond* – a 'safety net' versus a 'springboard' (#socialcarefuture, 2019). In some of the documents, care is described as a list of formal interventions. For example, as the *Prepared to care* document in Northern Ireland puts it, '[Social care] comprises a number of services, ranging from residential and nursing care homes and the provision of aids and adaptations to domiciliary or home care support' (COPNI, 2015: 3). However, elsewhere care is given a more expansive definition linked to support as a means to other ends, as in the English *Caring for our future* White Paper: 'seeing friends; caring for our families; and being part of our communities' (HM Government, 2012: 13). The 2021 Feeley Report in Scotland makes this point explicitly: 'Social care support is the means to an end, not an end in itself. The end is human rights, wellbeing, independent living and equity, as well as people in communities and society who care for each other' (Feeley, 2021: 19).

Many of the more recent documents do acknowledge this more expansive definition, although doing so does raise questions about the scope of policy, and when and how social care blends into tasks undertaken as part of family ties or friendship. In some of the literature, it is suggested that there is a continuum from informal to formal support (Bulmer, 1987). However, Abrams describes this as 'misleading and dangerous', arguing that it is not a continuum but a 'frontier': 'we ought instead to start out by envisaging a discontinuity, a principled antithesis almost between the formal and the informal' (1978b, in Bulmer, 1987: 175). Gingrich notes that the state has an ambivalent relationship with unpaid care, wanting to support carers to a degree, but also mindful that 'eschewing private or informal care might leave the state with a heavy bill or low capacity to deal with citizens' needs' (Gingrich, 2011: 178). In the UK, Understanding Society data shows that around 1 in 5 people provide unpaid care each year, making unpaid care a much bigger part of care provision than anything done by the state or market (Zhang and Bennett, 2019).

As well as the question of what *is* social care, there are also uncertainties about its boundaries with other public services. As the Dilnot Report in England puts it,

> Social care is part of a wider care and support system, which includes social care, the NHS, the social security system, housing support and public health services. It also includes the services provided by third sector organisations, and the invaluable contribution made by carers and volunteers. The state pension and private financial products also provide income that is used for care and support needs. (Dilnot, 2011: 4)

These boundaries are set differently in each of the four nations of the UK, given their different social security entitlements and the differential approaches to integration with health. In Northern Ireland, social care has been part of an integrated health and care system since the 1970s, whereas in the other jurisdictions, integration with health is newer and less developed. Social security entitlements and spending also differ across the nations. Since 2020, social security benefits have been devolved to the Scottish Government with a £3 billion budget allocation, whereas most benefits in England, Wales and Northern Ireland still sit with the UK's Department for Work and Pensions (DWP).

A final layer of complexity relating to what *is* social care concerns the multiplicity of agencies and organisations working in the social care space. As the *Rebalancing care and support* White Paper in Wales puts it:

> Complexity is the overriding feature of the care and support landscape. Social care in Wales is provided through a market place of over 1,000

providers, mostly from the independent sector, who often compete for the same contracts. People's care and support is commissioned through local authorities, local health boards or directly by themselves. It is funded through national and local government and through fees and charges people may pay to their local authority or directly to a care provider. (Welsh Government, 2021b: 7)

Although the number of providers and the degree of outsourcing varies between the nations – which we discuss in the next chapter – the complexity of commissioning and provision does not. During the COVID-19 pandemic it became clear that governments themselves did not fully understand the complex supply chains, highlighting that the question of what is social care, who delivers it and who is responsible for it, is much more complex than in health services (Daly, 2020).

What should social care policy do?

Despite the definitional ambiguities and boundary issues, policy documents from the four nations have a very similar vision of what social care policy is aiming to achieve. The overarching principle in all four systems is that care policy should maximise individual and collective wellbeing. It will do this by being fair, rights-based and high-quality – and ensuring these goals are achieved for everyone in the system (people who require support, unpaid carers and care workers). These elements combined are expected to deliver sustainability. We look in turn at wellbeing, fairness, rights, quality and sustainability, as well as at the tensions that can arise when all of them are in focus at once.

Wellbeing

All four nations have placed wellbeing at the centre of care policy and indeed, broader society. Wellbeing has become a central concept in public policy in many countries, exemplified by the adoption of the United Nation's (UN) Sustainable Development Goals (SDGs) in 2015 in which 'wellbeing' is a key pillar (Joseph and McGregor, 2019; Austin, 2020; Keating et al, 2021). Gray and Birrell (2013: 2) note that placing 'wellbeing' at the centre of social care is to take an expansive view of care as something that is an essential human need and important fabric of society; this is very different from the view of care as a list of tasks for a residual group of vulnerable people. The concept of wellbeing has several elements, which Joseph and McGregor (2019) separate into three dimensions of wellbeing: material (what a person has), relational (what people are able to do with what they have) and subjective (how people feel about what they have, can do and can be).

Renewed interest in wellbeing in the UK from 2010 led to the development of a national wellbeing measurement framework that included objective and subjective measures (Bache and Reardon, 2013).

Wellbeing as a central pillar of social care policy has much older roots (Hamblin, 2019). The 1968 Seebohm Report, which recommended the creation of local authority social services departments across the UK, aimed to 'enable the greatest possible number of individuals to act reciprocally, giving and receiving service for the well-being of the whole community' (Ministry of Housing and Local Government, 1968). Seebohm has since been a reference point for many policy documents about social care (Gray and Birrell, 2013: 2). In England, the incoming Conservative-Liberal Democrat coalition government in 2010 published a consultation document, *A vision for adult social care* (DH, 2010), which explicitly evoked Seebohm and the sense of adult social care being underpinned by reciprocity and wellbeing. Since then, care policy in all four nations has set wellbeing as the goal of its services. Seebohm's theme of reciprocity also remains an important concept, which we return to later in the chapter.

The Care Act 2014, applicable in England, defines wellbeing as including outcomes such as physical and mental health, dignity, protection from abuse, control, relationships, participation in activities and the community as well as social, emotional and economic wellbeing. It gave local authorities an overarching duty to promote individual wellbeing. In the Social Services and Well-being (Wales) Act of the same year, these aspects of wellbeing were included and joined by 'securing rights and entitlements'. In Scotland and Northern Ireland, wellbeing has not had the same flagship legislation but is an important principle across care policy. In Scotland, mental wellbeing is included in its National Performance Framework (NPF). The Carers (Scotland) Act 2016 places a duty on local authorities to prepare an adult carer support plan that must consider the impact of caring on the carers' wellbeing. In Northern Ireland, the concept of 'social wellbeing' has been used by the Department of Health (Hamblin, 2019). In the Northern Ireland documents there is also recognition of 'the shadow of our recent history in NI, particularly in the mental wellbeing of the citizenry' (Health and Social Care Northern Ireland, 2011: 1).

To some extent, and particularly in the earlier documents, wellbeing is seen as the aggregation of individual outcomes, as, for example, in the 2006 Wanless Report, which has a strong utilitarian thread:

> The aims of social care fall into two broad groups: first, ensuring that people are able to live in safety and to satisfy personal care needs, including feeding, washing, dressing and going to the toilet; second, enhancing well-being and social inclusion, so that older people are able to engage socially, and maintain their self-esteem. The larger the

number of people for whom these goals are attained, the higher the overall outcomes. (Wanless, 2006: 16)

Other articulations, and particularly more recent ones, focus more strongly on collective wellbeing – for example, Welsh Deputy Health and Social Services Minister Julie Morgan's Foreword to the 2020 *Connected communities* strategy: 'It is the strength of the links between people, within families, neighbourhoods, workplaces or wider communities, which gives us our sense of belonging and well-being' (Welsh Assembly Government, 2020: 4). The Well-being of Future Generations (Wales) Act 2015 legislated for place-based wellbeing plans to be developed by Public Services Boards, giving a more explicitly collective orientation to wellbeing (Hamblin, 2019).

The elasticity of the term creates doubt about whether wellbeing is being used in the same way across policy domains and jurisdictions. It is a multi-dimensional concept, and policy documents have often left implicit which of the dimensions they are focusing on. As Keating et al note, 'the application of wellbeing to particular policy spheres has been patchy, and the language used has been imprecise' (2021: 615). This aligns with Paun et al's assessment (2016: 29) that use of 'wellbeing' vocabulary in the four nations does not mean they are talking about the same thing. Paun et al summarise a round table of senior civil servants from all four nations, at which one participant said: '"While we [all] use the word wellbeing, our concepts are incredibly different".' Paun et al go on:

> Specifically, it was argued that in Scotland and Wales the approach to the issue is 'based on wellbeing as a very broad and holistic concept' whereas in England (including the What Works Centre for Wellbeing) there is a narrower focus on 'subjective wellbeing' as measured in standardised questions in the Labour Force Survey. (Paun et al, 2016: 29)

A common strand of wellbeing in the care policy documents across the four nations includes the opportunity to stay at home, or in a home-like environment, for as long as possible. As New Labour's White Paper, *Building the National Care Service*, puts it, 'By creating the right support and incentives to keep people in their own homes, we can begin to support people to live the lives they want to' (HM Government, 2010: 3). This goal is seen as paramount for older people, whereas for working-age adults it is one of a broader set of aspirations about being able to exercise control and participate in work and other activities (Welsh Government, 2021b). In Scotland's Feeley Report, wellbeing is about independent living: 'Independent living means people of all ages having the same freedom, choice, dignity and control as other citizens at home, at work, and in the community' (Feeley, 2021: 9).

Wellbeing also includes an absence of fear, an aspiration associated with NHS founder Aneurin Bevan, whose essays are entitled *In place of fear* (Bevan, 1952). The 1999 Sutherland Report on funding reform, which covered the whole UK, stated: 'If our proposals are accepted, the nation will have demonstrated that it values its older citizens and is prepared to give them freedom from fear and a new security in old age' (Sutherland, 1999). The 2010 English White Paper, *Building the National Care Service*, evoked the language of Bevan in saying that a reformed care system will ensure 'no one needs to live in fear of losing their home or savings to pay for care' (HM Government, 2010: 12). A decade on, the Conservative government's proposals for a care cap used much the same language (prior to delaying the reforms): 'From October 2023, no one will be forced to pay unlimited and unpredictable costs for their care, giving them the certainty and peace of mind that this government will step in and look after those most in need of support' (DHSC, 2021b: 6).

Establishing the promotion of wellbeing as a duty on public bodies, as the English and Wales legislation did, is an important step in moving beyond functional accounts of social care. However, doubts have been raised about how this duty is discharged. From a legal perspective, Sloan (2021: 39) notes, 'Even at the time the [English] 2014 Act was being implemented, however, the Government admitted that the principle was not designed to require a local authority to "undertake any particular action in ... itself"'. What is also not always clear in the debate about care and wellbeing is whether care leads to wellbeing, or whether it facilitates the conditions for wellbeing. We return later in the book to the extent to which the role of social care policy is to set up services that 'deliver' wellbeing, or to contribute to the conditions in which people can flourish (see Chapter 7).

Fairness

In all of the nations, a key aspiration of care policy is to make the system fairer. New Labour's 2010 White Paper, *Building the National Care Service*, linked a fair system to the core values of Britishness:

> In Britain we don't just look out for ourselves, we also look after each other. It is part of the soul of our nation, underpinned by our core values of fairness and responsibility. ... Millions of people provide care and support at home for a family member or friend. It is the hallmark of a civilised society. (HM Government, 2010: 2)

Fairness here is given both a timeless quality – part of the 'soul of our nation' – as well as a temporal location in progressive modernity ('the hallmark of a civilised society').

Three elements of fairness are commonly invoked in the policy documents. The first (and most common) is about who pays, including how to ensure that the system is fair to people with different levels of assets, and fairly distributed across the generations. The second is about access to care, which, it is felt, should not be based on geography or health condition. The third is reciprocity: fairness is linked to responsibility – everyone has to do their bit. In all of these the aspiration is to end the 'lottery' on who pays what, who gets what, and who does what.

Looking at these in turn, the first relates to distributional fairness in who pays for care, and the need to address the unequal distribution of care costs. The New Labour government appointed Sir Stewart Sutherland to lead a Royal Commission on Long Term Care for the Elderly. Its report concluded: 'Responsibility for provision now and in the future should be shared between the state and individuals – the aim is to find a division affordable for both and one which people can understand and accept as fair and logical' (Sutherland, 1999). In moving towards the implementation of the Sutherland proposals, the Scottish Executive commissioned a report entitled *Fair care for older people* (2001), highlighting the centrality of fairness to the reforms. The report of the 2011 Dilnot Commission into funding reform in England was entitled *Fairer care funding* (Dilnot, 2011).

There is common acceptance that no one should be denied access to care on the grounds of ability to pay, as part of 'a shared commitment to social justice' (HM Government, 2007: 5). Yet, there is also an understanding that some people pay high fees for care whereas others pay nothing – an inequity not seen in arrangements for other welfare goods, such as health and education, which are free at the point of use. As the Dilnot Report put it, 'Care is the one major area of our lives where, at the moment, there is no way for people to protect themselves against the risk of high costs' (2011: 2).

In developing a new model for funding care, the policy documents emphasise the need to ensure that people who have saved over their lives are not penalised. As the Wanless Report states: 'It is a common complaint that the existing system penalises those who have saved for their old age' (2006: 21). In the public consultation that accompanied the development of New Labour's care proposals it was noted: 'Although people agreed that those who could not afford to pay for themselves had the greatest need for state support, they also felt it was unfair that people who had worked hard and made sensible decisions to save were less eligible for state support' (HM Government, 2009: 14).

A key part of this fairness argument is the claim that people with assets should be able to pass on their homes to their children. This protection of assets has often been a key part of the political rhetoric of care reform: 'The way in which charges are made for care, particularly residential care which in some circumstances can mean using the value of a person's home to pay for it, is widely viewed as unfair' (Boyce, 2017: 20). Protecting people's housing assets was an important part of England's care cap reforms, and linked to a Conservative Party manifesto promise that no one would 'need to sell their home' to pay for care (The Conservative and Unionist Party, 2019). This claim later had to be corrected since a care cap still requires people to contribute up to the level of the cap, which may require selling property if other assets are not available (Tallack and Sturrock, 2022).

One of the challenges of reforming care funding to make it fairer, however, is that some versions of fairness consider that it is entirely appropriate that those with more assets (such as a house) should use those to pay for care. As Gingrich puts it, 'extensive care funding might effectively underwrite middle-class inheritances rather than improve equity' (2011: 178). This alternative account of fairness is evident in the *Power to people* report, which seeks to steer Northern Ireland *away* from free personal care at home (or domiciliary care, as it is sometimes called). This is a position that runs counter to the direction of reforms in England and Wales; in Scotland the free personal care reforms have explicitly sought to make fewer people pay for their care. In Northern Ireland, the *Power to people* report gave the following rationale:

> [T]he current charging arrangements in Northern Ireland are unfair and create unintended consequences. It does not feel equitable that, if you need the support of a care home, and have sufficient funds, you have to pay the whole cost, whilst someone with the same assets and income can receive domiciliary care for no cost. ... By giving free domiciliary care to people who could afford to contribute simply means you have less available for those who can't or to invest in new services. (Kelly and Kennedy, 2017: 65)

Although the proposals in *Power to people* have not been implemented as yet, they highlight the contending views of fairness and equity within care. In England, Wales and Scotland, the focus has primarily been on why people should have to pay for care when they do not have to pay for health (particularly given that, to many people, health and care seem almost interchangeable; see Sussex et al, 2019). In Northern Ireland, the focus is on why affluent people should benefit from a state subsidy in home care that is not available for residential care.

Fairness also relates to the intergenerational distribution of costs and the balance between what older people should pay versus the contributions of working-age taxpayers. Although around half of social care spending is on people of working age, the framing of care funding is usually in relation to paying for people in old age, who are certainly more numerous (comprising about two-thirds of the people receiving long-term care in 2019/20; see

The King's Fund, 2021). The question sometimes asked is whether care should be paid for by older people themselves or by younger taxpayers. The 1999 Sutherland Report stated: 'The Commission's recommendations represent a unique opportunity for a new contract between Government and people and between all generations of society. This will ensure that the nation's resources which are spent on the care of older people are more effective and will promote increased social cohesion and inclusiveness' (Sutherland, 1999).

A decade later, New Labour proposed a commission to 'determine the fairest and most sustainable way for people to contribute', which would ensure 'fairness to all including between generations' (HM Government, 2010: 9). In Wales, the intergenerational aspect of funding has a particularly high profile as a result of the Well-being of Future Generations (Wales) Act 2015, described by the UN as 'groundbreaking' (Nesom and MacKillop, 2021: 432). The summary of the Act states:

> The Well-being of Future Generations (Wales) Act is about improving the social, economic, environmental and cultural well-being of Wales. ... It will make the public bodies listed in the Act think more about the long-term, work better with people and communities and each other, look to prevent problems and take a more joined-up approach. (Welsh Government, 2015a: 3)

This Act has continued to be a reference point for future care policy statements in Wales, such as the 2021 *Rebalancing care and support* White Paper (Welsh Government, 2021b). Others note, however, 'the Act is vague, open-ended and aspirational, expecting prompt local implementation without much national guidance or support' (Nesom and MacKillop, 2021: 432).

A second framing of fairness relates to *access to care*, and the extent to which people are able to get the care that they need. Often this is discussed in terms of geography, as it felt to be unfair that people receive different care depending on where they live, the so-called 'postcode lottery' (invoked in New Labour's *Building the National Care Service* [HM Government, 2010], and *Prepared to care*, 2015, in Northern Ireland [COPNI, 2015]). New Labour's 2009 consultation paper on care reform highlighted the tensions between geographical diversity and fairness:

> People told us that they could see the advantages of a system which allows areas to be flexible and respond to local needs. But the majority of people were more concerned that a system which varied a person's level of care and support because of where they lived was unfair. (HM Government, 2009: 14)

In Wales, fairness of access to care relates also to 'responding to the Welsh language needs of service users and carers' (Independent Commission on Social Services in Wales, 2010: 7).

The language of a National Care Service has been used at different times to capture the need for a fair and consistent approach to social care. The 2021 Feeley Report in Scotland set out the case: 'A National Care Service must ensure that people have equity of access to social care supports, and experience a similarly high quality of care, wherever they live in Scotland' (Feeley, 2021: 39). A decade earlier, New Labour made the same promise in England (just before losing power): 'In the new National Care Service, everyone should be able to get really good care wherever they live and whatever they or their family need' (HM Government, 2009: 9). Wales is now also considering developing a National Care Service (Welsh Government, 2021a).

Of course, what is left unexplored in this discussion of the postcode lottery or a National Care Service is why fairness necessitates consistency across, say, Scotland or Wales, but not across the UK (despite remaining a single state in law). Tolerance of inequities of access between the four nations, experienced most acutely by those in the border regions, requires a strong sense of political community and separateness from the neighbouring territory. Katzenstein's (2016) work on small states suggests that a sense of a common opposition to a neighbour, especially a large one, helps in this. Keating and Wilson (2014) draw on survey findings in applying territorial identities across a range of subnational territories, classifying Scotland as having a strong territorial identity, Wales as medium and Northern Ireland as strong/divided. The themes of political identity within each of the nations are further discussed in Chapter 6.

Besides its geographical dimension, fairness of access also relates to care conditions. The dividing line between the NHS and social care in the UK makes a big difference here, as 'health' conditions are treated free at the point of access, whereas services and support for 'care' conditions are means tested. In 2022, people in England with assets over £23,250 paid for their own care, both at home and in residential care. In Wales, the means test threshold for residential care has been increasing since 2016 (to £50,000 in 2022), and there is a maximum weekly charge for home care of £100. In Scotland, free personal care is provided both at home and in residential care, and people pay only for the food and accommodation costs of residential care (which is free for people with assets below £28,500). In Northern Ireland, personal care at home is free for all who meet the needs threshold, but residential care is paid for by those with assets above £23,250.

In all jurisdictions, there may be an NHS contribution to costs if someone requires nursing care, and this may be provided in a nursing home (with a qualified nurse on-site) rather than a standard residential care home.

The boundary between (free) health and (means-tested) care needs is a notoriously difficult one to judge. If people are able to establish that their needs are primarily health-based, they may be eligible for NHS Continuing Healthcare, otherwise support will be means tested. A 2014 think tank report into the future of care in England (the Barker Commission) highlighted the tensions at the interface between free care through the NHS Continuing Healthcare system and means-tested support available from local authority adult social care services:

> [W]hether an individual qualifies for NHS Continuing Healthcare is in effect an 'all or nothing' assessment. Pass the assessment and all health and care, including accommodation costs, become free. ... Fail it, and the means tests kick in for both care and accommodation, with large financial implications for those who do not qualify. ... Passing or failing the Continuing Healthcare assessment has too many parallels with winning, or not winning, a lottery. ... There are wide regional variations in who qualifies and who does not. (Barker, 2014: 18)

For people with dementia in particular, there has been concern that they face very high costs, which someone with a medical condition such as cancer would not have to pay. This issue became high profile at the 2017 General Election, with the Conservative Party proposing social care reforms that were dubbed a 'dementia tax' because of penalising people with long-lasting care conditions (BBC News, 2017). As Bell put it, highlighting the continued lack of progress on this issue:

> [This] brings us back to the equity argument about the contrast between those health conditions, such as cancer, which the government is willing to fully insure against and those, such as dementia, where government funding support is much more limited. These arguments stand in stark contrast, but the UK political system has repeatedly failed to generate any significant change in England to a system which is generally viewed as fundamentally unfair and unsustainable. (Bell, 2018)

A third version of fairness in the documents relates to reciprocity, whereby people are expected to take more responsibility for self-care and supporting others, and to rely less on provision by the state. Reciprocity has been described as one of the few 'social agreements that have been found to be universal among societies across time and cultures' (Ouchi, 1980: 137), although how far it necessitates a symmetrical exchange between people has been a discussion within care ethics (Tronto, 2013). In many of the policy documents consulted, reciprocity is about individuals taking responsibility for their health. The Welsh Assembly Government commissioned a report by Derek Wanless about health and social care in Wales, which argued, 'A step-change in individuals' and communities' acceptance of responsibility for their health is needed. No amount of effort by the health and care services can be a substitute for this' (Welsh Assembly Government, 2003: 2). New Labour's White Paper also argued that self-care has a role to play, with individuals responsible for making healthy choices that will 'minimis[e] the chances of certain types of care need arising' (HM Government, 2010: 79). In Northern Ireland, individuals are to become '"informed and expert patients" who take individual action to manage their own health and well-being' (Bengoa, 2016: 37).

A greater role for self-help is often linked to a focus on prevention. This is a key theme in all the documents relating to the idea that keeping people embedded in families and communities helps keep them out of statutory services for longer. As *Power to people* in Northern Ireland puts it: 'We have to work out how to make a fundamental shift away from a crisis dominated system into a long-term solution focusing on prevention and early intervention in which care and support is based initially around people and their communities' (Kelly and Kennedy, 2017: 46).

The 2021 White Paper in Wales – *Rebalancing care and support* – gave a clear steer on the importance of prevention to its reform agenda:

> Prevention is at the heart of the Welsh Government's programme of change for social services. There is a need to focus on prevention and early intervention to make social services sustainable into the future. It is vital that care and support services do not wait to respond until people reach a crisis point. (Welsh Government, 2021b: 25)

Similarly in Scotland, prevention was described as a key policy commitment across the policy papers. The *Changing lives* report (Scottish Government, 2006), reviewing the future of social work, made prevention its first recommendation. Prevention was to be 'everyone's job', with the development of 'anticipatory services to improve outcomes for people with predictable needs' (2006: 45). The carers strategy of the same year called for more prevention and early intervention to prevent carer illness (2006a: 26). The Feeley Report, 15 years on, similarly called for 'a new narrative for adult social care support that replaces crisis with prevention and wellbeing' (Feeley, 2021: 2).

Over time in the documents prevention is increasingly linked to a greater focus on individual and community *assets* rather than deficits. (In earlier documents, the language of assets tended to refer to people's housing and capital.) The Feeley Report talked of '[seeing] people who need some support for their assets, their experience, and their potential rather than as passive' (2021: 20). According to *Power to people* in Northern Ireland:

> We have argued in other parts of this paper for interpretations of adult care and support to be expanded into a much wider, broader, community-centred and asset-based approach to individuals and their support networks. One in which prevention and wellbeing are the primary focus, together with reablement and the promotion of independence. ... All these models have slightly different methods, but fundamentally they all strive to move away from a 'medical model', dominated by a deficit approach to age and disability and thereby move to a more people-orientated, relationship-centred way of working. (Kelly and Kennedy, 2017: 62)

This expansion of social care into approaches designed to keep people active in communities and focused on their relational capabilities is distinctive from, and sometimes at odds with, more 'functional' understandings of social care, as a set of services. Specific policies on prevention are discussed in more detail in Chapter 4.

A further aspect of fairness in care policy relates to the paid workforce and the need for a 'fair price' for care and a 'fair wage' for care workers. The Feeley Report in Scotland includes a chapter on 'fair work' and draws on Scotland's Fair Work Convention, calling for implementation of its 2019 recommendations (Feeley, 2021). These demanded urgent interventions by policy makers to improve the quality of work and employment for the social care workforce in Scotland, and the creation of a new national body to guarantee minimum standards regarding terms and conditions (Fair Work Convention, 2016). In Wales, the 2021 *Rebalancing care and support* White Paper cited the work of Wales' Fair Work Commission. The Commission recommended the establishment of a Fair Work Forum in social care, including trade unions, and implementation of regulations to protect workers delivering commissioned services. The White Paper noted that, 'In response to the recommendations of the report, the Welsh Government has recently convened a Social Care Forum which is considering how best to improve pay and other conditions of employment in the social care sector' (Welsh Government, 2021b: 20).

Northern Ireland has announced similar plans to establish a Social Care Fair Work Forum composed of care bodies, employers, trade unions and others, tasked with generating proposals to improve terms and conditions. There is no equivalent strategy for England, although the 2021 *People at the heart of care* White Paper for England notes: 'We want the adult social care workforce to feel recognised and to have opportunities to develop their careers' (DHSC, 2021b: 7). Other stakeholders in England have called for a cross-sector approach to fair work similar to that taken in the other nations (Dromey and Hochlaf, 2018; TUC, 2021).

Rights

A related but separate articulation of the aims of care policy is to enhance or uphold human rights. Gray and Birrell (2013: 21) note that anti-oppressive practice and a 'rights' agenda have slowly acquired a higher profile within social care, having been largely ignored in 20th-century care policy. Growing awareness of the rights of people using social care services stimulated and reinforced other changes within social care, including the passage of disability discrimination laws, while the UN Convention on the Rights of Persons with Disabilities (2006) was influential in creating an international profile for rights-oriented approaches to care (Series, 2019a).

In all four nations, policy documents indicate that rights is an important framing for social care, as shown by the extracts in Box 2.1. In Scotland, Wales and Northern Ireland this remains important, including in the most recent documents. In England, although 'rights' was a key focus in New Labour documents, this has been less evident since 2010. Chaney's analysis of party manifestos in the four nations finds that rights tend to be a concern for left of centre parties (in power since 1998 in Scotland and Wales) whereas right of centre parties (in power in England since 2010) put more emphasis on fairness (Chaney, 2022: 162).

Several elements of rights are articulated in the documents: an emphasis on equal rights regardless of impairment; the right to choice and control; geographical equality; and information as a pre-requisite for claiming rights.

Box 2.1: The centrality of rights-based approaches to social care in the policy documents

- England: 'People with care and support needs should be treated as citizens with rights, rather than having to fight to get services. Everyone who receives care and support must be treated with dignity and kindness, and their human rights must be respected' (HM Government, 2009: 25).
- Scotland: 'In order to maximise the potential of social care support we have to change our perspective of what is social care support. We need to shift the paradigm of social care support to one underpinned by a human rights based approach' (Feeley, 2021: 4).
- Wales: 'People's rights must be at the heart of action and decisions about what happens in our care homes, in the wider social care system and in our communities' (Welsh Government, 2021b: 12).
- Northern Ireland: 'The Expert Advisory Panel wishes to emphasise at the outset the fundamental importance of a human rights approach in which people with care and support needs enjoy the same entitlements to quality of life and wellbeing as all other citizens' (Kelly and Kennedy, 2017: 25).

There are clear parallels with the fairness debates. However, rights discourses are often about absolutes, and can sit awkwardly with the balancing and reciprocity inherent in the concept of fairness. Rights are also usually held by individuals, and this can create tensions with communitarian accounts of care that emphasise how people are located within and constituted by community identities (Mulhall and Swift, 1992; Etzioni, 2012).

A key element of recent legislative reform on social care has been an emphasis on people with care needs being entitled to equal citizenship with others. Recent policy has also focused on equalising entitlements across different groups of people. Rather than having distinctive approaches for older people, people with physical and learning disabilities and people with mental health problems, policy has focused on being inclusive of all groups. The *Putting people first* report argued that 'Older people, disabled people and people with mental health problems demand equality of citizenship in every aspect of their lives, from housing to employment to leisure' (HM Government, 2007: 1). This 'de-differentiation' approach, in which all adults requiring social care support are part of one care system, contrasts with many other parts of the world in which working-age and older people are considered separately. It can be linked to a discourse of rights, inclusiveness and collective advocacy, although also to a form of individualisation (Bigby, 2020). Legislation in England, Wales and Scotland has further extended this inclusiveness by bringing the rights of carers into line with people with care needs.

New entitlements to advocacy, intended to protect the human rights of people with care needs and carers, have been advanced in England, Scotland and Wales. Wales and Northern Ireland both have an Older People's Commissioner, whose role includes ensuring rights are protected (Welsh Government, 2021b). The Feeley Report in Scotland also puts human rights at the heart of the proposed new National Care Service: 'We believe we cannot improve social care support and people's health and wellbeing if we do not ensure their human rights are upheld. A human rights based approach has been central to the creation of the report and we believe that it needs to be central to its implementation' (Feeley, 2021: 22). The Scottish Government's consultation on the National Care Service proposed a charter for rights and responsibilities and a Commissioner for Social Care (Scottish Government, 2021: 43).

A key right articulated in many documents focuses on a person-centred approach, in which people have choice and control over the support they receive. This relates in particular to budgetary control, with all four jurisdictions making it possible for people funded by the state to take their support as a cash allocation (Ungerson and Yeandle, 2007). As *Putting people first* puts it for England: 'Over time, people who use social care services and their families will increasingly shape and commission their own services.

Personal Budgets will ensure people receiving public funding use available resources to choose their own support services – a right previously available only to self-funders' (HM Government, 2007: 2).

This initiative aimed to give further impetus to older legislation: the Direct Payments Act 1996 applied UK-wide and gave local authorities the power to make cash allocations to some groups of social care users under 65. This was subsequently widened to become a duty and to encompass all people with social care needs and unpaid carers (Glasby and Littlechild, 2016). In developing individualised funding, Scotland and Wales have deliberately avoided the language of personalisation and choice and control that are associated with the English policy. Scotland has introduced 'self-directed support' rather than personalisation. Similarly in Wales, policy documents have emphasised 'voice and control', as a discursive shift away from the English framing of 'choice and control'. Pearson et al (2020: 290) note that in England and Wales the law expressly gives preference to direct payments, whereas in Scotland and Northern Ireland the law and guidance sets out four options with no preference for one over another.

The underpinning principles remain very similar across the four nations despite the differences of language and emphasis. As the *Self-directed support national strategy in Scotland* put it: 'there is a recognition that individuals are best placed to say what would make a difference to them and their families or carers, and a desire to move away from the strict definitions of what can and cannot be funded to achieve social care objectives' (Scottish Government, 2010b: 11).

Much has been written about the extent to which these reforms are 'consumerising' or are part of a move to enhanced citizenship rights (Clarke et al, 2007; Ferguson, 2007; Needham, 2011). The structure of the care market in different parts of the UK (explored in Chapter 3) also shapes the extent to which it is possible for people to meaningfully exercise their rights to self-direction or personalisation. In Northern Ireland, the *Power to people* report noted that 'consumer power' was particularly weak: 'many care providers see themselves as having only one customer: the Trusts. ... There is very little choice. It's either domiciliary care or a care home and in some places the market has so failed that there isn't a willing provider to give a service' (Kelly and Kennedy, 2017: 63).

Deploying choice and control also relies in part on having a right to access information and advocacy. This right is protected by law in England, Wales and Scotland. However, Needham et al (2022) found that implementation of the Care Act 2014 in England had been poor, and that the lack of information or advocacy undermined choice and control. The 2021 English White Paper *People at the heart of care* reaffirmed the importance of information and proposed a new national information service (DHSC, 2021b). In Wales, the *Sustainable social services* White Paper made the point: 'Knowing who and where to go to for help is necessary in any system' (Welsh Assembly Government, 2011: 22).

Quality

A further aim of care policy in all four nations is to assure the quality of care provided. What constitutes a high-quality care system is often constitutive of the other principles discussed in this chapter – that is, it is one that enhances wellbeing, promotes fairness and protects rights. In many of the documents there is an implicit logic that people who require support are experts on their own lives, such that giving people choice and control over their support improves quality (as well as having a rights-based rationale). As the *From vision to action* report in Wales puts it, 'More personalised services promote better outcomes, greater user satisfaction and can often be more resource efficient' (Independent Commission on Social Services in Wales, 2010: 7).

The 2021 Feeley Report in Scotland notes the proliferation of standards and quality definitions in social care, and proposes reducing these down to six quality criteria: accessible; personalised; integrated; preventative; respectful; and safe (Feeley, 2021). The Welsh White Paper from the same year gives a somewhat different emphasis: 'The quality of people's experience of care and support is impacted by the behaviour of those providing services, such as warmth, kindness, empathy, respect, genuineness and love' (Welsh Government, 2021b). As discussed earlier in the chapter, such differences of emphasis depend in part on the understanding of what care is: an expansive relational account versus the narrower, more functional definition.

Each nation has a formal and standardised inspection regime. In England, the Care Quality Commission (CQC) inspects social care services (as well as health), and has recently acquired a new power to inspect local authority commissioning of care services, set out in the *People at the heart of care* White Paper (DHSC, 2021b). Regulation is undertaken by the Care Inspectorate Scotland and the Care Inspectorate Wales, and in Northern Ireland by the Regulation and Quality Improvement Authority (which also regulates health services). Each adopts quality measures based in part on functional aspects of care and translated into outcome measures (discussed in Chapter 5). Unlike England, Wales does not issue a quality rating for care providers. In all four nations, there has been a shift to measuring quality using subjective measures such as 'I' statements. This means, for example, defining accessibility in terms of: 'I get the support I have a right to receive when and how I need it' (Feeley, 2021: 5). In Wales the guidance accompanying the Social Services and Well-being (Wales) Act 2014 notes that, 'The Quality Standards are intended to be aspirational, and not a check list to be met. They are designed to challenge local authorities, to raise ambition and to encourage innovation' (Welsh Government, 2019: 5). Regulatory bodies are often required to assess quality and keep people safe without restricting the positive risk-taking necessitated by choice and control, a potential tension that we return to later in the book.

Sustainability – for all?

Many of the documents make clear that the ultimate goal of social care policy is sustainability. Through enhancing wellbeing, achieving fairness in costs and benefits (and in working conditions), protecting rights and assuring quality it is possible to achieve a care system that moves from perpetual crisis into sustainability. This can be 'whole system' sustainability, as the *Integration and innovation* White Paper envisages (DHSC, 2021a), or apply to specific parts such as sustainability of the market (Care Act 2014), sustainable use of NHS resources (Welsh Government, 2021b) or ecological sustainability to protect future generations (as in the Well-being of Future Generations Act in Wales).

Sustainable care arrangements are a matter of social justice – their absence intensifies the inequalities of care (Tronto, 2013). They have to be sustainable for all parties in the care system – crucially, people using services, carers and paid care workers (Keating et al, 2021). Often the interests of these groups will pull in the same direction. Indeed, often social care will be constituted by the relationships between them: 'no judgement about whether care is good can be accomplished from a singular perspective, not that of caregivers or care receivers' (Tronto, 2013: 40). It is also important to note that these categories themselves are not fixed: 'The world is not divided into carers and cared-for as separate and permanent classes' (Noddings, 2013: 21). Kirkegaard and Andersen (2018) and Bartels (2013) make the point that categories such as 'cared for' and 'carer' only come into being through the social encounter, and are therefore relational categories.

Relational accounts imply that what is good for one party is good for another. What is left unsaid here (and also in the policy documents) is whether sustainability can be achieved for all of these groups at the same time, or whether trade-offs are required. For example, it may not be possible to reconcile rights with some understandings of fairness. As discussed earlier, making the system fairer might entail reducing the rights of people to pass on their assets to their children. Alternatively, equalising the care spend across the generations may involve reducing the allocations made to working-age adults so that more is spent on older people to bring it up to parity. Much of the care literature highlights reciprocity as a principle underpinning care (Bulmer, 1987; Mansell and Beadle-Brown, 2004) and an alternative to the 'gift' model (Fox, 2018: 82), but Kittay critiques the kind of reciprocity that underpins social contract theory and instead advocates 'nested dependency' (Kittay, 2013). Some people receiving care resist securing a more professionalised care workforce because of the way it limits their choice and control (see the debate in Gerlich and Farquharson, 2020). This theme of trade-offs is discussed in Chapters 4 and 5 in relation to the specific mechanisms that are being used to move the care system towards the goals of enhancing wellbeing and sustainability.

Conclusion

In this chapter we have looked at how policy documents in the four nations have framed social care, focusing on the extent of discursive convergence and divergence. Within the policy documents we found a high degree of convergence across the four nations on what the problems of social care are, and on the values that should underpin a new approach. There appear to be few differences in what each nation considers good social care to be. Some documents focused more on functional accounts of care, whereas others were more expansively focused on care as a route to wellbeing. However, the importance of wellbeing was growing in all four nations over time. All four were pursuing prevention and advocating a more asset-based approach. In all four nations, fairness was an important framing for social care. In Scotland, Wales and Northern Ireland, this was accompanied by rights, whereas in England, there was less emphasis on rights, particularly after New Labour left office in 2010.

In later chapters of the book we look at 'decisional', 'practice' and 'outcome' convergence, aspects that are clearly related to the discursive framing discussed here. Setting out what social care *is* and what it is *for* are important precursors to deciding how social care should be reformed. One Health and Social Care Board interviewee in Northern Ireland was sceptical about how far this had been done in relation to care funding:

'I don't think we know what we ultimately want the social care service to do. Therefore, if we don't know what it's to do, I don't think we know who should pay for it. Should the state pay for it, or should the individual pay for it, from their resources? Because unless we answer the question, "What's it for?", I don't think you can answer, "Who pays the buck?" I don't think we have had that debate in Northern Ireland.'

Even in the three other nations, where legislation has set out a path for the state's role in social care, it is recognised that implementing change brings its own difficulties. This Welsh interviewee from local government explained:

'I've not met anyone who's disagreed with the direction and the ambitions of the Social Services and Well-being Act. The idea of putting the citizen at the centre, working co-productively, focus on wellbeing, absolutely the right direction. Actually, implementing it is a whole other challenge, and it's a change of culture, its resources.'

We move in later chapters to consider issues of implementation and outcomes, as well as exploring differential resources between the four nations. In the next chapter, we look at the extent to which demographic changes are increasing demand for care and support. Using the care diamond framework, we consider the respective contributions made by the family, state, market and community to the 'quantum of care', and what it means to say that each of these is 'in crisis'. We then go on, in Chapter 4, to look at the policy changes that have been made, which we characterise as the 'mechanisms' of change.

3

What is in crisis? The context of care policy in the four nations

In Chapter 2 we considered the extent of discursive convergence between the four nations as part of setting the context for the policy analysis presented in this book. We noted the similarities in the four nations in their focus on wellbeing, fairness, rights, quality and sustainability. In this chapter we look at the characteristics of the four nations that are 'care-relevant', to provide further context and draw out the contextual divergences that sit alongside discursive convergence. We use Razavi's (2007) 'care diamond' as a heuristic device that identifies four 'supply-side' components of care – family, state, market and community – in order to explore the contribution that each makes in the four nations. We explore different aspects of care, for example, levels of unpaid care and the degree of marketisation. Alongside these, we also consider the legitimacy of different points of the diamond, such as the contested role of state and market, or the appropriate roles for family and community. We look at how the values identified in the previous chapter – wellbeing, fairness, rights, quality and sustainability – give emphasis to particular ways of arranging care.

One of the clear themes from Chapters 1 and 2 is that adult social care in the four nations has been under strain for the last two decades. All the documents we analysed converged on a view that *something must be done*. As set out in Chapter 1, this has gone from a sense of 'slow collapse' to one of 'urgent crisis'. We structure this chapter around five 'crisis claims', namely, that there is:

- a crisis of *demand*, created by population ageing;
- a crisis of *family*, created by changing family structures and/or overloading of unpaid carers;
- a crisis of *the state*, with historic failings exacerbated by underfunding and inadequate policy;
- a crisis of *the market*, with unstable or inadequate provision due to underfunding and/or profit extraction;
- a crisis of *community*, with not-for-profit providers struggling to stay afloat and broader community resources undervalued.

Key descriptive indicators and our own interview data provide evidence of fragility in all of these domains, which we discuss in this chapter. However, we also recognise that claims of crisis invoke competing normative views about what is meant by care, who should provide care, and under what conditions. Some will expect families to play the largest role, whereas others may prioritise the state or the market. The language of crisis can be a route to fatalism rather than reform (O'Neil et al, 2017; Crowther, 2018). We nevertheless see it as an important way to explore the different facets of strain in the four nations' care systems.

The care diamond

A useful model to aid comparative analysis is the 'care diamond', which Razavi (2007) developed from the broader concept of a 'welfare diamond' (Jenson and Saint-Martin, 2003; Jenson, 2015). Razavi explains the concept as follows: 'The institutions involved in the provision of care may be conceptualized in a stylized fashion as a care diamond, to include the family/household, markets, the public sector and the not-for-profit sector (including voluntary and community provision)' (Razavi, 2007: 66).

The care diamond can be seen as providing different points towards which care can tip, in the way a ball might move around in an old bagatelle game. Crisis claims are often about whether one point in the diamond is doing too much or not enough relative to another. However, it is important to stress that there is not a fixed quantum of care, such that when there is more state involvement, there is necessarily less of a contribution from families or market. Different aspects can be additive rather than substitutive: for example, family care may increase at the same time as more state activity (Lemmon, 2020). The state works through other institutions as well as within its own domain (Razavi and Staab, 2012: 1111), and leads on system design as well as provision. Writing about the broader concept of a welfare diamond, Jenson and Saint-Martin (2003: 81) argue, 'That which the state does not take on is left to markets, families or communities'. While this may be true in relation to some aspects of the welfare state – health, education and employment support – it seems a misrepresentation of the balance in care, given the dominant and continuing role for families. Rather than being a residual category, for when the state cannot provide support, families are likely to be a foundational source of care, albeit one that requires support from other points of the diamond. We also note that countries may shift the balance between different points of the diamond over time, rather than pursue a consistent pattern from more 'traditional' forms of care (families, community) to more 'modern' (state, market) (Razavi, 2007).

What constitutes 'the 'crisis'?

There are several aspects of contemporary society that are deployed when talking about crisis, which we look at here in turn: the crisis of demand, of family, of the state, of the market, and of community. We use these as lenses through which to consider the context of care in the four nations.

The 'crisis of demand'

The number and profile of those who need care and of those who provide care has changed, impacting the quantity and quality of caring relationships. The crisis is often framed as a consequence of an 'ageing society' (Burke, 2021). This perception is driven by downward trends in fertility and mortality in the post-war era in 'developed' nations, due to public health improvements alongside social changes associated with 'modernity' or 'post-modernity' (Archer, 2012). This is not only seen as a crisis of now, but also of the future, given predictions of rising numbers of older people (Keating et al, 2021). Future trends are often presented in the bleakest terms: for example, predictions of numbers of people with dementia in the future are described as a 'rapidly growing threat' (Gregory, 2022).

There is debate about the future impact that ageing will have on the proportion of people who will need care and support (Fine, 2007: 126–37). Healthier ageing has softened (or delayed) the relationship between these, and some argue that care needs will be compressed into the final years of life, whatever the lifespan may be. There is particular resistance to the framing of increased longevity in negative terms, as a 'timebomb' or 'threat'. As New Labour's care White Paper put it: 'we must also stop seeing an ageing society as a burden, and see instead the positive contribution that everyone can make to society and their community, whatever their age' (HM Government, 2010: 88). There is a broad consensus, however, that ageing is related to growing rates of disability, as people age with multiple long-term conditions (Wittenberg, 2016). Reed et al (2021: 8) note that over a quarter of adults have more than one long-term health condition, and that this share is expected to double between 2015 and 2035. Trends for men and women are also projected to diverge; men are predicted to experience a higher level of compression of dependency than women (Kingston et al, 2018).

Their demographic profiles mean that this will be experienced differently in the four nations. Figure 3.1 shows people over 65 as a percentage of the total population. Wales has the highest proportion of people over 65, and Northern Ireland has the lowest. With regard to disability, Wales again has the highest rates, with the lowest levels in England and Northern Ireland, as shown in Figure 3.2

The implications of population ageing and rising rates of disability in terms of demand for specific care services remain unclear. As indicated in Chapter 2, all four nations are committed to enabling people to live in their own homes for as long as possible. This means residential care placements are increasingly reserved for those with the highest levels of acuity, and often

Figure 3.1: The percentage of the population over 65 in the four nations, 1990–2020

Source: ONS (2021a), derived from Office for National Statistics, National Records of Scotland, Northern Ireland Statistics and Research Agency – population estimates

Figure 3.2: Disability prevalence in the four nations, 2010–19

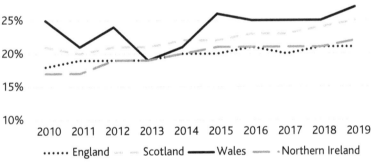

Source: derived from the Family Resources Survey 2010–2019. The survey defines a person as having a disability if they have a physical or mental impairment that has 'substantial' and 'long term' negative effects on their ability to do normal daily activities, https://www.gov.uk/government/statistics/family-resources-survey-financial-year-201819.

used only in the last year of life, with implications for what kind of provision is needed (Gori et al, 2016).

Analysis by the Institute for Government of the balance of public spending on residential and home care shows that Wales spent proportionately more than the other three nations on residential care in the 2000–20 period. By the end of the period it was still shifting spending towards residential care, which Atkins et al (2021) attribute to the higher means test for residential care in Wales, suggesting that it has led to more state-funded residents in care homes. There is no comparable Northern Ireland data, and methodological changes over time in England inhibit clear comparison, but it seems that in England and Scotland over time the balance of spending has been tilting away from residential care towards home care (Atkins et al, 2021: 43).

Some interviewees emphasised the changing nature of demand for residential services in social care, with the profile of care home residents becoming older and more frail: "In 1990, just going into a care home, there were individuals in there, convalesce is probably too strong a word, but you know, people who were very much able. ... The support that's being provided in care homes is very different to what it was 20 years ago" (Wales, care commissioner).

Another commented that this was leading to changes in the design of care homes:

'When I go to care homes that were built in the 70s and early 80s, the thing that hits you is the size of the car park. And that's because about 10 per cent of people who went into those care homes had their own cars and were able to engage in going into town and meeting friends and all that. If you compare that with a population of social care, particularly older people's services now, they're really high-end intervention points.' (England, national provider representative)

This shifting pattern in residential care is complemented by changing patterns in home care services. Research by the Institute for Government notes:

In all four countries, hours have been increasingly concentrated on fewer people, as more care intensive clients have been accommodated at home, rather than in care homes. The number of people receiving home care has fallen in both Scotland and England since 2010, but the number of clients receiving intensive home care has increased. (Atkins et al, 2021: 49)

Higher levels of acuity in home care have implications for the services provided. As one interviewee put it: "[When I started] ... social care ... it was fire lighting, shopping. ... [Now] I manage domiciliary care service, a lot of those healthcare tasks, for example, like catheter care, personal care, stoma care, medications, that has all moved over to what's known as the social care world" (Northern Ireland, local care provider).

As well as constituting a change in demand, such shifts have implications for the skills and professional identity of social care staff, a point we return to in Chapters 4 and 5. The intensity of work has also changed, now that support is mostly provided to people with 'critical' or 'substantial' rather than 'moderate' or 'mild' needs (Health and Social Care and Housing, Communities and Local Government Committees, 2018). One interviewee noted:

'When the local authority also commissioned moderate needs, it was a different job, because a half-decent employer would put some moderate needs on every round. So there was somewhere that you went where you could have a conversation, have an interaction and you could make a positive difference and it was just different. It was almost like the downtime. That's not there anymore and I don't think, as a system, we recognise that actually what we're asking people to do is a health care assistant's job.' (England, local provider)

The issues created by rising demand and the changing patterns of provision link to the discussion of fairness in Chapter 2. This relates to who should bear the costs of increasing care provision – the balance between individuals and the state, as well as between generations – and how far people are looking after their own health. It also creates questions about who should provide care to meet the rising demand. Growing rates of disability and age-related frailty are perceived as a looming crisis in part because the 'supply-side' of care is seen as insufficient. This has a number of components, which, following Razavi (2007), we identify as family, state, market and community, albeit recognising the overlaps and interdependencies between them.

The 'crisis' of family

Discussion of the crisis of family tends to focus on one of the following: first, family changes that have eroded traditional patterns of informal care provision, raising concerns for some that families are doing *too little*; and second, the continued and unsustainable pressures on unpaid (usually family) carers, generating concerns that families are doing *too much*. Looking at the former, the UK has experienced a shift in the structure of families and their ability to provide care for family members. Drivers for this include internal (within-country) and international migration, and the reduction in multi-generational family relationships due to changes in fertility, dubbed the 'beanpole family' by sociologists (Bengtson and Martin, 2001; Greenhalgh, 2002).

Internal and international migration has increased, although less so for older people (ONS, 2015). The 2011 Census for England and Wales showed that 3.6 per cent of older people in England and Wales moved house during 2011, compared to 14 per cent of under-65s (ONS, 2016). When younger people move away from older family members, more caring has to be done at a distance (White et al, 2020). Another change in family structure, driven by increased longevity and lower fertility, is that more families have multiple generations, but there are fewer family members per generation: hence 'beanpole'. In addition, more couples have no children and on average people have fewer 'vertical' kin: no surviving parents or grandparents, or no viable relationship with those kin (Berrington, 2017). The combination of multi-location and geographically dispersed family structures with fewer members makes intergenerational interaction rarer than it would have been in the past. This trend has an obvious impact on the availability of family care (Bell and Rutherford, 2013).

The rise in female workforce participation over the last 50 years has also affected the availability of care within the family (Heitmueller, 2007; Ferrant et al, 2014). Only 57 per cent of women of aged 25–54 were in paid employment in 1975, but by 2017 this figure was 78 per cent (Roantree and Vira, 2018). This change has reshaped the division of labour outside of formal employment. Caring labour once performed in the family may be organised through external means: the state, the market and in communities by neighbours and friends, although many women continue to limit their working hours in order to provide care (Moussa, 2019). Our focus is on the care of disabled people and frail older people rather than children, although, of course, changes in female workforce participation and gendered roles in the family have profoundly affected childcare as well.

Whether family care is considered to be 'in crisis' is both subjective and normative, depending on what one considers the role of families to be. The extent to which this is experienced differently in the four nations can be looked at from a range of perspectives. Survey data on the proportion of people who say 'you can rely on family' shows that people in Northern Ireland and in Scotland are a little more likely than those in England and Wales to say you 'can rely on family a lot', as shown in Table 3.1. This is not specific to care, although care is likely to be encompassed within this.

In the interviews, participants from Northern Ireland and Wales were most likely to invoke the importance of familial responsibilities. Several interviewees in Northern Ireland made points like the following interviewee:

'Families very unquestionably step up and support, particularly older people, but also children with learning disability who mature into adulthood. It's families and there are discussions in families. "Mum and dad aren't here. Who is going to look after you? Will it be this sister or that brother?" Those kind of family decisions are made.' (Northern Ireland, social worker)

Interviewees felt that traditional care values persisted in relation to gender roles, multi-generational care and the lack of geographical family dispersion within Northern Ireland:

'The traditional values … are still held here in Northern Ireland, that it is a woman's role to stay at home and to look after the house and the family. As a daughter or a wife it's my job, it's my duty then to give up my work and look after them. I think here we're not as far down the road as England, maybe Scotland and Wales would be, in that we would still have family settlements within a particular area.' (Northern Ireland, carers' organisation)

Table 3.1: Percentage of people saying they can rely on family in the four nations

Country of residence	% not at all	% a little	% somewhat	% a lot
England	5.4	13.2	25.0	56.3
Wales	5.1	13.7	23.7	57.9
Scotland	4.8	11.5	24.6	59.1
Northern Ireland	3.4	11.1	24.9	60.7

Source: University of Essex, Institute for Social and Economic Research (2021). Understanding Society: Waves 1–11, 2009–20 and Harmonised BHPS: Waves 1–18, 1991–2009 [data collection], 16th edn. UK Data Service, SN: 6614, http://doi.org/10.5255/UKDA-SN-6614-16.
Question asked: 'Thinking about your immediate family, how much can you rely on them if you have a serious problem?' (www.understandingsociety.ac.uk/documentation/mainstage/dataset-documentation/variable/scrrely)

Family responsibility for care was thought to be more enduring in Northern Ireland than elsewhere in the UK: "I mean, I think as compared to the rest of the UK, Northern Ireland still has a strong family backbone, I mean it does. I think more than anywhere else probably, Northern Ireland families, nieces, nephews, even distant relatives are involved in giving them help and support" (Northern Ireland, third sector).

A similar perception of being different from other parts of the UK was evident in some of the Welsh interviews, although with a sense that this might be changing:

'I do think there's something in Wales about being very close-knit communities. I think that there's an expectation perhaps in Wales, maybe more than other areas of the UK, that the expectation is that the family will look after you; the community will look after you. … I think that role is slowly changing in that less people of working age are around during the day than what they were in the 1980s.' (Wales, carers' organisation)

People tend to move out of urban areas in the 10 years before and after retirement (Future Care Capital, 2018: 11), and this can change the dynamic if people are ageing away from family. One Welsh social worker noted:

'There's more and more people moving in who have maybe had holiday homes here over the years and come here to retire. They manage okay while there's a couple, a husband and wife living together. But if something happens to one of them, then they're left alone. And they don't have that social network around them, because they've lived together and sustained themselves greatly when there were two of them. But when they're left alone, they then have difficulties because their extended family maybe live far away, in England possibly.'

While these points were particularly raised by Welsh and Northern Irish interviewees, unpaid care (predominantly by family members; see Brown, 2021) continues to be the main source of care in all four nations. Office for National Statistics (ONS) data show the share of people providing unpaid care in the four nations. Slightly higher levels are found in Wales and Northern Ireland, as shown in Figure 3.3.

These figures show the proportion of carers at any one time. Analysis based on longitudinal studies (Zhang and Bennett, 2019) shows that across the UK over a seventeen-year period, two-thirds of adults have been a carer, with women particularly likely to be providing intense rates of care (over 50 hours a week). By the age of 46, half of women had been a carer. Half of men had been a carer by the age of 57. Table 3.2 breaks this down by the four nations, with caring highest in Wales (which also has the oldest population).

Where the state does not provide support and people have 'unmet needs' in relation to the Activities of Daily Living (such as washing, dressing and eating) the pressures on carers are particularly acute. Data on unmet needs are not available across the four nations, but we know that in all four there are concerns that people are not receiving formal help where they struggle with Activities of Daily Living (Age UK, 2019). Vlachantoni (2019) used figures from the English Longitudinal Study of Ageing (ELSA), showing that about 55 per cent of older individuals with a difficulty in Activities of Daily Living reported not receiving any support.

Figure 3.3: Percentage of the population providing unpaid care in the four nations

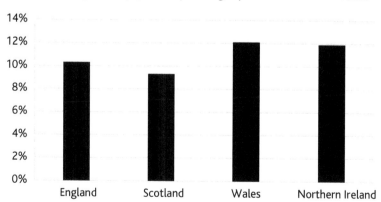

Source: Atkins et al (2021: 43), Institute for Government analysis of 2011 Census

Table 3.2: Percentage of adults who were carers in the four nations, 1991–2018

Nation	All carers	Women	Men
England	63	69	58
Scotland	65	70	60
Northern Ireland	66	69	62
Wales	70	73	66

Source: Zhang and Bennett (2019: 11), data from the British Household Panel Survey and Understanding Society

The prevalence of unpaid care generates concerns about whether families are doing too much. Some interviewees felt that too many carers do not seek support, and that some end up 'burning out': "The challenge for us, then, is in relation to carer burnout because there are lots and lots of hidden carers. Family members delivering this care, supporting the individual. They actually only come into our system at the point of crisis and breakdown" (Northern Ireland, Health and Social Care Board).

A Welsh politician drew attention to the differential support for parents of young children compared to those who care for older and disabled relatives and friends: "We're much better at supporting people with maternity and paternity leave, but I really don't think we do enough for people who are caring" (Wales, Assembly Member).

A local care commissioner in Wales made a similar point when discussing the seeming disparity between support for older and disabled people and for children:

'It seems absolutely right that society as a whole pays for those three hours of nursery because it's right that the parents go back to work, etc. But yet, somehow, when it comes to care for people who are disabled and who are older, there's some sort of issue. I think there must somehow be some discrimination or unconscious bias going on in how society's thinking about that: a 55-year-old leaving work to look after her 85-year-old mum, that's fine; [but] we don't want to lose a 25-year-old from the workforce.'

There is evidence that COVID-19 has further intensified pressures on carers; a survey conducted in autumn 2020 found that eight out of ten carers had increased their caring during the early months of the pandemic (Carers UK, 2020). Another report notes:

It has been estimated that unpaid carers have saved the UK £530 million of care costs per day during the pandemic. ... [T]here have been 4.5 million new carers since the start of the pandemic. ... Compared to men, women were more likely to provide care and were more likely to provide more hours of care. One in three women were providing some form of care (35%) and women accounted for 68% of those providing 20+ hours of care per week. ... Bangladeshi, Caribbean, Indian and Pakistani groups had the highest proportion of respondents providing 20+ hours of care per week. (Alarilla et al, 2021)

These COVID-19 pressures further highlight the importance of carers to social care, and also the ways that they are patterned by gender and ethnicity. Cheshire-Allen and Calder draw on interviews with carers in Wales to record the damaging impact of the pandemic on the subjective, material and relational aspects of carer wellbeing: 'Inequalities have been exacerbated because of the withdrawal of support services, leaving carers alone and without support, in many instances, putting themselves and the person cared for at increased risk of negative wellbeing states' (Cheshire-Allen et al, 2022: 61). As one interviewee from a carers' organisation in Wales put it, in a COVID-19 context: "At the moment there are no breaks. You know, for the past year, there have been no breaks for carers."

Pressures on unpaid carers across all four nations are often immense. They relate strongly to the issue of sustainability, discussed in Chapter 2, and its link to social justice. Supporting families to provide care in ways that do not entrench or worsen inequalities is a key element of ensuring that the care sector remains sustainable. In Chapter 4 we discuss the policy approaches in each nation to provide more effective support to unpaid carers.

The 'crisis' of the state

As Razavi (2007: 20) points out, the state occupies a distinctive position in welfare arrangements: '[It] is not just a provider of welfare, but also a significant decision maker about the responsibilities to be assumed by [others].' As in the previous section, we can differentiate between concerns that the state is doing *too much* and that it is doing *too little*. In the post-war era, the UK-wide National Assistance Act 1948 widened the role of the state in relation to care, creating a safety net for people who, through circumstances such as old age or disability, could not pay into national insurance. Local authorities were given a legal duty to provide suitable accommodation for those for whom support was not available elsewhere, and it was this legislation that underpinned care for older people, people with learning and physical disabilities, and people in need of ongoing mental health services (beyond NHS crisis care). The Act was implemented by local government, marking a clear separation from the centrally managed NHS.

Despite hopes that the National Assistance Act would end the stigma of the Poor Law, the post-war settlement retained intrusive means testing, inadequate financial support and forced institutionalisation. In all four parts of the UK, incarceration was the fate of some disabled people and people with mental health problems, often in asylums converted from workhouses or poor law hospitals. These institutions – large, isolated, alienating – came to be synonymous with the problem of the state doing *too much*. The de-institutionalisation movement from the late 1960s was prompted by abuse scandals in the media and activism by people living in institutions, making demands for independent living (Morris, 1993). Professional authority was challenged by radical user- and family-led initiatives such as 'normalisation', person-centred planning and direct payments (Zarb and Nadash, 1994; Cambridge and Carnaby, 2005).

The discussion in Chapter 2 about the goals of adult social care highlighted the centrality of person-centred approaches in contemporary care policy – and the break with the more paternalistic narratives of the past. Nonetheless the transition from institutional provision has been repeatedly acknowledged as being too slow (DH, 2012) and remains incomplete (Knapp et al, 2021). Scandals in closed institutional settings continue, often exposed by undercover journalists rather than regulatory inspection (Triggle, 2019). The state's role continues to be contested in relation to professional power and deprivation of liberty (Fox, 2018; Series, 2019b).

The National Assistance Act was supplemented by additional legislation in relation to older and disabled people in the 1960s and 1970s. However, sufficient resources were not provided to match growing levels of need, particularly when the NHS began to divest itself of long-stay geriatric wards from the 1980s (Hudson, 2021). The period from 1990 marked a period of state withdrawal, as provision of care was increasingly outsourced to the private and not-for-profit sectors, especially after the NHS and Community Care Act 1990. The Act shifted social care funding into a block allocation to local authorities, which, as Glasby (2007) notes, made local rather than central government responsible for containing the ballooning costs of care. Social workers became care managers, responsible for assessing need and arranging care rather than directly delivering it (Hudson, 2021). This was the beginning of privately provided home care for people funded by their local authority, and the reversal of 50 years of expansion in residential provision of care (Knapp et al, 2001). It required local authorities to commission 85 per cent of services from external providers. This was pursued most assiduously in England, a difference we discuss in more detail in the 'market' section later in this chapter.

Gray and Birrell (2013) note that the White Paper preceding the 1990 Act was unusual in including separate sections for Scotland and Wales, reflecting their different care arrangements (Northern Ireland had its own policy paper). The chapter on Scotland acknowledged that local authorities in Scotland were more likely to remain providers of care than their English counterparts, although they were to be encouraged to pursue outsourcing as a direction of travel (Gray and Birrell, 2013). The chapter on Wales noted its relatively underdeveloped mental health services and services for disabled people (Gray and Birrell, 2013: 16). Northern Ireland's equivalent paper – *People first: Community care in Northern Ireland in the 1990s* (Department of Health and Social Services, 1990) – confirmed the ongoing integration of health and care services, which has been a distinctive feature of Northern Ireland since the 1970s. Overall in Northern Ireland, there was 'no prescribed purchaser-provider divide and less independent sector involvement in domiciliary, day and respite care' (Gray and Birrell, 2013: 17).

In England, Scotland and Wales, the 1990 Act also ended social security benefits as a source of funding for residential care, and introduced means testing and charging for care (Gray and Birrell, 2013). It increased the power of local government over social care, but limited the resources available (Hudson, 2021). There was hope that the growth of a private home care market and the scaling back of state-provided residential care would reduce the costs of care, and enable families to play a larger role (Gray and Birrell, 2013). The state's role became that of commissioning and regulating care with a much reduced role in directly providing it. Following the Act, as new care provision developed, this came to mean commissioning day centres, supported living and home adaptations as well as residential and home care (Gray and Birrell, 2013). This was followed by the development of more respite provision, intermediate care, sheltered housing and housing with support (Knapp et al, 2001). Reablement followed, as a separate, short-term and often in-house service (Beresford et al, 2019).

State spending on these various models of care increased in the first decade of the 21st century, under a New Labour government committed to increased investment in public services (Gray and Birrell, 2013). Since 2010, however, the retrenchment of spending has been a key aspect of social care policy and practice, particularly in England. During the period of 'austerity', the percentage change of spending in adult social care was radically different in the four nations; Northern Ireland and Scotland actually increased their expenditure, as discussed in Chapter 1 (see Table 1.1). Data for 2017–18 show that England's public expenditure was the least generous, spending on average £303 per head (Oung et al, 2020) (see Figure 3.4). Scottish spending per head was £428 (Oung et al, 2020). The Scottish Government abolished charges for 'personal care' for over-65s in 2002 and in 2019 for disabled people of working age. Northern Ireland was the most generous system according to per head spending (£461 per head) (Oung et al, 2020) and has the largest proportion of state support for older and disabled people (Atkins et al, 2021). The Northern Irish system provides personal care at home free at the point of access (Oung et al, 2020). Wales spent £396 per head, some way above England, but still less generous than Scotland or Northern Ireland.

Figure 3.4: Total public expenditure on social care, 2017/18, per head

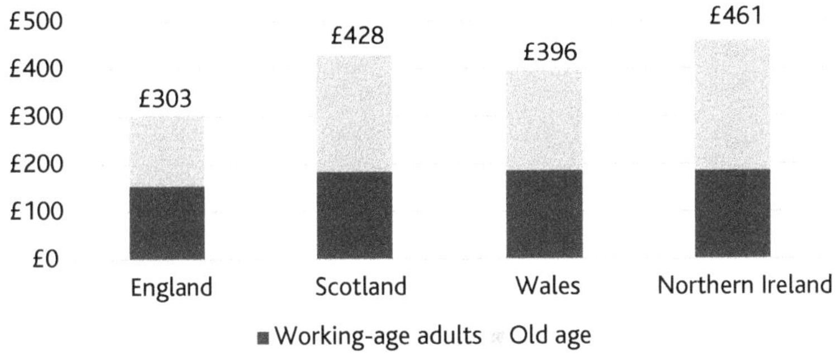

■ Working-age adults ░ Old age

Source: Oung et al (2020). Nuffield Trust analysis of HM Treasury Public Expenditure Statistical Analyses 2019. Adult social care expenditure is defined as personal social services spending on sickness and disability and personal social services spending on old age.

Longitudinal data shows state spending has changed over time in the four nations, highlighting again England's low spend in this area, as indicated in Figure 3.5.

Figure 3.6 gives the proportion of the total population in each of the four nations receiving funding from the state for residential or nursing home places. It affirms the higher spending of Northern Ireland on state support, particularly given that it has a younger population than other parts of the UK.

The administration of state welfare benefits is an important area of support for disabled and older adults in the UK. For most of the devolution period, this has remained the responsibility of the UK-wide Department for Work and Pensions (DWP). However, following the Scotland Act 2016, administration of some benefits, including Personal Independence Payment, Attendance Allowance and Carer's Allowance were devolved to the Scottish Government. Attendance Allowance and Personal Independence Payment are not means-tested benefits, and may be spent as the beneficiary sees fit. About 2 million people receive one or both of these benefits, far outstripping the numbers receiving adult social care services or support. The DWP provides payments to five times as many older adults living at home as receive adult social care services (Oung et al, 2020). Figure 3.7 shows expenditure on key benefits in each nation. This spending is most generous in Northern Ireland and least generous in England.

Combined figures for average spending per person on people eligible for social care in 2019–20 (combining old age, sickness and disability spending) highlight the overall differences in public expenditure in the four nations (Reed et al, 2021: 11), as indicated in Table 3.3.

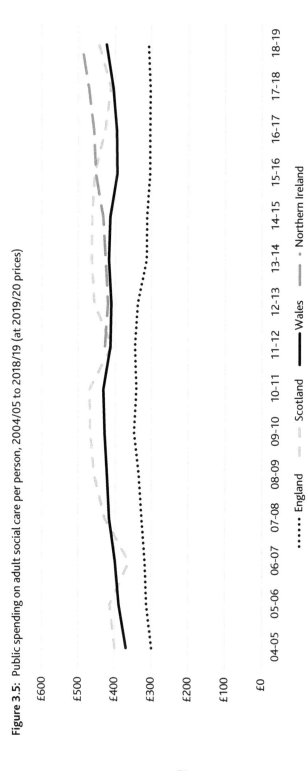

Figure 3.5: Public spending on adult social care per person, 2004/05 to 2018/19 (at 2019/20 prices)

Source: Atkins et al (2021: 41), data from Institute for Government analysis of HM Treasury Public Expenditure Statistical Analyses (PESA) ONS mid-year population estimates

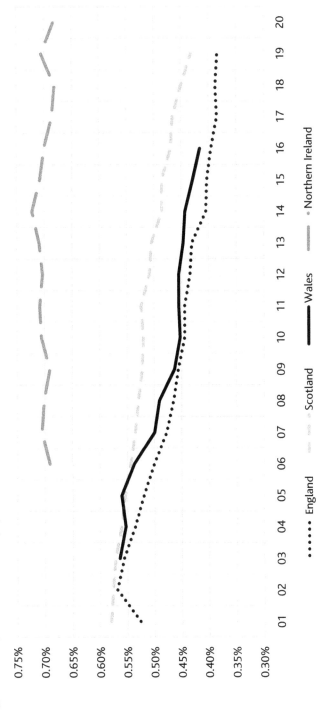

Figure 3.6: Proportion of the overall population who are fully or mainly state-supported care or nursing home residents

Source: Atkins et al (2021: 48), data from Institute for Government analysis of: NHS England, Adult Social Care activity and finance report and community care statistics; Northern Ireland Department of Health statistics on community care for adults and care package in effect; Scottish care home census; StatsWales, adults receiving social care services

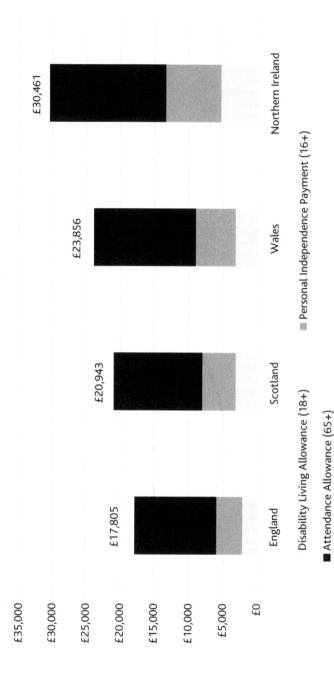

Figure 3.7: Spending on care-relevant benefits in the four nations per 100,000 of the population

Source: Oung et al (2020), data from Nuffield Trust analysis of disability living allowance, personal independence payment and attendance allowance data (2019) as a per 100,000 population rate (age standardised, 2018 population mid-year estimates)

Table 3.3: Spending per person combining old-age and sickness and disability spending in the four nations, 2019/20

Nation	Spend per person, 2019/20 (£)
England	318
Wales	416
Scotland	476
Northern Ireland	521

Source: Reed et al (2021: 11), data from HM Treasury (2016), ONS (2021b), ONS (2022)

The extent to which there is a crisis of the state in terms of 'doing too much' or 'spending too little' depends on what the state is expected to do. Many disability rights campaigners have welcomed the shift away from state-determined care to person-centred support. However, there have also been calls for more state funding and commissioning of care, and for better support for the care workforce. In relation to the values discussed in Chapter 2, the state's role has been to bestow duties and to protect rights, although its broad jurisdiction over the funding, commissioning, delivery and regulation of care means that it also influences quality and fairness, which in turn shape wellbeing and sustainability.

The 'crisis' of the market

A third 'supply side' element of care is the market, by which we mean the provision of care by non-state providers. From the early 1980s a series of legislative changes shifted formal care provision from the state to the market (Gingrich, 2011). As discussed earlier, the NHS and Community Care Act 1990 was a key intervention for market development, given its requirement that 85 per cent of care money be spent outside the state (Knapp et al, 2001). Private residential care had grown during the 1980s due to advantageous social security funding. The 1990 Act withdrew this funding, and a private home care market developed at scale for the first time (Lewis and Glennerster, 1996). Contracting out was also introduced for mental health and learning disability services (Knapp et al, 2001). Local authorities were given 'every incentive to make use of the independent sector' and 'to avoid local authority "empire building"' (Gingrich, 2011: 186).

The term 'care market' is usually used to refer to all non-state providers (for-profit and not-for-profit), recognising that both types of provider play a role (NAO, 2021). There is very little state provision in England, slightly more in Scotland and Wales and considerably more in Northern Ireland through the provision of free personal care at home (much of which is offered by HSCTs) (Gray and Birrell, 2013; Oung et al, 2020).

Table 3.4: Proportion of care homes owned by local authority or HSCT

Nation	Proportion of care homes owned by local authority or HSCT (%)
England	3.2
Scotland	15.3
Wales	13.5
Northern Ireland	9.9

Source: CMA (2017: 35), data from CMA analysis and LaingBuisson

In relation to care homes, the Competition and Markets Authority report (CMA, 2017) on competition in the care home market in the four nations found that the proportion of care homes owned by the local authority or HSCT was the lowest in England and highest in Scotland, as shown in Table 3.4.

In all four nations, the majority of care home provision is by the for-profit sector. In terms of non-state provision, the private sector has 87 per cent of provision compared to 13 per cent for the not-for-profit sector (Laing Buisson, 2022a). In England, the National Audit Office (NAO, 2021: 26) estimates that 14 per cent of care homes are run by the not-for-profit sector (2021). In Scotland, the equivalent figure is 23 per cent (Public Health Scotland, 2021) (comparable figures for Wales and Northern Ireland are not publicly available). Scotland and Wales have particularly emphasised the importance of fostering not-for-profit provision, giving local authorities explicit duties to engage and promote non-profit service providers' (Pearson et al, 2020: 287). In contrast, the Care Act 2014 (covering England) did not privilege any type of provider. A stronger role for the voluntary and community sector than for the market has historically been associated with the left, and Scotland and Wales have had left of centre parties in government for the whole devolved period. Chaney analysed care policy statements in the manifestoes of political parties in all four nations over 20 years, and found that, 'Right-of-Centre Parties' manifestos place greater emphasis on a role for the private sector. In contrast, Left-of-Centre parties place greater emphasis on a delivery role for third sector organisations (and cooperatives and social enterprises)' (Chaney, 2022: 165).

As in the shifting role for the state, the NHS and Community Care Act 1990 was again crucial, as this interviewee from the third sector in Scotland comments:

'The big impact of that [Act] on the third sector was that we became providers and the third sector was then able to put its money where its mouth was and get involved in quite significant and substantial areas of publicly-funded service provision. Whereas previously, it had been very much about kind of innovation, pioneering, showcasing, filling in the gaps, volunteer-led stuff. That Act was where it became the market, in effect.'

This development has led to greater differentiation within the sector between large charitable providers (which may operate in similar ways to private providers) and small, local and more informal bodies, with much in between. Some third sector organisations have retained or newly prioritised their campaigning function, while for others a service provider role has prevailed (Macmillan and Paine, 2021). In delivering care, these providers experience many of the same challenges as for-profit providers in relation to staffing and low fees, adding to the sense that this is a crisis for the broad care system as a whole rather than for segments within it.

In characterising the care market that developed after 1990, Gingrich suggests that, 'The combination of the LAs' [local authorities'] inexperience in contracting and a weakly developed regulatory environment created a logic of control that delegated much power to producers' (2011: 182). She identifies a 'trifurcated market': 'Wealthy users could buy high-quality care at high prices from exclusive private providers, low-income users received public funding for low-quality care, while middle-income users were stuck paying high fees while receiving the same low-quality care as the publicly funded users' (2011: 183–4).

Ten years on, this characterisation is a reasonable summary of patterns of delivery. A substantial market for adult social care services operates independently of state funding. Self-funders pay substantially more for care than is paid on their behalf by people funded by local authorities. The CMA found that the self-funder differential was highest in England, where self-funders paid on average 43 per cent more for care than people funded by local authorities (CMA, 2017: 33). Figures for Scotland and Wales were 38 per cent and 36 per cent respectively. Figures were not available for Northern Ireland.

Accurate statistics on the number of self-funders are difficult to gather as they are not collected, and the ONS is developing work in this area (2020). ONS data on care homes (2020) show big regional differences in rates of self-funding by care home residents. These are highest in the South East (45 per cent) and lowest in the North East (25 per cent) of England. The ONS Index of Multiple Deprivation also shows that 54 per cent of care home places in the most affluent postcodes were occupied by self-funders, compared with 22 per cent in the most deprived postcodes, while analysis by local authority shows the range varied from 78 per cent in the Cotswolds to just 4 per cent in the London Borough of Southwark.

Figure 3.8: Self-funders versus local authority/HSCT-funded in residential and nursing care

Self-funders ■ Local authority/HSCT-funded

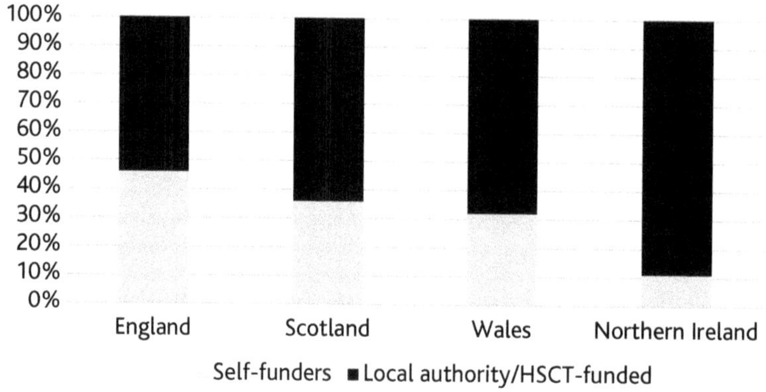

Source: Oung et al (2020), data from Skills for Care and Development reporting of Laing Buisson, 2018

Figure 3.8 shows rates of self-funding compared to state funding in the four nations (Oung et al, 2020). In Scotland, self-funders are estimated to make up 36 per cent of residential and nursing home residents and 25 per cent of recipients of home care or day services. Wales has a slightly lower number of self-funders, at 32 per cent in residential and nursing care and 21 per cent in home care. Northern Ireland stands out as a distinct system, with only 11 per cent of people in residential or nursing care self-funding and 7 per cent of home care users (Oung et al, 2020). Northern Ireland's relatively low numbers of self-funders was discussed by a number of interviewees. It links into free personal care at home as well as lower property prices in the province: "Although people do self-fund some of their care, to a far lesser extent than would be the case in the rest of the UK. Partly property is very cheap here, so even if you own your own property, it's not going to fund your care for that long" (Northern Ireland civil servant).

Interviewees in Scotland noted that free personal care placed a limit on the extent of self-funding: "The vast majority of people in care homes are publicly funded. And even those who are self-funded, are funded partially by the public purse because of free personal care" (Scotland, provider representative).

In areas with lower house prices people 'spend down' to the means test threshold relatively quickly, as this local interviewee in an English county explained:

'Nearly half of the social care market is privately purchased. But because people have low capital values in their houses, they become capital depleters a lot quicker. If you're in an expensive part of the country, okay, you might pay more for your care, but the point is, your house value might be three times more than it is here, so the number of years that you're paying for your care privately is longer.' (England, local councillor)

The prevalence of self-funding in England has affected the nature of the market for social care, and there is a risk in the future of increasing numbers of organisations catering only for private clients (CMA, 2017). Varying levels of affluence even within a locality affect investment decisions. One local care commissioner in England explained: "In the south [of the county], the [provider] view is very much, 'We know what our market is and our market isn't the local authority. The market is the person occupying the bed'."

Further, in more affluent areas, care homes can ask families to 'top up' care fees paid by the state: "When I started, very, very few homes had top-ups, very, very few. You see that across all the county now, but in the south of the county, south west, it's very difficult to get a bed without a top-up" (England, care commissioner).

This can lead to market provision being in the wrong place, as this civil servant in Northern Ireland highlighted: "Where the market wants to build a provision isn't necessarily where the greatest need is, or the greatest funds are. We've too many nursing homes, for example, around former sort of coastal seaside towns, not enough in remote rural areas and particularly not enough in the west."

Within the English local site, providers in more affluent parts of the county had the option of selling their properties: "If you're in [affluent town] and you've got a care home that isn't fit for purpose, you'd sell it, bulldoze it. Build three houses, buy a new one. If you're in [deprived town] with a half-full care home, you're really in a very difficult place" (England, provider).

Self-funding is less prevalent in Scotland than in England, although one interviewee expressed concern about the direction of travel: "But what we are in danger of seeing is Scotland becoming more like the rest of the UK with an increased high-quality provision for those who can pay for it and those who can't pay for it have what's left" (Scotland, provider).

Claims that the market is in crisis (Curry and Oung, 2021) can be countered by the view that, given its share of social care provision and the higher fees it charges self-funders, and the scope to move profits off to parent companies, parts of the for-profit sector are flourishing (Kotecha, 2020). It is clear, however, that many providers are struggling to maintain provision; they report staff shortages and the low fees paid by local authorities as key strains (Curry and Oung, 2021; Needham et al, 2022). Where profit margins are narrow, issues outside of the scope of commissioners or providers can affect the viability of provision. As one local councillor in England put it: "Every week in [this county] there are 64,000 homecare visits. ... If the price of petrol goes up, that's 64,000 visits a week affected by the cost of petrol. We, the council, cannot compensate for that."

Brexit and COVID-19 have disrupted an already insufficient supply of staff across a number of industries, including social care (Alberti et al, 2021; Holmes, 2021; Turnpenny and Hussein, 2022). Cross-subsidisation by self-funders is a key element of market sustainability (CMA, 2017: 13), and has equity implications; in England, it is likely to be partially phased out if proposals regarding a care cap are implemented (DHSC, 2021b). Scotland has had a National Care Home Contract since 2006. This sets a standard local authority fee rate for care homes, although viability of the market remains an issue, as the Feeley Report noted (Feeley, 2021).

The interdependence of different types of provision is a further important aspect of the care market. There is evidence of some 'cycling' between different types of provision, with the state taking over some failing services, one example being an NHS trust in Northumbria delivering social care to speed up hospital discharge (Rennie, 2022).

An interviewee in Wales offered this perspective on related issues there:

'You've had some cases where – domiciliary care is a good example – as people's needs become more complex, as it becomes more difficult to recruit domiciliary care workers, particularly Welsh language [speakers] or rural parts of Wales, those providers have had to hand back packages to the authorities. Authorities have then realised they have to grow more of their own. They can pay more because they're on standard local authority terms and conditions. It's a major factor and the Welsh government now are actively trying to support local government to take more back in.' (Wales, regulatory/oversight body)

In some areas in-house (that is, state) provision has been retained because external providers are considered too unstable or are unwilling to cover certain geographical areas. A Scottish interviewee reported a cycle of market entry followed by failure:

'You get all of these firms popping up every so often. … They might do it for a couple of years and then … the whole bureaucracy of registration and inspection, and complaints … starts to drive these firms, where it becomes uneconomic to continue. And then they fail and then the mainstream have got to pick up the cycle all the time, of firms setting up and then failing.' (Scotland, provider)

Alternatively, in Northern Ireland we heard concerns that pressures on external providers were in part *due* to in-house provision, as a result of the higher wages paid by the HSCTs. Obviously, higher wages are a positive development within social care, but some private providers reported feeling trapped in a downward spiral if the rates at which the state commissions services do not allow for higher wages. As we were told in our local site in Northern Ireland:

'The [HSCT] terms and conditions are very favourable. There's no question of that. They are favourable. I mean the things like sick leave and pensions, all the terms and conditions that would be appealing ... and that, again, is a difficulty for the independent sector because they would often tell us that we are taking their staff. And which is probably in many cases right.' (Northern Ireland, Director of Adult Services)

To address limitations in the market, steps have been taken in all four nations to improve market oversight. To date, however, market management has been poor (Needham et al, 2022). England's *People at the heart of care* White Paper acknowledged the need to improve local authorities' market oversight (DHSC, 2021b). As the DHSC puts it,

[I]n many local authorities, we see low fee rates and cross-subsidy between care home residents paying for themselves, and those who are funded by their local authority. Uncertainty over future funding stifles provider investment and, along with low fee rates, can result in poor workforce conditions, inadequate quality care, market fragility and pose a threat to continuity of care. (DHSC, 2021b: 26)

It proposed new requirements for local authorities, requiring them to work with providers to establish 'fair costs of care' and 'market sustainability' statements (DHSC, 2021b).

The crisis of the market relates in part to how well it delivers care and support, and how far local authorities and trusts are able to support and facilitate this. It also relates to normative claims about the extent to which there should be a for-profit element in the sector. The extent of profit extraction by private equity companies with a stake in care has been a particular concern (Burns et al, 2016). For-profit providers are estimated to make up about 60 per cent of the English care market; most are small and medium enterprises. Large providers constitute just 2 per cent of the organisations in the sector, but employ almost half of the workforce (Skills for Care, 2021).

Some commentators ask if there should be *any* for-profit provision in social care (Turbett, 2021). This is a concern particularly expressed in Scotland and Wales, where the debate about 'rebalancing' delivery towards in-house provision has been more active than in the other nations. A Welsh interviewee noted:

'There is certainly a shift to wanting to provide more provision in-house. I guess, part of the conversation in Wales was started under Mark Drakeford, the current First Minister, his manifesto to become First Minister talked about rebalancing. … And we had a recent White Paper called, "The Rebalancing of Care and Support in Wales". But, I guess, the conversation we're having is more about that: how do we get an optimum, I suppose, mixed market? And how do we spread some of the risk that we've seen in previous years, when the care home providers have gone under. … And certainly, I think there's a number of local authorities who are looking at: how do you in-source? Recognising that that comes with some significant costs as well.' (Wales, local government representative)

This shift to considering in-sourcing is part of a more statist tone to politics in Wales, which we discuss in Chapter 6.

Since 2020, COVID-19 has intensified the pressures facing the market, as some delivery models – such as staff working across multiple locations – were considered an unacceptable infection risk (Curry and Oung, 2021). For some interviewees, the pandemic raised new questions about what type of provision should be on offer, reflecting the sense of greater risk in larger care facilities:

'I think Covid has raised big questions that many professionals in the system already had, and many, actually, families and service users had, "Is an 80-bed nursing home the unit for me, in the last couple of years of my life? Is an 80-bedded, 100-bedded group care setting, a choice I want to make?"' (Northern Ireland, social worker)

The crisis of the market is thus primarily about whether the market is doing *too much*, rather than *too little*. Like the other crises discussed, the market crisis is different in the four nations. England has the most outsourced system; policy concerns here are about how to make the market work better, through market sustainability statements and greater market oversight by local authorities (DSHC, 2021a; NAO, 2021). In Scotland, the Feeley Report called for better market management rather than a reconfiguration of provision, to the disappointment of people hoping that a National Care Service might mean nationalisation of provision (Common Weal Care Reform Group and Smith, 2021). In Northern Ireland, with its low levels of self-funding, the *Power to people* report (Kelly and Kennedy, 2017: 63) found that too much of the market was oriented towards the priorities of the commissioning trust. This monopsony model was thought to limit choice and diversity and put too much emphasis on cost cutting. In Wales concern has focused on how to 'rebalance' provision, considering whether and how in-sourcing or alternative models might be more appropriate.

One interviewee warned against focusing too much on 'in-house' versus 'outsourced' in considering social care provision:

> 'Even if a Labour socialist government really wanted to reinvest in local government and take services back in-house, the sort of change of ownership of those services doesn't change the fact that the vast majority of care is still out there in communities. So figuring out how you support those individuals, so that they don't fall over – because if and when they do, that creates a whole bunch of further challenges for stretched public services – is just the reality of it anyway, I think.' (Wales, civil servant)

The continuing importance of family has already been discussed; in the next section we look at the role of community.

Of the values discussed in the previous chapter, it is quality that is most relevant to the role of the market in care. The extent of market involvement in care depends on how far local authorities and trusts or individuals can purchase good quality care from external providers. In all four nations, there is an assumption that this is possible, although the limits in doing so in the context of cash-constrained services are recognised. Regulation is expected to play a key role in assuring the quality of outsourced care, and the extent to which quality can be maintained through regulation is a point we return to later in the book.

The 'crisis' of community

Of all the 'supply-side' elements, community is perhaps the one where there is most optimism, despite some sense of crisis in relation to its survival at the edges of family, state and market. Community means many different things. It can be a companion with family care, as part of the informal provision of support for people. It can also be a term for the formal services provided through the not-for-profit sector, which includes charities and social enterprises, which are also part of the market of providers as discussed earlier (Razavi, 2007: 21).

Like the family, the various elements of community pre-date state (and market) involvement. Community did not go away during the post-war phase of state expansion or the later expansion of the market. Community as a place and as a set of relationships – loosely defined as a locality in which people live that is distinct from the institutions that the state may provide for them – was a strong theme in the de-institutionalisation phase of social care policy in the UK (Barclay, 1982). The focus was often on the community as a set of affective and reciprocal relations that could replace formal care provision. Reviewing the concept of community in relation to care, Bulmer highlighted two elements: 'the focus upon local social relations within a geographical area and the sense of belonging which is also entailed in the concept' (1987: 29). This 'belonging' element of community is the one often emphasised in contrast to the 'institution'. Fox describes a defining feature of the asylum as 'its abhorrence of love' (2018: 9). In place of the institution was to be the community – defined by Roberto Ungar as 'the political equivalent of love' (quoted in Plant et al, 1980: 203).

The 1968 Seebohm Report included a chapter on the notion of community. It was framed in a holistic sense, as 'a network of reciprocal social relationships, which among other things ensure mutual aid and give those who experience it a sense of wellbeing' (Ministry of Housing and Local Government, 1968). The 1982 Barclay Report into the roles of social workers similarly emphasised the role that community could play in care services. It recognised that 'the bulk of social care in England and Wales is provided, not by the statutory or voluntary social services, but by ordinary people who may be linked into informal caring networks in their communities' (Barclay, 1982: 199). However, in a minority report from the Barclay Commission, Robert Pinker was scathing about the way that the report had mobilised the term 'community': 'It seems that when our policy makers reach an intellectual impasse they cover their embarrassment with the fig leaf of community' (quoted in Barclay, 1982: 241).

Community can be associated with nostalgia for an era of closer ties. One of our interviewees commented on de-industrialisation and the loss of physical infrastructure vital for social support:

'[This] was very much an industrial place. ... They had [the factory] and their kind of social clubs, and bowls clubs and all that. It was a community around the working place. ... And that was part of the ongoing support for people. So they had a natural social context in which to continue post-retirement, because they still had those connections to those industries ... as those big industries have closed, so also those social clubs have met their demise as well.' (Scotland, provider)

In Northern Ireland, interviewees spoke of the continued importance of differences between communities, noting that these fostered close community support within, but not between, them:

'So, you'll have the Catholic community all working very closely together to support everybody in that community, and the Protestant community working very closely there, and the Chinese community are down here. ... And part of the problem is the historical issues here, where you didn't go outside your community. ... That's still is an issue in some cases for people.' (Northern Ireland, carers' organisation)

Another Northern Irish interviewee from the Health and Social Care Board noted:

'You have this really strange dynamic as a context of people thriving and surviving through conflict and trauma. [They're] actually really strong communities, because if you live in a situation where you have been fearful of what would happen to you or your loved ones, or you've been fearful of what will happen to where you do your shopping, or where you do your business, that creates a level of trust and dependency within your own community.'

As in Scotland, with the closure of social clubs, the physical infrastructure is relevant here. This interviewee continued:

'I think some of the fabric − I mean built fabric − of Northern Ireland actually plays into social inclusion. ... You have churches. You have chapels. All of which have halls, which are meeting places for communities. You also have the Loyal Orders, which have halls, particularly in rural areas. You have Orange halls which are meeting places for communities.' (Northern Ireland, Heath and Social Care Board)

Another interviewee commented on another legacy of Northern Ireland's past, in terms of provision of community services:

'I think the other thing that the Troubles did for us, as well, is it meant that we have a lot of duplication of services, which you would not have had in other parts of the UK. So, for instance, in a very small geographical area, you would maybe have a day centre which would have been for, say, learning disability, and one would be for one part of the community, and literally half a mile up the road you'd have another day centre for the other community. And never the twain would meet. So that's something that we're struggling with, because we have duplicated resources. As you know, when people have resources, they don't want to get rid of them. They don't like to let go quickly. And yet we recognise that that need is no longer there; that same need to be separated has changed, thankfully, because of our situation.' (Northern Ireland, social worker)

The Northern Irish experience is a reminder that community isn't always a unifying or inclusive dynamic. In Scotland some similar views were expressed by an interviewee: "Certainly in central Scotland, there are manifestations of community that are frankly not positive. By that I mean things like. ... Orange walks, the marching of people with bands celebrating events in Ireland many hundreds of years ago, and that sort of thing" (Scotland, NHS).

A Welsh Assembly Member commented on continuity and change in a locality, and the dangers of overstating the settled nature of communities:

> It is a traditional Welsh village, and the population speaks Welsh and everyone else has been there since the Middle Ages. ... The local chapel and church and stuff, offers communities lots of voluntary sector stuff centred on those faith communities. ... [But] the same family fractures [are] happening in Wales as everywhere else. [I'm] trying to dissuade you of any sort of romantic notion of tight-knit communities everywhere, back to very romantic ideas of coal-mining valleys and everybody standing together and all this sort of stuff because, well, there's no mines left now anywhere.'

There is a clear sense here of the value of community, and also a wariness of overstating its durability or inclusiveness.

Despite the social and economic changes that have disrupted and challenged community, and its potentially divisive elements, it continues to be important concept within care. The 2010 Conservative-Liberal Democrat coalition government White Paper located social care within 'the Big Society', a concept loosely defined as enhancing community action and voluntarism (Hudson, 2011). It emphasised that communities as well as individuals needed to step up: 'Communities and wider civil society must be set free to run innovative local schemes and build local networks of support. ... Care must again be about reinforcing personal and community resilience, reciprocity and responsibility, to prevent and postpone dependency and promote greater independence and choice' (HM Government, 2010: 4).

The Welsh government similarly set out an expansive view of community in relation to taking a more preventative approach:

> If public services are to meet need, we have to change the terms of the debate. The answer is not a return to the 'prevention role' for social services, but recognition that the whole local authority has a responsibility for leading community services and promoting community wellbeing and that it should galvanize the communities'

own commitment to enable its citizens to play a full part. (Welsh Assembly Government, 2011: 17)

In all four nations, co-production has emerged as an important principle in developing the role of community within public service reform. This approach has been given particular prominence in Scotland and Wales. In Scotland it was a key theme in the 2011 Christie Report, which set out the Scottish Government's broad approach to public services: 'Reforms must aim to empower individuals and communities receiving public services by involving them in the design and delivery of the services they use' (Christie, 2011: 6). Both Cairney et al (2016) and Housden (2014), in drawing out the underlying principles of the 'Scottish approach', highlight the centrality of co-production. Similarly in Wales, co-production has been a central principle of public service reform more broadly (Phillips and Morgan, 2014; Llewellyn et al, 2020), with a distinctive emphasis on mutualism and cooperatives (Hayes et al, 2019). In Northern Ireland, co-production in health and care services was a key theme of the Bengoa Report (Bengoa, 2016), and was included as a commitment across 'the Programme for government, budget and strategies' in the new power-sharing agreement in 2020 (Northen Ireland Executive, 2020: 29). Co-production has also been a principle within care reform in England (Needham and Carr, 2009), but without the broader aspirations found in the other nations to make it a general principle of public services.

Along with the increased prominence of strengths-based approaches and a focus on individual and community assets, discussed in Chapter 2, the emphasis on co-production enhances the role of community in social care. In fact, we might argue that community is less in crisis than the other elements that we have looked at, at least in retaining its normative legitimacy. While there are those who critique over-reliance on the family, the state or the market, most would argue for the centrality of community in providing not only practical support but also as a vital source of wellbeing and sustainability (Unwin, 2018). The extent to which people feel they can rely on community is not evenly distributed. In her report on kindness in public services, Unwin's (2018) research into kindness in communities in the four nations (see Table 3.5) found that Scotland scores highest on all indicators, and England the lowest.

Disaggregated data from this report show that perceptions of kindness are higher among women than men, and among those living in rural, compared with urban, areas (Unwin, 2018). People from higher social grades report experiencing more kindness than those in lower grades, and in England (the only jurisdiction where ethnicity data was available), Black and minority ethnic people were less likely to report experiencing kindness in their neighbourhood.

Table 3.5: Percentage in the four nations strongly agreeing with statements about kindness in communities

% strongly agreeing that ...	England	Northern Ireland	Scotland	Wales
People in this area are kind	36	49	52	44
I have helped someone in this area who needed it in the last 12 months	37	43	64	49
I make time to speak to my neighbours	43	51	59	53
If my home was empty, I could count on someone in this area to keep an eye on it	51	61	72	63
I could turn to someone in this area for practical help if I needed it	41	49	60	54
I could turn to someone in this area for emotional support if I needed it	27	38	47	41
Base size: all	1,253	1,032	1,050	1,011

Source: Unwin (2018: 16), data from Carnegie Trust survey of 5,000 people across the UK in 2018

Conclusion: a differentiated crisis?

In this chapter we have explored the context of care in the four nations, using the lens of crisis to look at key aspects. These include the pattern of state versus non-state provision of care and the levels of state expenditure. We have discussed the extent to which there is a differentiated crisis between the four nations, with important background conditions – such as the extent of self-funding or of market provision – varying between them. The crisis in England is often portrayed as a crisis of public service cuts, exacerbated by COVID-19 and Brexit. The crisis in Scotland and Wales relates more to rising demand. In Northern Ireland, the crisis has partly been one of policy inactivity as political stasis has hampered important legislative changes. Responses to these 'crisis claims' involve different responses from policy makers in each of the four nations. In Scotland, for example, there is more optimism about the role of the state in crisis reversal, whereas in England the government expects the market to drive the move from crisis to sustainability.

In focusing on family, state, market and community, we have compared contextual elements of care provision in the four nations. Using the care diamond approach to distinguish different elements of provision enabled us to consider how these have changed over time. There are historical 'moments' in the 20th century when the diamond 'tipped': towards the state after the Second World War; towards the market from the 1990s;

and towards the community, in the de-institutionalisation phase of the 1970s, and more recently, with co-production and asset-based approaches. These patterns should not be over-stated, however, given the sustained importance of family throughout, and the interdependence of all four types of provision.

Whether families, the market, the state or communities are in crisis (and how these issues should be addressed) is in part a normative claim. Some argue that families should 'step up' and acknowledge their responsibilities (Asthana, 2017; Fraser, 2019). Our interviewees did not share this view; many noted the enduring contribution of families as the main site of care, and the need to better support unpaid carers. Others saw the failings of social care as lying with neoliberalism and the market, and the state as needing to step in and replace marketised care, alongside more community (that is, not-for-profit) provision (Smith, 2021). Many interviewees were pragmatic, arguing that a mix of provision was needed to ensure sufficiency of supply and to support choice for people using services. In England, the continued dominance of the market was taken for granted, whereas in Scotland and Wales there was more interest in a 'rebalancing' of provision. In Northern Ireland, it was assumed that HSCTs would continue to play a major role in the provision of care.

The state was seen as having a central role in resolving the crisis in all four nations, given its position as lawmaker, funder and commissioner. Increased funding for care was seen as crucial in the context of rising demand, and the state was viewed as having a unique role to play in addressing this. However, it is important to emphasise that the impact of austerity – in the form of major cuts to local government budgets – has been much greater in England than elsewhere, with a significant impact on the nature of the crisis there, affecting self-funding levels, unmet need and pressure on both providers and unpaid carers (Glasby et al, 2021).

There was more optimism in some nations than others about the potential for the state to take social care out of crisis. Scotland's National Care Service is premised on a core role for the state in centralising and standardising care, as discussed later in the book. Northern Ireland already has a state-dominated system, given the integration of social care into the NHS in the 1970s. By contrast, in England – the most marketised social care system – the state itself is reluctant to assume this role. The 2021 *People at the heart of care* White Paper assumes that, with support and favourable conditions, the resolution of the crisis will come from the market (DHSC, 2021b). In Wales, there is a dual narrative, emphasising a strong role for the state and for co-production through new forms of ownership, such as mutualism. The extent to which these tendencies sit within broader patterns of policy-making in the four nations is explored in Chapter 6.

Along with Chapter 2, this chapter has provided the contextual background for the chapters that follow. In Chapter 4 we explore the key policy mechanisms used to address perceived failings in the care systems of the four nations, such as greater integration with health and the professionalisation of the workforce, before considering care outcomes in Chapter 5.

4

The mechanisms of social care reform

To realise the values articulated in Chapter 2, in the context of the supply and demand pressures set out in Chapter 3, policy makers in the four nations have instituted a series of reforms. These have focused on questions such as:

- How should care be *funded and allocated* (including more individualised approaches)?
- Who should *access* it and when (including efforts to delay or slow down formal access to care through preventative and asset-based approaches)?
- How should it be *integrated* with health?
- How should people *providing care* (unpaid carers and the paid workforce) be supported?

In this chapter we look at what Pollitt (2002) calls 'decisional convergence' around adult social care in the four nations. In Chapter 2 we looked at discursive convergence on what social care is for, highlighting the goals of wellbeing, fairness, rights and quality as the basis of a sustainable care system. In focusing here on decisional convergence, we look at the following mechanisms that have been used in all four nations across the previous 25 years. These are:

- redistribute the costs of care
- personalise support
- support unpaid carers
- invest in prevention
- integrate with health
- professionalise the workforce.

All of these policies are priorities in the four nations, but the balance between them and the specific policies introduced vary. Chaney (2022), in his analysis of 20 years of manifesto commitments on social care in the four nations, finds that the manifestoes of English parties focus on funding solutions, whereas in Wales the foremost issue is integration with health. Addressing care worker pay and conditions is the lead social care issue in party manifestoes in Scotland and Northern Ireland. We discuss these issues and the balance between them in the sections that follow.

Redistribute the costs of care

The question of who should pay for social care has been one of the big unresolved public policy issues of recent decades. Whereas health is provided free at the point of use by the NHS, social care has to be purchased privately by individuals who have assets above the means test threshold. In all four jurisdictions, it is recognised that the funding system requires reform, as set out in Chapter 2. The lack of risk pooling for social care along the lines of health means that people potentially face very high care costs that undermine fairness, wellbeing and sustainability. The Labour-appointed Sutherland Commission in 1999 recommended a tax-funded system, ruling out private forms of risk pooling: 'Private insurance will not deliver what is required at an acceptable cost, nor does the industry want to provide that degree of coverage' (Sutherland, 1999). In 2011, the Dilnot Commission, appointed by David Cameron's Conservative-Liberal Democrat coalition government to look at care funding, again concluded that a private insurance model was not appropriate for social care (Dilnot, 2011).

With private insurance off the table, two main options for redistributing the costs of care have been considered. The first, which gained the highest level of support in New Labour's 2009 public consultation on social care, was what they called the 'comprehensive offer'. This was defined as: 'people get their care free when they need it in return for a compulsory contribution' (DH, 2009: 12). Such an approach would bring social care funding into closer alignment with the way that the NHS is funded and was in line with the recommendation of the 1999 Sutherland Report. The second option was a cap on private care costs, which was recommended by the 2011 Dilnot Report and was passed into law in the Care Act 2014 (although not implemented). These approaches are looked at in turn.

Free personal care

The majority report from the Sutherland Commission (1999) recommended 'free personal care', with the state paying the costs of activities such as personal washing, dressing, eating and drinking for anyone who met a needs threshold. Even in this 'comprehensive offer', accommodation costs in residential care were to be paid for privately, subject to a means test. Nonetheless, this proposal was rejected for England and Wales, with the Westminster government agreeing with the minority report from the Sutherland Commission, which said it was unaffordable (Brindle, 2009). It was also noted that ending private payment for social care would mainly benefit the better-off. Bosanquet and Haldenby put it this way in a letter to *The Guardian* in 2021 when options for funding care in England were again being considered: '[Free care] would be a massive subsidy to the longer lived, mainly the more affluent in the south-east – ie an end to levelling up before it had started' (Bosanquet and Haldenby, 2020).

In Scotland, in the first major policy divergence from England and Wales after devolution, the Sutherland proposals were accepted (Hassan and Shaw, 2020). Free personal care was introduced initially for people over 65 (in 2002) and later (2019) for disabled people of working age. People in Scotland who meet needs assessment criteria are entitled to 'free personal care' (including support with washing, dressing and eating). Local authorities are still able to charge people for other types of care (including meals on wheels, transport, day services, laundry, alarms and aids and adaptations). A fixed rate was established for personal care and nursing costs in residential care homes in Scotland (£212.85 and £95.80 respectively per week in 2022), with accommodation and food costs for people in residential care chargeable for people with assets above the means test threshold (£28,750 in 2022). It is estimated that free personal care meets about 25 per cent of the total weekly cost of a residential care home place (Bell, 2018). Withdrawal of Attendance Allowance for Scottish care home residents following the introduction of free personal care meant they lost up to £86 per week in social security benefits.

The Health Foundation (Bell, 2018) has warned against seeing free personal care as central to Scotland's care system, noting that it only constitutes 20 per cent of total public expenditure on care homes (the remainder is spent on people whose income and assets are below the means test threshold). The Feeley Review (2021) noted that the amount paid for personal care and nursing care for self-funders had fallen behind what was paid for state-funded residents, recommending that these should be brought into line.

A funding cap

A second option for funding care, recommended by the Dilnot Commission (2011) and passed into law in England's Care Act 2014, was to 'cap' lifetime payments for care to a fixed maximum amount. The Dilnot Commission proposed both a lifetime limit on care contributions of £35,000 and raising the means test threshold for individuals to £100,000 (based on income and assets). Drafting of the Care Act 2014 took inspiration from its report but did not take all its calculations on board. It legislated for a lifetime cap of £72,000 and left the means test threshold unchanged. This was a big step forward in terms of limiting the liabilities faced by private individuals. In practice, however, this cap was never implemented. Following a warning from English local authorities that they could not administer the cap amid other financial pressures facing them, this part of the Care Act was postponed and eventually abandoned (Foster, 2021).

There have been various efforts since to revive or reinvent the Dilnot Commission's cap on care costs for individuals. The Conservative Party's incoherent and unpopular reforms proposed in the 2017 General Election (a 'floor' on spending enabling people to keep £100,000 of assets and incorporating the value of their housing assets into the means test for home care) are one such example. These were quickly dubbed a 'dementia tax' by opposition parties and the tabloid press, and effectively abandoned after several days of negative coverage (BBC News, 2017). The perceived damage done to the Tories' poll rating during the rest of that election campaign was a reminder of how politically toxic care funding reform can be. It draws attention to new winners and losers, often failing to remind people how many people are already losers in relation to care expenditure.

Boris Johnson became Prime Minister in 2019 and promised that he had a social care plan ready that would fix social care 'once and for all' (Campbell, 2019). However, it was another two years before the plan emerged (with some of this delay being due to the COVID-19 pandemic). In relation to paying for care, the key element turned out to be a revival of Part 18(3) of the Care Act 2014, which had legislated to introduce the cap. The new proposals put the maximum care contribution at £86,000 for care expenditure incurred after October 2023, with plans to make the means test more generous so fewer people would be required to fully self-fund their care. New 'fair costs of care' proposals were set out by the Department of Health and Social Care (HM Government, 2021). These would require local authorities to work with providers to set realistic fee levels and ensure self-funders could have their care purchased for them by their local authority, ending the self-funder subsidy (HM Government, 2021). As the detailed proposals emerged in autumn 2021, however, it transpired that they were less generous than those in the Care Act, and likely to hit people with assets close to the £86,000 threshold harder than the more affluent (Tallack and Sturrock, 2022). During preparations for these reforms ahead of implementation in 2023, major concerns emerged from local authorities and care providers about the investment required and rapid implementation timetable (CCN, 2022). In autumn 2022, the Chancellor announced that implementation of the cap would yet again be postponed, at least until 2025 (HM Treasury, 2022).

Incremental change

Wales has made some progress on reforming care funding, although developments fall well short of Scotland's commitment to free personal care. The Welsh Government had planned to follow England's intended 'care cap' route, but plans were put on hold after England failed to implement the cap (Boyce, 2017). An interviewee from local government indicated that the lack of progress on reform in England continued to influence discussions in Wales: "The conversation keeps coming back to: well, shall we see what England's doing? And until we resolve that bit of it, I think that's the big stumbling block."

In place of wider-ranging reform, the Social Services and Well-being (Wales) Act 2014 introduced a cap on the maximum weekly charge for home care (£100 in 2022) and raised the means test threshold for free care in residential settings (set at £50,000 in 2022). These changes were designed to be short-term fixes ahead of a longer term settlement. An interministerial group on paying for care was established in 2018, and the Welsh Government has commissioned a number of reports on options for reforming the funding of social care (Holthman, 2018; LE Wales, 2020). The new Welsh income tax powers that came in 2019 create a context in which the Welsh Government can consider raising additional funding for social care (LE Wales, 2020). Following the Scottish route is one of the options being considered: "We're certainly looking at free personal care, we're looking at workforce options, we're looking at some of those cliff-edge costs and how they can be possibly smoothed a little, or the kind of things that have been on the table like Dilnot" (Wales, civil servant).

Following the 2021 elections the governing Labour Party signed an agreement to work with Plaid Cymru on a number of agreed items (Welsh Government, 2021a). This included setting up an expert group to create 'a National Care Service, free at the point of need, continuing as a public service', with an implementation plan to be in place by the end of 2023 (Welsh Government, 2021a: 3).

Ending risk-pooling

Northern Ireland is in a different position to the three other nations in relation to care funding reform. Progress on this, as on other issues, has been hampered by the broader lack of legislative activity on social care. The long-standing integration of health and social care means that funding arrangements differ from elsewhere in the UK. Care is arranged through Health and Social Care Trusts (HSCTs), with no charges made to individuals for personal care at home. As a result of this and Northern Ireland's socioeconomic profile, there are very few self-funders (as discussed in Chapter 3).

Our exploration of convergence and divergence indicates that in England, Scotland and Wales the focus has been on limiting individual liability for care costs through a cap or by risk-pooling. As discussed in Chapter 2, in relation to fairness, the policy debate in Northern Ireland has been focused on reform in *the opposite direction*, with proposals to introduce private payment for home care (Kelly and Kennedy, 2017: 65). However, the difficulties of policy-making in the region have contributed to policy inaction on this issue, as on others. As one interviewee put it:

> 'Now, politically, within Northern Ireland, there are two things that our politicians know probably need to happen. And because of the way Northern Ireland is, whether any politician will ever put this on the table to do it, I don't know. One is charging for domiciliary care and two is introducing water rates. And they have been kicked around for so long and I don't know if they can ever do it.' (Northern Ireland, care commissioner)

One interviewee suggested that, as in Wales, a lack of progress in England had contributed to this stasis: "We do this thing here in Northern Ireland – and we don't just do it on care, we do it with a lot of things – wait and see what happens over there" (Northern Ireland, regulatory/oversight body).

We have focused in this section on who pays for care at the point of use, rather than how funds are brought into the system, a related, but separate, issue. Given the extent to which austerity has intensified the care crisis in parts of the UK, clearly more investment is needed. In England alone, the Health Foundation has estimated that an extra £1.9 billion is needed by 2023–24 to meet demand, without addressing quality or unmet need (The Health Foundation, 2021). Government funding for care (in the form of a block grant to local authorities) has reduced in England and Wales, although it has increased in Scotland and Northern Ireland, as previously discussed. The devolved nations have some capacity to raise funds through taxation and to decide how much to allocate to social care within their block funding. In December 2021 the Scottish Government's budget included a substantial increase in spending on social care, from less than £400 million to more than £1.1 billion, making it the policy domain with the biggest increase. Some of this money will go to local authorities to improve the pay of care workers and some to fund the creation of Scotland's planned National Care Service (Scottish Government, 2021). The UK Government's planned health and social care 'levy' (from October 2023) would have introduced a hypothecated tax, designed to increase care funding across the UK (DHSC, 2021b). However, the levy plan was abandoned in 2022, with the government reverting to short-term influxes of cash (HM Treasury, 2022). Critics have highlighted the missed opportunity to put social care on a sustainable, long-term, financial footing (Laing Buisson, 2022b).

Personalise support

Making social care more person-centred has been a key reform principle in all four parts of the UK, albeit with some differences of emphasis. The 'personalisation agenda', as it is sometimes called, has been a feature of decades of campaigning by disability rights organisations for choice and control over how people are supported. Since the 1980s, the human rights-oriented message demanding greater recognition of personhood (linked to the UN Convention on the Rights of Disabled Persons) has chimed with the increased 'individualisation' of a more consumerist welfare agenda (Needham, 2007). The Independent Living Fund, introduced in 1988, provided disabled people with cash allocations enabling them to pay for personal assistance (Glasby and Littlechild, 2016). Some local authorities were very receptive to experimenting with new, more individualised, ways of providing support, such as 'direct payments' (Glasby and Littlechild, 2016). Sustained campaigning by disabled people, and the framing of individualised funding as a way to minimise state spending, led to direct payment legislation being introduced by John Major's Conservative government (Zarb and Nadash, 1994; Pearson et al, 2020). The Community Care (Direct Payments) Act 1996 gave local authorities the power to allocate funds directly to older people (and from 2000, to disabled people). This became a duty for local authorities in England and Wales in 2001, in Northern Ireland in 2002 and in Scotland in 2003 (Glasby and Littlechild, 2016).

Take-up was low and geographically patchy, however, leading to initiatives to broaden the reach of the policy (Pearson, 2000). In England, the *Putting people first* concordat was signed in 2007 by central government, local government and the social care sector, giving new momentum to this agenda. The concordat widened the focus beyond individualised funding (HM Government, 2007) to include early intervention, prevention, social capital and improved access to universal services. However, it was personal budgets – which expanded direct payments to include new forms of individualised funding that could be managed by a local authority or third party – that drew most attention and follow-up.

The Care Act 2014 reaffirmed the government's commitment to personalisation in England. Expectations were set out in statutory guidance accompanying the Act:

> Local authorities should facilitate the personalisation of care and support services, encouraging services (including small, local, specialised and personal assistant services that are highly tailored), to enable people to make meaningful choices and to take control of their support arrangements, regardless of service setting or how their personal budget is managed. (DHSC, 2022: Section 4.46)

The person-centred approach was further endorsed in the 2021 *People at the heart of care* White Paper: 'Person-centred care is a key theme running through this [10 year] vision. Genuine choice and control about personalised care and support can enhance quality of life and promote independence in a way that matters to individuals' (DHSC, 2021b).

The Social Care (Self-Directed Support) (Scotland) Act 2013 similarly emphasised principles of choice and control through individualised funding. Pearson (2004) notes that in Scotland the original direct payment legislation of the mid-1990s was viewed with some suspicion, as a form of 'backdoor privatisation'. The 2013 Act was broader than this, offering a range of ways in which people with an assessed care need could direct their care (Pearson et al, 2018). The Act states that all councils must offer self-directed support, through a direct payment, a managed budget, a third party or a mix of these options. As with personalisation arrangements in England, the legislation weaves together responses to disability rights campaigns for independent living and co-production with concerns for cost-efficiency and effectiveness (Pearson and Ridley, 2017).

In Wales, the 2006 *Beyond boundaries* review of local service delivery called for more personalised services, and for 'citizens (to) receive high quality, personalised, joined-up services, planned across organisational boundaries'. Nonetheless, it warned against 'relying on a simplistic version of choice between service providers, whereas what citizens may value most is different forms of choice, personalisation and the opportunity to express preferences and influence provision' (Beecham, 2006: 5). As in Scotland, the language of personalisation was later dropped. The *From vision to action* report used the language of 'citizen directed support' (Independent Commission on Social Services in Wales, 2010: 54), while other documents focused on 'voice and control', in contrast to the 'choice and control' approach favoured in England. The Welsh Government's White Paper *Sustainable social services* explained the choice of vocabulary: 'We believe that the label "personalisation" has become too closely associated with a market-led model of consumer choice' (Welsh Assembly Government, 2011: 15). The Social Services and Well-being (Wales) Act 2014, implemented from 2016, made a clear commitment to voice and control through 'citizen centred support', although Llewellyn et al (2020) note that what is meant by 'voice and control' isn't clearly defined in the Act.

Northern Ireland has had the same direct payments legislation as the rest of the UK since 1996, although it lacks the more recent legislative endorsement of self-directed support and personalisation seen in the other three nations. Northern Irish policy documents confirm the importance of this agenda. The *Transforming your care* review states the first key principle of social care reform as being, 'Placing the individual at the centre of any model by promoting a better outcome for the service user, carer and their family' (Health and Social Care Northern Ireland, 2011). However, in 2015, a detailed analysis of home care (*A managed change*) noted: 'relatively modest progress when compared to other areas of the UK. In recent years the rate of uptake has reached a plateau and there have been small reductions in some Trusts/programmes of care' (Health and Social Care Board, 2015: 31). The document then went on to reaffirm the commitment to self-directed support: 'Self-directed support is regarded as one of the HSCB's [Health and Social Care Board] major reform projects in the delivery of community based care and support for older people and those with disabilities' (Health and Social Care Board, 2015: 31). In using the language of self-directed support, Northern Ireland has drawn on the Scottish model (Pearson et al, 2018). As in Wales and Scotland, some avoid the language of personalisation. As one interviewee put it: "Personalisation is not a word that I come across too often here. To me, it is a very English word" (Northern Ireland, carers' organisation).

Conversely, Northern Ireland's *Power to people* report (one of whose authors, Des Kelly, has worked in England for many years) used the term 'personalisation' liberally, alongside self-directed support, talking also of the importance of 'consumer sovereignty' in social care – a concept that contrasts with the perspective adopted in Scottish and Welsh documents (Kelly and Kennedy, 2017). Just as the care funding debate evokes contested accounts of fairness, we can see in debates about person-centred care the underpinning tensions around rights and markets. These play out differently in the four jurisdictions. We can also see some reluctance in the devolved nations to use language too closely associated with England, a point of divergence we return to in later chapters.

Support for unpaid carers

In all parts of the UK, there has been increased formal recognition of the role played by unpaid carers. Their contribution is crucial to a sustainable care system, and they are increasingly recognised as needing, and being entitled to, support themselves (Yeandle et al, 2012). COVID-19 in particular was seen to magnify the strains on carers across all four nations. The UK nations, with the exception of Northern Ireland, legislated to improve the support provided to carers in the 2010s. In England, the Care Act 2014 gave carers the right to support following an assessment. A Carers Action Plan to support implementation followed (DHSC, 2018). The 2014 Act also aimed to make support for carers more consistent across local authorities (Marczak et al, 2022). Improved support for carers was a key element of the Social Services and Well-being (Wales) Act 2014. As in England, it gave carers the right to support following an assessment, and established in law that they had the same rights as those they care for. The Carers (Scotland) Act 2016 gave all carers in Scotland the right to a support plan and to having their eligible needs met, as identified in their plan. The Feeley Report noted that relatively few unpaid carers receive statutory respite support and recommended a 'right to respite' (Feeley, 2021), which the Scottish Government (2021) was considering as part of its National Care Service consultation.

Northern Ireland has not enacted specific legislation on carers since the Carers and Direct Payments (Northern Ireland) Act 2002. The 2017 *Power to people* report proposed bringing Northern Ireland's rights for carers into line with those for England in the Care Act 2014, but this has not yet happened. HSCTs in Northern Ireland have a duty to inform carers of their right to an assessment, but (unlike other parts of the UK) no duty to meet needs identified by that assessment. Northern Ireland also lacks a legal definition of a carer (which other UK nations have). The definition in the Care Act 2014, for England, is 'An adult who provides or intends to provide care for another adult'; the Welsh definition is similar; and the Scottish definition includes care for disabled children as well as adults. Wales and England have national eligibility criteria for carers' support, whereas in Scotland this is decided by local authorities, and in Northern Ireland, it is at the discretion of HSCTs. Carers who meet the eligibility criteria for Carer's Allowance, a welfare benefit first established in 1976 (when it was entitled 'Invalid Care Allowance'), can receive this weekly amount in England, Wales and Northern Ireland, provided they are not receiving other 'overlapping' payments from the state (such as State Retirement Pension). In Scotland, since 2019 (following devolution of social security arrangements to Scotland) this benefit has been increased, with a Carer's Allowance Supplement designed to align its value with the unemployment benefit 'Jobseeker's Allowance'.

As we have shown, there is clear divergence in legal and financial entitlements for carers. The Scottish approach is the most generous financially. Northern Ireland lags behind on carer legislation. Implementation of legislation intended to support carers has been patchy and problematic in England, Scotland and Wales, as we discuss in the next chapter, but the existence of a formal definition and of specific rights in law is nonetheless recognised as an important achievement in these three nations in the last decade.

Invest in prevention

Supporting people *before* they need statutory social care services has also been a central part of social care policy in all four nations. As Miller et al note:

[T]here is growing recognition that the system has too often concentrated only on those with the greatest and most complex needs, leaving fewer and fewer resources, financial and otherwise, to meet lower-level needs. Early intervention and prevention are seen as an essential component of achieving a more personalised social care system through ensuring that service users are supported to retain independence for as long as possible. (Miller et al, 2013: 120)

However, whereas the areas of reform already outlined have clear mechanisms for change (for example, a funding cap, a direct payment, a carer's assessment), prevention remains ill defined. It aims to stop something happening, and less progress has been made in specifying what that means and how it could be achieved.

In England, Tew et al (2019: 10) highlight the importance of the Care Act 2014 in increasing the ambition of preventative approaches. Whereas prevention activity was underway before the Act, this focused on a relatively narrow set of interventions such as reablement, falls prevention and signposting. In contrast:

'Second wave' approaches to prevention and capacity building ... have become more prominent since the implementation of the Care Act 2014. ... This has involved more fundamental revisioning of the role of local services and the relationships between services, citizens and communities – and a more positive and holistic focus on enhancing wellbeing, opportunity and social connectivity, as opposed to a more defensive focus on mitigating risk and providing services in response to identified needs. (Tew et al, 2019: 10)

With this 'second wave' has come an interest in asset-based and strengths-based approaches that focus on people's skills, capabilities and networks rather than their needs and deficits (Milne et al, 2021). Models include 'Local Area Coordination', the 'Three Conversations' approach and 'Asset-based Community Development'. A scoping review by Milne et al (2021) found that strengths-based approaches are increasingly mainstream within local authorities. Definitions remain fluid, however, and it is unclear how their effectiveness and feasibility should be evaluated.

Cairney et al (2016) highlight prevention as a key pillar of the 'Scottish approach'. The Christie Report of the Commission on the Future Delivery of Public Services (Christie, 2011) formed the basis for Scotland's public services strategy, and placed a strong emphasis on prevention. In its response to Christie, the Scottish Government talked of developing a 'decisive shift towards prevention' (Christie, 2011: 1). The subsequent National Care Service consultation reaffirmed this focus:

Done well, a focus on early intervention and prevention avoids the need for more costly action at a later stage. For example, supporting unpaid carers so that they can continue their caring relationship, supporting families to prevent family breakdown, or ensuring appropriate care to prevent deterioration or falls resulting in a need for hospital treatment, all result in benefits for individuals and families, and for our health and care services. (Scottish Government, 2021: 6)

Similarly in Wales, the 2003 report into the health and social care system placed a strong emphasis on prevention: 'There should be a strategic adjustment of services to focus them on prevention and early intervention. Potentially this offers significant long-term cost and quality of life gains' (Welsh Assembly Government, 2003: 2). The Well-being of Future Generations (Wales) Act 2015 gives a particular focus to its ambitions around prevention, requiring public bodies to take account of prevention as one of the 'ways of working' required by the Act. Guidance to accompany the Act indicates:

> Understanding the underlying causes of the problems people and communities face can help us find different solutions, intervene early and prevent problems from getting worse or arising in the future. But this is not just about addressing problems – it is about finding enabling solutions and early interventions at the right time to make progress in achieving the well-being goals. (Welsh Government, 2015a: 23)

In Northern Ireland, investing in prevention is identified as a key principle in *Transforming your care* (Health and Social Care Northern Ireland, 2011), and has been restated subsequently. The Bengoa Report in 2016 described a prevention focus across the heath and care system as vital to avoid system collapse (Bengoa, 2016). However, the 2017 *Power to people* report highlighted the lack of a prevention focus to date:

> [O]ur system is currently focused almost entirely on 'Failure Demand' defined as demand caused by a failure to do something or do something right for the customer. ... We have to work out how to make a fundamental shift away from a crisis dominated system into a long-term solution focusing on prevention and early intervention in which care and support is based initially around people and their communities. (Kelly and Kennedy, 2017: 45–6)

Technology is seen as playing a key role in relation to prevention and early intervention, particularly to enable people to live at home for as long as possible (Wright, 2020). All four nations have a digital strategy that incorporates social care. The Scottish Government's *Health and social care delivery plan* notes that, 'Digital technology is key to transforming health and social care services so that care can become more person-centred' (Scottish Government, 2016: 23). England's 2021 *People at the heart of care*

White Paper includes £150 million of investment, over three years, 'to drive digitisation across the sector; and unlock the potential of caretech innovation that enables preventative care and independent living' (DHSC, 2021b). Wales and Northern Ireland have invested in telecare and note its importance to future care systems, although Wright (2020) observes that the Welsh Government has been more cautious than elsewhere, calling for incremental rather than rapid growth. There has been recent enthusiasm about the scope for using data collected by digital devices in a proactive way as part of a broader preventative approach (Welsh Government, 2015b; Health and Social Care Board, 2016; Scottish Government and COSLA, 2021).

There is clear convergence between the four nations in relation to the prevention focus, recognising its potential 'win-wins' in improving people's quality of life and wellbeing while reducing reliance on state services. Nonetheless, as we discuss when considering policy successes in Chapter 5, it has been hard to keep focused on prevention at a time of fiscal pressures (particularly in England), and the challenge of evidencing progress on prevention remains significant.

Integrate with health

People who use social care often also use primary, community and acute health services. The NHS and local authorities that purchase and provide care services share a number of goals: keeping people well in their own homes for as long as possible; improving system efficacy; and promoting a more person- (or patient-)centred approach. However, the experience of using both NHS and care services can often be fragmented, frustrating and sometimes detrimental to wellbeing. For instance, people may find themselves in hospital unnecessarily due to insufficient coordination between hospital discharge and local authority assessment processes for social care. Integrating these services to provide a more coordinated service has been a key policy goal for all four nations for at least two decades.

There have been a number of different approaches to this challenge. These include pooled funding and the joint planning and purchasing of services, as well as merging organisations, colocating staff and centralising information systems. Miller et al (2016) differentiate between micro, meso and macro forms of integration. Micro integration describes the interactions of practitioners, for instance home care workers and district nurses. Meso integration describes joint teams of practitioners from different organisations or the development of targeted services such as integrated discharge teams. Macro integration describes the systems-level integration at play in joint boards and shared policy-making across localities. Across the UK, recent integration policy has mainly focused on macro-level changes: systems-level funding and strategies for particular localities, with meso and micro initiatives greatly varying from place to place (Miller et al, 2016).

Northern Ireland has had structural health and social care integration for much longer than the other nations. In 1972 a Health and Personal Social Services Order established joint health and social care bodies in the province. Despite its longevity, integration remains an incomplete goal of the Northern Irish system, as evidenced in the 2011 review *Transforming your care*: 'Services provided by different parts of the health and social care system should be better integrated to improve the quality of experience for patients and clients, safety and outcomes' (Health and Social Care Northern Ireland, 2011: 40). Responding to the recommendations of this report, Northern Ireland established Integrated Care Partnerships (ICPs) that identify high-intensity users and attempt to design 'wraparound care' led by clinicians (Malone and Hayes, 2017). The 2020 Northern Ireland Executive *New decade, new approach* statement (following re-establishment of power sharing in Northern Ireland) noted that policy proposals relating to integration needed to be implemented (Reed et al, 2021: 23).

In Scotland, the government has taken a more direct legislative approach to integration. The Public Bodies (Joint Working) (Scotland) Act 2014 placed a duty on NHS organisations and local government to delegate health and care functions and budgets to new integrated authorities, with a view to making these new authorities the joint commissioner of health and care. Five years on, recognising limitations in what had been achieved through this approach, the 2021 National Care Service (NCS) consultation document put forward further structural reforms:

> [W]e propose that IJBs [Integration Joint Boards] will become Community Health and Social Care Boards (CHSCBs) and will be the local delivery body for the NCS, funded directly by the Scottish Government. This will be the sole model for local delivery of community health and social care in Scotland. The functions of CHSCBs will be consistent across the country and will include all community health and social care support and services that the Scottish population requires. (Scottish Government, 2021: 90)

In Wales, in 2009, Health Boards were established to coordinate health and social care across regions, but stopped short of full integration:

> We are not persuaded that some social services should transfer to the NHS. This would undermine the integrated support, protection and inclusion for the vulnerable provided by the local government family. There are faster and less disruptive ways to address the issues encountered at the interface between health and social care. We recommend that

social services and social care for adults and children should remain a local government responsibility. (Independent Commission on Social Services in Wales, 2010: 7)

The Social Services and Well-being (Wales) Act 2014 established a legal duty on local government to promote integration, implemented through seven Regional Partnership Boards (RPBs). The Well-being of Future Generations (Wales) Act 2015 established 19 Public Service Boards (PSBs) that are required to promote wellbeing in their local areas (Heenan and Birrell, 2018). Although the RPBs and PSBs are expected to work in coordinated ways, in practice there has been confusion about their operational distinction (Reed et al, 2021: 43). In 2021, the *Rebalancing care and support* White Paper proposed to put RPBs onto a legal footing, enabling them to employ staff, hold budgets, undertake commissioning and shape markets (Welsh Government, 2021b: 19).

Integration has been a policy goal in England for several decades, but structures have not had a legal basis comparable to that in the other nations (Reed et al, 2021: 3). In England, the Better Care Fund, established in 2013, sought to transform local health and care systems using a joint pot of money spent on shared priorities. These local priorities are agreed and signed off at local Health and Wellbeing Boards – another macro integration intervention (enshrined in the Health and Social Care Act 2012) to develop joint health and care strategies. In 2015, NHS England announced a range of pilots to explore organisational alignment between different aspects of health and social care services. These 'vanguard sites' sought to develop new models of care based on new contractual structures, payment regimes and joint organisations (Miller et al, 2016). Since 2015, these new organisations and partnerships have developed 'place-based' approaches: collaborations that seek to manage demand into acute services and promote wellbeing and the prevention of ill health. NHS England developed these loose partnerships into 'Sustainability and Transformation Partnerships' and more recently into more formal 'Integrated Care Organisations' (Miller et al, 2021). In yet another development, in 2021 the Department of Health and Social Care introduced proposals for Integrated Care Systems, which are legal structures, bringing England into line with the other nations (DHSC, 2021a).

Professionalise the workforce

High staff turnover and rising vacancy rates are symptoms of problems within the social care workforce. Skills for Care data shows a pattern of growth in staff vacancies over time, with figures for England in 2020–21 showing vacancies at around 105,000 at any one time (Skills for Care, 2021). The report also showed that turnover rates were highest for people on zero-hour contracts. An All-Party Parliamentary Group (APPG) report on social care covering the four nations noted that half of care workers leave their job within the first year. A care provider giving evidence to its inquiry reported:

> There are simply too few people wanting to join and stay in adult social care roles. Despite regular efforts by government, Skills for Care, and employers, including a recent national recruitment campaign in England, the tide has not been turned whilst the demand for care continues to grow. ... The inability to access enough qualified, motivated and values-based carers and nurses is the biggest single threat facing the sector. (Quoted in Hayes et al, 2019: 17)

Key issues reported to the APPG were low pay, availability of easier jobs in hospitality and retail, lack of training and career development and Brexit uncertainty. These point to clear problems for service user outcomes:

> The lack of funding, training and professionalisation evident across much of the social care workforce is clearly a major factor in negative service user experiences, and during the course of this inquiry, we have heard accounts of the use of multiple care workers to support someone, and the associated unfamiliarity with people, insufficient time allocated for care duties, a lack of continuity of care, and indeed a lack of any kind of care worker at all. (Hayes et al, 2019: 33)

New Labour's 2010 White Paper, *Building the National Care Service*, indicated its intention to introduce a licensing scheme for all social care workers (encompassing residential care, homecare and personal assistants [PAs]) (HM Government, 2010). The change of government later that year meant these changes never happened. In 2011, the coalition government Health Minister Andrew Lansley announced:

> The risk to service-users and the general public posed by groups of unregulated health and social care workers is not considered to be such that regulation of individual workers is necessary ... the Government does not believe that the extension of statutory regulation to all workers in the health sector across the UK and the social care sector in England would be a proportionate response. The emphasis should be on employers of unregulated workers to take responsibility for the quality of services provided. (Cited in Hayes et al, 2019: 31)

A decade on, the 2021 White Paper, *People at the heart of care*, appeared to revive earlier plans, and included proposals for a voluntary 'skills passport' that would be used for 'establishing a foundation for registration of staff in the future' (DHSC, 2021b: 76).

In Scotland, worker registration is mandatory in some care settings. The Scottish Social Services Council (SSSC) has a remit for adult day care and residential care, care at home and housing support services. The majority of the social services workforce must register with the SSSC within six months of starting work. Workers are not required to have a relevant qualification in order to register, but must acquire one within five years; most are paid the Scottish Living Wage, and are entitled to travel time, holiday and sick pay and sleepover payments (Hayes et al, 2019). The Resolution Foundation found that Scottish care workers were the best paid in the UK (Cominetti et al, 2020). As one of the interviewees working in the third sector in Scotland put it:

'[W]e now have the bones of an adult social care reform programme, which is going to tackle all of these things that I've been talking about in the workforce. Living wage, sustainability, different service models, they've accepted, totally, that is where they should be focused. I'm kind of moaning about how terrible everything is, but actually, in policy terms, it's pretty bloody good! Actually, it really is, it really is, comparatively.'

In Scotland, as elsewhere, the PA or directly employed workforce is unregulated and operates outside state visibility:

'So I guess we didn't really know how big our PA workforce was until Covid happened and we tried to pay them the £500 payment or get their ID card and their PPE. We realised, oh we don't really know where they are and what they do or how they're trained.' (Scotland, civil servant)

The National Care Service consultation in Scotland (Scottish Government, 2021: 130) is looking at whether a register and national minimum employment standards for PAs should be introduced.

The Northern Ireland Social Care Council is the regulator for the social services workforce there. People working in social care in Northern Ireland have been required to register with the Council since the end of 2017. Registration in Northern Ireland covers residential care workers and is being extended to home care workers. No qualifications are required to join the register. Given the relatively high proportion of in-house staff in social care, an issue for Northern Ireland is the pay differential between care staff employed by a Trust and those employed in the private sector, as discussed in Chapter 3.

In Wales, social care staff in domiciliary and care home settings are required to register with Social Care Wales. To be eligible for registration, they must have suitable qualifications and agree to abide by professional standards. The Welsh Government describes registration as 'serving the dual purposes of professionalising and raising the status of the social care workforce, and reassuring service-users and their families that workers have the qualifications and skills required to perform their work professionally' (Hayes et al, 2019: 20).

England is, therefore, alone among the four nations not to have mandatory registration (beyond professions such as social workers and nurses). Oung et al (2020) point to the difficulties of introducing registration in England:

> One of the biggest challenges with the professionalisation of the English social care workforce is its size, as well as the vast number of settings in which the workforce operates. Developing mandatory registration as a first formal step in professionalising the workforce would require large amounts of planning and resources, especially if registration is to increase the attractiveness of working in the sector. (Oung et al, 2020)

A further complexity arises where staff work across the England–Wales or England–Scotland borders and would become subject to separate registration frameworks. The APPG report called for recognised compatibility standards between England, Wales, Scotland and Northern Ireland (APPG on Adult Social Care, 2019: 12).

Many of the interviewees made the case for professionalisation, seeing it as crucial to increasing the skills and prestige of the sector:

> 'I want also some proper remuneration recognition for social care staff, because these people are dealing with very complex people and very complex issues and they should not be seen as people who do a minimum wage job. They are people that should be on a career pathway, because they are professionals, they should have acknowledgement of that. They should also have the qualifications for that. And also I think registration would help with the status because it would also help us to be really clear about the support that is offered to the worker, but also the worker's responsibility and accountability for the quality of the service they provide.' (England, provider representative)

For many it was also an important way to acknowledge and recruit for the level of expertise required. Comparisons to other parts of the NHS were common:

> 'I want proper career pathways and escalators for social care, just as we have them in other parts of the system around the NHS.' (England, provider representative)

'You can go in, now, and start working in a nursing home or for a domiciliary care provider. Maybe you're looking after people who are terminally ill, for example. You maybe worked in a garage the week before. ... They're put through training and stuff once they start but if you compare that to what someone who wants to be a GP or a doctor has to go through, it's two completely different things. Then we're surprised when people complain about the standard of care in the nursing home or they refuse domiciliary care because it's not good enough.' (Northern Ireland, third sector)

Professionalising care workers is about more than just registering them. The title of an APPG on Adult Social Care (2019) report on care workers in 2019 identified three strands: elevation, registration and standardisation. Hayes et al (2019: 3) note that addressing aspects of professionalisation and sector reform cannot be done effectively if this happens piecemeal: "Training, occupational registration, concern for safeguarding, terms and conditions of work and funding are intricately connected and improvements must be made on all fronts to recognise and reward the skills and professionalism of care workers."

Hayes et al (2019) also highlight that other changes in care systems, such as the trend towards personalised or self-directed support, have implications for the workforce that need to be considered. As the *Domiciliary care workforce review* for Northern Ireland (2016–21) put it: 'In line with the principles of personalisation, the role of the professional and the care worker within SDS [self-directed support] will become less about being a "fixer" of problems and more about being a co-facilitator of solutions working in collaboration and co-production based on power sharing and mutual respect' (DH, 2018: 30).

There is also a need to recognise how diversity across the four nations in relation to affluence and diversity and urban and rural factors affects workforce availability and the sorts of issues that are required to attract staff. Interviewees in Scotland emphasised the challenge of getting sufficient providers and staff in rural and remote areas:

'Attracting providers into some remote and rural areas is quite challenging, because of the problems with actually recruiting the workforce and all the issues around about things like travel time. ... Some of the island communities in particular have issues in attracting providers, and quite often have to pay additional subsidies in terms of hourly rates.' (Scotland, local government representative)

Similarly, interviewees in Northern Ireland highlighted the rural and urban divide:

'If you're in the city … [it's] not the most stable of workforces, but providers would tell us that they find it easier to get the staff to work in the cities. There is the turnover, but you can get the people. In rural areas, obviously the pool that you're recruiting from is shallow, but also there are additional difficulties. The contract price, particularly for domiciliary care, is low and a lot of providers squeeze their staff in terms of payment of travel time, or travel expenses, mileage. Now, that's less significant if you're able to work by walking to and from a dozen streets, surrounding the street you live in. But if you have to have a car and you have to drive to your clients that becomes an issue.' (Northern Ireland, civil servant)

It can be particularly hard to find social care staff in areas where wages are high and there are plentiful alternative forms of employment. One of the local councillor interviewees from England noted that the lack of this dynamic in their area made recruitment easier: "The fact that we have a low wage-base economy means that we can afford to keep [social care] going pretty well, actually, when compared to some other places."

In Wales, the Welsh language is an important aspect of staff recruitment, particularly in the areas where Welsh speaking is most prevalent. The right to speak Welsh was added to the definition of wellbeing in Wales in 2017 (Hamblin, 2019), but, as has been pointed out, 'just 16 percent of staff working in regulated services and 10 per cent of staff working for commissioned care providers can communicate effectively through the medium of Welsh' (Hayes et al, 2019: 15). This may in part be because Welsh speaking is unevenly distributed across Wales (Jones and Lewis, 2019). One of the interviewees from the NHS in Wales commented:

'I don't get a double decker bus arriving in [the local town] with 16 [occupational therapists] on it who can speak Welsh. So you've always got to be thinking outside the box. You've got to have good links with the universities, offer placements for students, encourage people when they do go away to train that they're more than welcome to come back.'

Addressing workforce challenges requires recognition of these different aspects of diversity, and the ways in which different levers will be required in different localities.

Assessing progress

As is evident from the range of issues discussed in this chapter, reforming the care system is a daunting task, equivalent to the foundational work that went into constructing a comprehensive welfare state in the UK after the

Second World War. We identify two groups among the four nations: those with a wide-ranging care act (a 'big bang' approach, adopted in England and Wales) and those that have reformed their care system in more gradual way (Scotland and Northern Ireland). England had a large set-piece Act – the Care Act 2014 – which was the most wide-ranging care legislation since the National Assistance Act 1948, codifying over 50 years of care policy and guidance (Spencer-Lane, 2011). The breadth of the Care Act 2014 has been seen by some people as a disadvantage. As an English civil servant in our study put it, "The Care Act is quite kind of aspirational in its drafting and therefore probably is going to be true for all time that if you ask user representative charities, do you feel that the Care Act has been beautifully delivered over the country, they're always going to say no".

In England a new Health and Care Act was passed by Parliament in 2022 to further progress integration between health and social care and give the Care Quality Commission the power to inspect local authority commissioning (DHSC, 2021a).

The Social Services and Well-being (Wales) Act was seen by Welsh interviewees as the key legislation, albeit alongside other Acts that established new approaches:

'We had new legislation with the Social Services and Well-being (Wales) Act. That was all about the design of the system, if you like, the expectations, more voice and control, more collaboration. Looking at early intervention, focusing more on safeguarding, so that was the policy principles. The sister Act was RISCA, Regulation and Inspection of Social Care. That established new responsibilities for [the] Care Inspector of Wales. That's the service regulator – and new responsibilities for us as the workforce regulator.' (Wales, regulatory/oversight body)

The Well-being of Future Generations (Wales) Act 2015 was also seen as important legislation, supporting and taking further the Social Services and Well-being (Wales) Act. A Welsh civil servant described it as a 'top of the tree' Act in terms of shaping the context for other policies. However, another respondent noted that the links between the legislation were not always clear:

'So you've got the Future Generations Act. … Then you've got *A healthier Wales*, which is just a sort of policy document, but that's the road they want to go down. And you've got all these people then working in Welsh Government, in their different little silo departments, not understanding these other policies, and these other pieces of legislation, might actually fit into the future sort of direction of their

work. So you've got departments there who don't talk to each other.'
(Wales, carers' organisation)

Scotland has no equivalent to the wide-ranging Acts in England and Wales, but has pursued an iterative approach to care reform, developing a series of new laws for different issues in the care system. In contrast, Northern Ireland has lacked legislative change in social care. As one interviewee put it: "Legislation is a blunt tool but, well, we don't have an adult safeguarding bill ... and every other part of the UK does. ... We haven't got the care bill or any equivalent" (Northern Ireland, regulatory/oversight body).

There is a sense of 'playing catch up' (Chapman, 2018). As another Northern Irish interviewee from the Health and Social Care Board put it: "It is very outdated, the legal framework underpinning the delivery of social care [in Northern Ireland]. It was in the '72, '73 order here ... and to support there has been circulars produced by government with particular 2010 circulars that everyone kind of still relies on."

In Northern Ireland, the 2020 power-sharing agreement re-establishing the Executive indicated an intention to implement the proposals in the *Transforming your care* and *Power to people* reports (Northern Ireland Executive, 2020). In January 2022, the Department of Health announced that it was consulting on its response to the *Power to people* report (DH, 2022a). Proposed actions by the Executive included the introduction of comprehensive legislation on social care and a review of charging arrangements, although it remained a draft consultation framework rather than a clear plan for change.

Conclusion

In this chapter we have set out the six mechanisms that have been used to advance care reform in the four nations, noting areas where they are converging and diverging in decisions being made. Much as we found when looking at care values in Chapter 2, the broad goals of reform across the nations are very similar. All six of the mechanisms we have looked at here are being attempted, although the tactics through which this has been done are different. Scotland is the nation that has made most progress on care reform. We can summarise the findings presented in this chapter in the following way:

Active: Scotland has pursued an iterative approach to care reform, developing a series of small pieces of legislation for different issues in the care system. It has: introduced free personal care for over-65s, later extending it to working-age adults; introduced care worker registration and improved pay and conditions; developed a more centralised infrastructure for integration than exists in England; and brought in a standard national fee rate for care homes.

Emergent: Wales had weaker powers than Scotland following devolution and had to overcome public ambivalence about the new institutions. This led to delays in pursuing a distinctive social care agenda from England. The Social Services and Well-being (Wales) Act 2014 was a large and ambitious piece of legislation. It introduced new rights for carers, a maximum weekly charge for home care and an increase in the means test threshold. Wales has also introduced mandatory care worker registration.

Symbolic: the wide-ranging Care Act 2014, applicable to England, was seen at the time as a new settlement for care, equivalent to the National Assistance Act 1948. However, it has only been partly implemented. Successive prime ministers have talked about the importance of reforming care spending, with a particular focus on protecting people's homes (a bigger issue in England than elsewhere, due to higher levels of self-funding). An adapted version of the care cap model from the Care Act 2014 has also been passed into law in the Health and Care Act 2022 but its implementation has already been postponed from 2023 to 2025.

Stalled: much of Northern Ireland's care settlement was shaped by its structural integration of health and care in the 1970s (itself in part a response to the political violence of that era). As a result of this long history of integration, it has some features that other parts of the UK are seeking to emulate, for example, *de facto* free personal care at home; registration of the workforce; and a strong civil society. However, its lack of policy capacity over the last 25 years (with repeated suspensions of the Northern Ireland Assembly) has prevented progress on key issues such as carers' rights. Much of its legislative framework for care is still derived from the National Assistance Act 1948.

In the next chapter, we focus on how reforms in each of these areas have fared, in order to understand the practice and results element of convergence and divergence (Pollitt, 2002). We explore this through the lens of outcomes, starting by discussing the growth of an outcomes orientation in all four nations, and then looking in detail at outcomes for the six mechanisms discussed in this chapter.

5

The outcomes of social care reform

In the previous chapters we discussed the context and mechanisms of social care in the four nations, focusing on Pollitt's (2002) criteria of discursive and decisional convergence. Here we consider the extent to which we are seeing convergence or divergence in relation to outcomes. We draw on what Pollitt calls 'results convergence'. This is a measure of success: how far has the policy achieved what it set out to achieve? In assessing results convergence we also consider Pollitt's criteria of practice convergence – in other words, how have the discourses (Chapter 2), contexts (Chapter 3) and decisions (Chapter 4) translated into practice?

As we discussed in Chapter 1, perceptions of success depend on attitudes to the original policy. They require a realist willingness to accept that while some aspects of success can be measured, interpretation and perception will play a key role. We start by looking at how each of the four nations has made outcomes a much more explicit part of their social care reform efforts. We then go on to consider what has been achieved in the areas we identified in Chapter 4 as the key reform mechanisms of all four social care systems:

- redistribute the costs of care
- personalise support
- support unpaid carers
- invest in prevention
- integrate with health
- professionalise the workforce.

We look at each of the mechanisms in terms of practice convergence and producing desired outcomes. We then discuss how the reforms have impacted differently, recognising the need to consider success in terms of benefits for different target groups (in this case, people who require support, families, care workers and the broader community). In doing so we also suggest that some of these mechanisms are in tension, meaning that it is unlikely that they can all meet their objectives and desired outcomes at the same time. For example, the introduction of free personal care may be in tension with the prevention agenda and with the move towards more personalisation.

Focus on outcomes

All four nations of the UK have made strong policy commitments to becoming more outcomes-focused, by measuring and funding care on the basis of end goals rather than processes. This has been part of a broader trend to orient public service performance measurement away from activities and outputs and towards outcomes (Bovaird, 2014; Birrell and Gray, 2018). Outcomes are presented as more sophisticated than outputs (such as the number of care visits or the numbers of people discharged from hospital), which can hide poor-quality service. In relation to social care, outcomes are 'the valued consequences of social care support for service users and other people'; they include quality of life and wellbeing (Caiels et al, 2010: 1). As Caiels et al point out: 'measuring wellbeing outcomes, rather than units of service *output* (eg numbers of care home placements) gives us a much better indication of *value*' (Caiels et al, 2010: 1, emphasis in original). Outcomes approaches tend to draw more heavily on subjective measures than other measures of performance, for example the satisfaction of people using the service. In that sense, they align with the subjective dimension of wellbeing.

Outcomes are much more elusive than output or process measures. They are compromised by attribution problems and the absence of counter-factuals (that is, what would have happened without the intervention) (Talbot, 2010). Public policy academics have used terms such as 'outcome theology' and 'fool's gold' to convey this sense that an outcome orientation in performance measurement relies on faith and wishful thinking rather than hard metrics (Tunstill et al, 2015; Bovaird, 2014). Bovaird cautions:

> [M]any 'outcome measures' are chosen by public agencies not because they really correspond to the quality of life improvements which the agency seeks but because they are easy to measure, fashionable, or sympathetically regarded by the controlling political group (or, we would add, in some cases because they are easy to game in performance management or evaluation). (Bovaird, 2014: 4–5)

Despite these concerns, policy makers' enthusiasm for outcomes has not dimmed. Birrell and Gray's comparative work on outcomes in Scotland, Wales and Northern Ireland notes the influence of Outcomes-Based Accountability (OBA), drawn from the work of Friedman (2005), and its application in the state of Virginia in the USA (Birrell and Gray, 2018). Scotland was the first mover – OBA was brought into government by the SNP after its 2007 election success. Outcomes were embedded in a 10-year National Performance Framework (NPF) that spanned public services, and had an explicit wellbeing focus (Arnott, 2019). Each local authority produces

'Single Outcomes Agreements' (SOAs) to set out how local priorities cohere with the NPF's overarching vision and strategy (Cairney et al, 2016: 6).

Similar attempts to embed a holistic outcomes approach across sectors and levels have also been a focus in Wales and Northern Ireland. In Wales, OBA was adopted following criticisms of the performance of public services in 2014, and in Northern Ireland it was agreed by the power-sharing Executive in 2016 (Birrell and Gray, 2018: 68–71). In practice, there have been criticisms in all three jurisdictions that outcomes are too vague and aspirational to be measured, or that they are focused on activities rather than outcomes (Birrell and Gray, 2018: 75). Risks of gaming and distortion or of over-simplification of attribution are also noted. However, Birrell and Gray point out that ambiguity has been helpful in Northern Ireland, 'where politically the outcomes approach facilitated compulsory inter-party power sharing by promoting very general agreed outcomes' (Birrell and Gray, 2018: 71).

What this outcome orientation means in relation to social care has been interpreted differently in different jurisdictions. Scotland's first NPF in 2007 included a target on keeping older people in their own homes, and reducing emergency admissions (McCormick et al, 2009). The *Beyond boundaries* report in Wales in 2006 called for local public services that were 'outward facing and focused on outcomes for citizens' (Beecham, 2006: 7). There is a specific NPF target relating to social care outcomes in Wales (Welsh Government, 2019). Outcomes are also important in England, although the specific OBA methodology has not been adopted. Rather, the Adult Social Care Outcomes Framework (ASCOF) has been developed as a way of measuring the experiences of people using publicly funded care.

Focusing on outcomes is thus a key element of social care reform in all four nations. These can be considered at the macro level, to identify how far each system is improving outcomes for people. Problems of data comparability nevertheless make it impossible to say which of the four nations is currently achieving better outcomes for people involved in the social care system. The Institute for Government's study on public services in the four nations noted that 'The four Governments measure very few social care outcomes, and those that they do measure are difficult to compare' (Atkins et al, 2021: 38). As Ed Humpherson, Director-General of the Office for Statistics Regulation, put it in a strongly worded blog: 'As data issues go ... there is not so much a gap as a chasm, with consequences to our understanding of social care delivery and outcomes' (Humpherson, 2021).

Some outcomes data relating to care services are available from the four nations, but there is a lack of comparability in the populations surveyed and questions asked. The Nuffield Trust synthesised available data to show satisfaction with social care (one of the subjective outcome measures) among people receiving services in the four nations. As Figure 5.1 shows, satisfaction

Figure 5.1: Satisfaction with social care services, 2013/14 to 2019/20

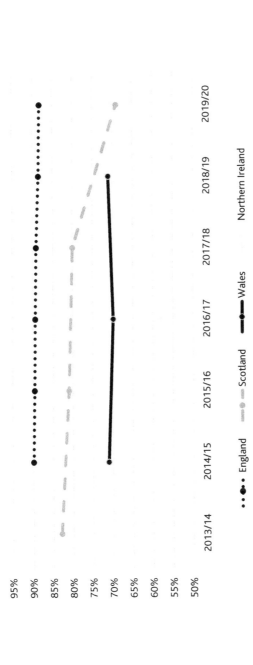

Source: Reed et al (2021: 28). For England: NHS Digital, 'Personal Social Services Adult Social Care Survey', https://digital.nhs.uk/data-and-information/publications/statistical/personal-socialservices-adult-social-care-survey. For Scotland: Scottish Government, 'Health and Care Experience Survey', www.gov.scot/collections/health-and-care-experience-survey. For Wales: 'National Survey for Wales', https://statswales.gov.wales/Catalogue/ National-Survey-for-Wales. For Northern Ireland: Department of Health, 'Tables from the health survey Northern Ireland', www.health-ni.gov.uk/publications/ tables-health-survey-northern-ireland.

is highest in England, but has fallen slightly over time. In Scotland it has fallen more sharply. Wales is at a lower level and has stayed relatively stable, and Northern Ireland has the lowest satisfaction (but only one data point). These data come with a number of health warnings, however, relating to different question wording in each dataset, a change of methodology in Scotland and a lack of data in Northern Ireland (Reed et al, 2021: 28).

Unwin (2018) offers another form of comparative data, based on research on kindness in which she polled people in the four nations to develop comparative insights about how they were treated when using public services. As Table 5.1 shows, people are less inclined to say that they strongly agree that there is kindness in social care than in GP and library services. Across the four nations, England is the nation where people say that they experience the least kindness (in care and in other public services).

As well as looking at these system-wide measures, we can also consider how an outcome orientation may be reshaping service design and delivery. In England, following the Care Act 2014, national government funded a programme to support local authorities to move to a more outcomes-oriented approach to commissioning. At a local level, some local authorities experimented with outcomes-based commissioning, awarding homecare contracts on the basis of a more holistic set of measures, rather than on the traditional 'time and task' model (Bolton, 2015).

Operationalising outcome-based approaches requires new approaches to commissioning and market management (Needham et al, 2022). There are different understandings of how an outcome orientation translates into practice. For some, it is a transformative approach, putting wellbeing and the priorities of people using services at the heart of the system, as in Northern Ireland's *Power to people* report (Kelly and Kennedy, 2017). It can also be

Table 5.1: Percentage in each jurisdiction strongly agreeing that they experience kindness when using key public services

% of which with direct or close experience strongly agreeing that people are treated with kindness when using:	England	Northern Ireland	Scotland	Wales
GP surgeries	40	50	55	44
Public libraries	33	44	56	45
Social care services	23	38	40	32
Police services	25	30	40	29
Public transport	20	34	34	30

Base size: all respondents, excluding those saying 'don't know' at each individual category

Source: Unwin (2018: 16), data from Carnegie Trust survey of 5,000 people across the UK in 2018

framed as a new form of performance measurement that sits alongside value for money. The 2021 *Rebalancing care and support* in Wales White Paper stated: 'We look to service commissioners to focus on specifying, scoring and measuring against providers' ability to deliver multiple outcomes against the overarching duties set out in the Act to achieve quality services and secure well-being, balanced against value for money' (Welsh Government, 2021b: 28).

For others, the process seems little different to previous ways of commissioning care. Northern Ireland's report on domiciliary care reform (*A managed change*) in 2015 suggested that traditional and outcomes-based approaches might be very similar if the same amount of money was available:

> The 'time and task' model of providing domiciliary care has come in for significant criticism in the media and is often articulated in the currency of '15 minute calls'. ... The alternative, referenced earlier, is the 'outcomes based approach' which theoretically starts with assessed need and care outcomes and thereby informs time allocations and costs. In reality there may be little difference between these options if the core budget remains the same. (Health and Social Care Board, 2015: 41)

The *Power to people* report in Northern Ireland is also cautious about the outcome approach: 'It is our view that the term "outcome-based" in the social care context has become familiar before there is a proper understanding of what it actually means' (Kelly and Kennedy, 2017: 28). The Feeley Report in Scotland notes that 'Previous attempts to establish a single set of outcome measures across adult health and social care have been hampered by complexity and duplication' (Feeley, 2021: 51). In setting out a new approach to health and social care in Scotland, Feeley recommended:

> [A] single, clear set of outcomes, process measures and balancing measures should be developed for the whole health and social care system. ... It should ... ensure a focus on outcomes for people using social care supports and healthcare services and should reflect the ethical and collaborative approach to commissioning that we recommend here. (Feeley, 2021: 51)

A key aspect of the success of outcomes-based commissioning is risk and benefit sharing (Needham et al, 2022). The complex nature of health and social care issues means that an outcomes approach will involve many actors. If there are successes or failures it will be more difficult to attribute success or blame to a specific area of the wider system. This is a stark departure from commissioning on a fee-for-services basis, where a specific provider is accountable for a service or activity line. Trying to improve the sophistication of the commissioning of services is the rationale behind changes in England to give the Care Quality

Commission powers to inspect local authority commissioning teams (DHSC, 2021b). In Scotland, it underpins proposals within the National Care Service to take commissioning away from local authorities and give it to centrally-appointed care boards (Scottish Government, 2021).

Overall, then, an outcomes orientation has been difficult to operationalise within the four nations and difficult to compare between them, given lack of data. In the rest of this chapter we assess how far the four nations have achieved what they set out to do across the six mechanisms (redistribute the costs of care; personalise support; support unpaid carers; invest in prevention; integrate with health; and professionalise the workforce).

Redistribute the costs of care

In Chapter 4 we set out the two main routes to reforming care funding in the four nations: the free personal care option and the care cap. After 20 years of free personal care in Scotland, it is possible to see how it has worked in practice. As Figure 5.2 shows, the number of older people supported by the state (per 100,000) in Scotland is higher than in the other three nations, followed by Northern Ireland, which also has free personal care at home. There is no similar pattern in support for working-age people, probably due to the relative recency of extending free personal care to under-65s in Scotland, and the relatively few people in this age group who had been self-funding before the change.

Figure 5.2: Number of state-funded clients (as organised by local authority or HSCT) per 100,000 of population age-group (2017)

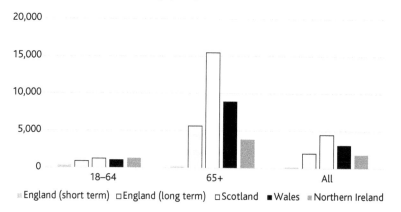

Source: Oung et al (2020), data from Nuffield Trust analysis of NHS Digital – Adult Social Care Activity and Finance Report, England (2017); Welsh government – Adults receiving services by local authority and age group (2018); NISCC – Social Care Matters (2017); HSCB – Statistical Report (2016); DoH – Statistics on Community Care for Adults in Northern Ireland (2017); ISD Scotland – Insights into Social Care in Scotland (2017); ONS Mid-year population estimates (2017)

Beyond the numbers receiving care, there has also been a large increase in Scotland in demand for local authority assessments, since people must have care needs at the requisite level if they are to quality for free personal care (Lemmon and Bell, 2019). When free personal care was first implemented in 2002, it had been feared there would be a reduction in unpaid care, as families looked more to the state for care funding. A 2015 study found no evidence of this, instead noting a complementary effect, with carers carrying on longer in providing 'non-personal' care (Karlsberg Schaffer, 2015). A 2008 review of the Scottish policy by Lord Sutherland (whose 1999 report had proposed free personal care for the whole of the UK) suggested that benefits may be felt in the 'quality' of care, with more scope for family to support people with social activities when the state provided increased support for tasks such as help with eating and bathing (Sutherland, 2008).

The commitment to free personal care has contributed to some centralisation of care policy in Scotland, with an agreed national rate for personal care and nursing care, and a National Care Home Contract. This standardisation in Scotland's care funding has required annual negotiation between key stakeholders, including care providers, local authorities and integrated joint boards, which may explain why it has gone further than others in its proposals for a National Care Service.

Many of the Scottish interviewees were supportive of the policy of free personal care, but noted that there had been unintended consequences for other policy ambitions within the system. In particular, the policy had increased the focus on categorising people according to their needs, rather than incentivising preventative or holistic approaches:

'It has made a major difference. What it negatively has done, however, has been to take our eye off a prevention orientation.' (Scotland, provider representative)

'So, whereas up, washed, dressed, fed and bed is not chargeable, all the other services that people receive are chargeable. Therefore we had to start categorising what it is we're doing to people, with people. Which then becomes a huge bureaucracy, which wasn't or isn't helpful. And personal care is just one aspect of care for the whole person.' (Scotland, civil servant)

Given the focus on meeting assessed care needs – that is, on care as a set of tasks – this more functional approach to care also creates tensions with the self-directed support policy within Scotland, which is about taking a more expansive view of what people need to support better outcomes.

Figure 5.3 shows how patterns of care in Scotland have changed over the period since implementation. After a decade, fewer people were receiving

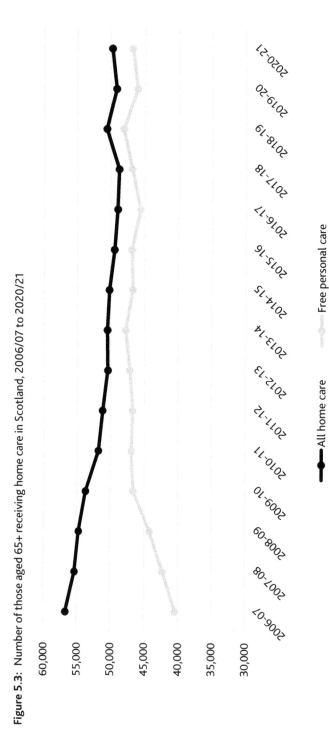

Figure 5.3: Number of those aged 65+ receiving home care in Scotland, 2006/07 to 2020/21

Source: Scottish Government (2013, 2022), data from Community Care Quarterly Key Monitoring Return

care, and almost all the care provided was free personal care, within its relatively limited scope (Bell, 2018).

Free personal care in Scotland has not dealt with all aspects of fairness discussed in previous chapters. Self-funders (one-third of those in care homes) paying their own accommodation costs pay over 40 per cent more than state-funded residents for accommodation (CMA, 2017). Self-funders in Scotland have also lost the Attendance Allowance that is payable to self-funders in other UK jurisdictions. The need for people to continue to pay for everything, apart from (narrowly defined) personal care tasks, is poorly understood by the public (Self Directed Support Scotland, 2020). As one interviewee put it: "I don't think the general public is fully aware about what the restrictions are, because they hear the words, 'Free personal care.' And think that's what it means, which is certainly does not" (Scotland, provider representative).

In Wales, reform of care funding became part of Labour and Plaid Cymru's *Co-operation agreement* after the 2021 election (Welsh Government, 2021a), and it is likely it will continue to form the basis of care policy discussions. A briefing on free personal care by the Wales Fiscal Analysis (2020) team at the University of Cardiff raises several issues regarding possible implementation. It highlighted the higher proportion of social care demand in Wales, compared to in Scotland, the different means-tested threshold (impacting the starting point for free personal care implementation), the difference in private provision availability and the possible impact of Attendance Allowance changes. Their rough estimate was increased expenditure of £305.2 million, and there were concerns that, in a post-COVID-19 situation, this figure might rise under the existing devolution settlement (Wales Fiscal Analysis, 2020).

The second approach to making care funding fairer is a care cap to limit private expenditure. This was expected to be introduced in England towards the end of 2023 (DHSC, 2021a) but has now been postponed until 2025 (HM Treasury, 2022). Introducing the care cap would mean people in England would, for the first time, have protection against very high care costs, although the high level at which the cap is to be set means it is only likely to affect people who live in a care home for several years (DHSC, 2022). Linked to the care cap are the 'fair costs of care' proposals designed to reduce the self-funder subsidy, as people can ask local authorities to purchase care on their behalf at the local authority rate (DHSC, 2022). If the care cap goes ahead, it is likely that some issues similar to those in Scotland will be encountered. The first is the mismatch between public expectations and reality, when people learn that the care cap will only apply to 'personal care' expenditure and not to their other expenditure, such as accommodation and food in care homes. Second, implementation is likely to be hampered by the same complexity that led to the abandonment (in 2016) of the initial

Care Act 2014 cap. Local authorities have to be able to identify self-funders, to assess that they have care needs that are eligible, and then start a 'meter' to track their care spending. It is expected that they will need to undertake many more assessments and reviews (HM Government, 2021), putting additional strain on an already pressurised local authority workforce. It is impossible to assess how the cap will work in practice, ahead of detailed implementation plans, or whether it will achieve the required results and make the system fairer, and its postponement until 2025 highlights that there are many practical difficulties ahead.

Personalise support

Personalisation (England) or self-directed support (other nations) means a focus on the person in receipt of care. It involves access to information and advocacy in order to provide choice and control and access to high-quality and flexible support. In practice, the focus of personalisation has mostly been on the roll-out of personal budgets, and their distribution as direct payments. The uptake of direct payments has varied between user groups and between the four nations, as shown in Figure 5.4. England has the highest level of public funds distributed as a direct payment (around 10 per cent). Wales distributes 6 per cent of its funds as direct payments. Scotland has the poorest performance on direct payments, distributing only around 3 per cent. Somewhat surprisingly, there has been a recent upswing in receipt of direct payments in the Northern Irish system, which, in 2018–19, distributed 7 per cent of its funds as direct payments (Gray and Birrell, 2013; Oung et al, 2020).

In line with the pattern shown in Figure 5.4, more recent data from England shows that the numbers of people holding a direct payment in England has fallen year on year since 2016/17 (The King's Fund, 2021).

Looking across the four jurisdictions, Pearson et al (2020) identify a lack of progress towards personalisation and self-directed support. Indeed, in England there was a sense of going backwards, 'a fundamental retreat from policy discourses around choice and control', with disabled organisations finding that they were losing ground that had been gained a decade earlier (Pearson et al, 2020: 292). Organisations such as Think Local, Act Personal (TLAP, 2019) in England have been highly critical of how measures such as the pre-payment cards have limited people's choice and control in some areas – a feature also found in Scotland (Pearson et al, 2020). A 2020 report on self-directed support (SDS) in Scotland heard from over 600 people with experience of using SDS (Self Directed Support Scotland, 2020). It found high levels of support for the principles of SDS and the freedoms that it had brought, but extensive problems with implementation. In relation to mental health for example, 'People were clear in stating that high quality

Figure 5.4: Spending on direct payments as a percentage of total care spending, 2000/02 to 2018/19

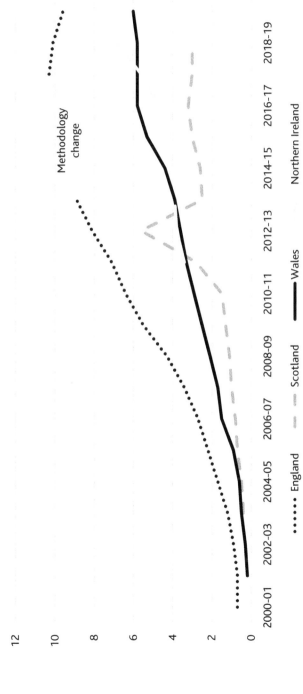

Source: Atkins et al (2021: 44), data from Institute for Government analysis of: NHS England, Adult Social Care finance reports, long-term care spending by activity; Scottish government data on expenditure on adult social care services, local financial return 03; Stats Wales, Social services revenue outturn, net expenditure by setting; Northern Ireland quarterly direct payments statistics December 2020 and PESA spending data

support via SDS is beneficial to their mental health. However, they were also explicit in outlining how inadequate assessment processes and reductions in support have a negative impact on their mental health' (Self Directed Support Scotland, 2020: 9).

Pearson et al (2018) used Freedom of Information requests and telephone interviews with local authorities in Scotland to explore implementation of SDS. They concluded that 'the introduction of SDS has resulted in little change in the way that social care is delivered' (2018: 667). They were particularly critical of the failure to engage meaningfully with co-production (2018: 663). They identified a number of reasons for slow progress on SDS, including policy overload, as the attention of the Scottish Government moved on to other agendas, rather than ensuring implementation of SDS; a lack of understanding of SDS within the health domain; and the impact of austerity. Too much focus on integration with health was also directing policy attention away from SDS.

Pearson and Ridley (2017) explore whether SDS was the right policy but 'at the wrong time', given the pressures of austerity, concluding that this was certainly a factor in creating an environment that was not conducive to implementation. Across the four nations, interviews with disabled people's organisations found that austerity had led to a loss of innovation and reduction to functional tasks, with pressures particularly acute in England (Pearson et al, 2020: 289). One of our Scottish interviewees, a civil servant from the SDS team within the Scottish Government, highlighted the tension with the free personal care policy: "I was at a review just recently of a lady who's 100 who lives on her own and has a small amount of payment to direct her own care and support. But the social worker's discussion was actually all about personal care."

Another interviewee set out broader frustrations with the implementation of SDS to date:

> 'The narrative in Scotland is, you know, well, you all must innovate, we need to find the solution, whether it's more family care, whether it's reducing paid support, whatever the hell it is and I keep saying to them, "Well you legislated for it, it's called SDS, why not try it?" Why not try and implement that first, see if it works. Really push the implementation of it and then that might be the answer to your problems. You've legislated for that and you're kind of just leaving it to rot.' (Scotland, third sector)

A new Framework of Standards to support SDS was published in 2019 to reinvigorate the policy, although since then attention has focused more on National Care Service development than on SDS per se.

In Northern Ireland, 6,411 people were receiving direct payments at the end of 2021 (DH, 2022a). As in Scotland, the existence of free domiciliary care in Northern Ireland is likely to act as a disincentive to moving towards a direct payment. Where direct payments seem to have played a role in Northern Ireland has been in rural areas, where commissioned services are unavailable:

'What we see more often now is that older people, because there's a dearth of provision of care, or providers of care and when people have specific needs, they can't be met by existing arrangements, they're offered a direct payment.' (Northern Ireland, regulatory/ oversight body)

'I would see a much higher incidence of direct payments in rural areas because the care staff aren't there, so they are paying family members.' (Northern Ireland, carers' organisation)

While the flexibility of direct payments does create opportunities here, their use to supplement 'thin markets' is a limited form of self-direction (Carey et al, 2018). A fuller approach requires that providers and commissioners create the conditions that enable person-centred support (Needham et al, 2022). One of the Northern Irish interviewees from the third sector highlighted that even where care is person-centred in terms of the relationships, it cannot be personalised when stuck within a rigid and underfunded system:

'And people say, "But I really like when Dolores comes in. Dolores is lovely and she does her best. She will make me a cup of tea even though she's not supposed to and she will bring a pint of milk". At a personal level, there is great value put on it. But we also talked to people who are being put to bed at 6:30 in the evening and their morning call is at 11:00 the next morning. And they're incontinent. ... Even though, "I really like the young woman who puts me to bed and I really like the young woman who gets me up", this is terrible. 16 or 17 hours in bed. Do you know?'

This point reaffirms the interdependency of different care mechanisms in which making care more person-centred and relational also requires attention to the adequacy of funding.

Much of the focus of personalised support has been on people living at home, although there is scope to develop the agenda within care homes (Ettelt et al, 2020; NIHR, 2021). The high prevalence of dementia in care homes means that initiatives here must be appropriate for people with cognitive impairments. Ballard led a study on people with dementia in care homes for the National Institute of Health Research (NIHR), and noted: 'In the case of personalised care, we know what to do and yet we can't make the system deliver what's needed' (Ballard et al, 2020). A number of challenges were identified, many of which related to the additional work, the lack of flexibility of team rotas and inadequate levels of staffing.

Overall, then, it is clear that approaches to personalisation are still very limited in all four nations, for a range of reasons that link to austerity, prioritisation of other agendas (for example, free personal care or integration with health), lack of appropriate commissioning or market shaping to facilitate choice and control, and system pressures such as lack of staffing.

Support unpaid carers

Analysis of the implementation of carer support in England found that the wellbeing commitments of the Care Act were being undermined by the challenging financial context facing local authorities (Marczak et al, 2022). The number of carers' assessments had fallen, and there had been a reduction in carer-related local authority expenditure since the introduction of the Act. One English interviewee, a former civil servant, suggested that carers' policy lacked ambition, focusing on incremental change rather than a more systemic approach:

> 'When you look at carers' policy, it does tend to be about very small marginal gains on the edges, kind of "Can we slightly improve Carer's Allowances by £5?" territory, where you think this is absolutely not reflecting the contribution and the pressure of being a carer. So, I think all the policy has really been about is minimising harm or damage to the carer by respite or health checks, etc.'

In Scotland, legal rights for carers are similar to England and Wales. However, carers' more generous benefit allowance marks a clear advance in comparison to the other four nations. An interviewee in an English carers' organisation noted: "Scotland is racing ahead with its carers' benefits policy – it's leaving England, Wales and Northern Ireland behind."

Nonetheless, the provision of statutory support to carers in Scotland remains limited. A Carers' Scotland report (Collie, 2019) found that the proportion of carers having an assessment or review in 2019 was 21 per cent, down from 31 per cent in 2016. In Wales, the impact of the Social Services and Well-being (Wales) Act on carers has been assessed through the *Measuring the mountain* project. Its final report noted: 'The most urgent conclusion however, is the need to provide better support for carers. Three in four of their experiences were negative, and their stories demonstrated more than any others, the impact of not treating people as partners and of not recognising their views, expertise or needs' (Cooke et al, 2019: 79).

In the Welsh local site, the local authority care commissioner made a positive case for the difference made in terms of access to Carer's Assessments ensured by the Act. They argued that recognition alone through the assessment is in itself an achievement:

'I think the fact that carers are allowed to be heard, to be seen as carers, to have that Carer's Assessment really has made a difference. I think it gives it a clearer definition that that person is a carer. They're acknowledged as a carer; they're known as a carer then. And, you know, I think it safeguards them as well. If anything was to happen to the carer, there's a plan there.'

However, other interviewees were concerned that while legislation provided rights to assessment and support, often carers had no knowledge of these rights, and were therefore not accessing them or getting their assessed needs met:

'Frequently, do they even know about the right to a carer's needs assessment? That's something since the Act that we've picked up and thinking, no, we need to do a publicity campaign. There was a push at the start, the carers' organisation is always keen to help and work with us. I talk with them very frequently to think about, well, how are we getting those messages out?' (Wales, civil servant)

In Northern Ireland, where carers have a right to an assessment (but not to have their needs met), participants felt similarly frustrated at going through the process of assessment, only to be denied access to any services that might meet their assessed need:

'Carers that we talk to or that contact us, will say, "Well, what's the point in having a carer assessment, they never do anything about it?" I had one three years ago, I said that I needed maybe one overnight a week, or whatever, and X, Y and Z, and they came back and said they didn't have the money to do it. There's a lot of unmet need in Northern Ireland, because some carers here just sort of say, "Well, what's the point in doing it in the first place?"' (Northern Ireland, carers' organisation)

In relation to supporting carers, therefore, there was widespread feeling that the policies had not met their objectives. As with the other reform mechanisms, austerity was felt to be a barrier in translating carers' rights into tangible support, even in the relatively well-funded Northern Irish care system.

Invest in prevention

The Care Act 2014 in England created a duty on local authorities to provide preventative interventions that help improve people's independence and wellbeing. The Social Services and Well-being (Wales) Act (2014) makes a similar commitment, as does the Scottish *Health and social care delivery plan* (Scottish Government, 2016), and *Power to people* (Kelly and Kennedy, 2017) in Northern Ireland. However, funding pressures have meant that they have needed to refocus attention on the provision of services for people with existing care needs, shifting attention away from prevention. This highlights a key paradox, which is that although prevention is likely to save money and improve outcomes in the longer term, it is seen as dispensable in the short term when budgets are tight (Tew et al, 2019). Cairney et al note that although prevention is highlighted as one of the key pillars of the 'Scottish approach', it is more of 'a normative policy ideal, a vague but important "communicative practice"' rather than a concrete policy (Cairney et al, 2016: 341–2).

Given the counterfactuals involved (measuring the interventions that have been avoided), it has been widely noted that measuring the success of prevention is difficult (Allen and Glasby, 2013). In England, Tew et al (2019) found that the financial challenges of austerity limited the capacity of local authorities to promote wellbeing and to prevent, reduce or delay the need to access social care services. Similarly, Marczak et al (2022) found English local authorities were defining prevention in different ways, failing to link up with health partners and struggling to invest in prevention given the challenges of austerity.

There was also a clear sense of things getting worse as financial pressures put more strain on the system:

> 'We haven't got the money and you can't spend what you haven't got. I think with the money that we have now got, we don't access them until they're at a critical point and that is a big difference to years ago, where you would get them earlier. Because we haven't got the money now.' (England, local councillor)

An Audit Wales report on progress on the Well-being of Future Generations agenda found a lack of joined-up working:

> For most of the steps we reviewed, public bodies had not identified a way of measuring the impact of prevention. ... This also needs to be a collective endeavour; public bodies can only really plan for and measure the impact of prevention across the delivery system. Benefits delivered by one partner may reduce demand for another. This underlines the

importance of linking prevention with integration. (Audit Wales, 2020: 29)

In all four jurisdictions, the rhetoric of taking a more preventative approach has clashed with other goals of the care system. One interviewee, a care provider from Scotland, linked the lack of preventative work to wariness around tracking unmet need in the system:

'There's a reluctance to record un-met need. Because that almost means that there's a sense of failure. There's a thing about keeping staff morale up, saying we're doing the best we can with the resources we have. But then a lot of staff are saying I know if I had more time with a person, I would actually be able to keep them in the community longer. And so there's a constant sort of battle about trying to prove a negative. How can you prove that something hasn't happened?'

In Northern Ireland, there has been a commitment to 'shift left' (Health and Social Care Board, 2015), in other words, to invest in early prevention to reduce or delay people's use of acute or long-term services. The *Power to people* report called for a fundamental shift to prevention (Kelly and Kennedy, 2017). However, in the absence of any implementation of the report's findings, this agenda remains stalled.

Although prevention continues to be a key priority in the most recent policy statements in the four nations, the ability to achieve this alongside other priorities has been limited. The scope for technology to transform the sector, and in particular to support more preventative interventions, currently remains underdeveloped. A review of technology preparedness within care services notes that local authorities are not well placed to make the most of the opportunities offered by technology, and are poorly prepared for the 'digital switchover' in 2025, which will affect analogue devices such as pendant alarms (Wright, 2020). There is too much 'pilotitis' rather than a strategic approach to technology-enabled care. Some citizens have access to consumer technology to support them in care – such as Amazon's Alexa; however, infrastructure can be poor, particularly in rural areas, and there is still a 'digital divide' in access to and skills in technology (Hamblin, 2020). Issues of privacy and data security have not been properly addressed (Hamblin, 2020; Wright, 2021).

Overall, prevention continues to be an aspiration rather than a clearly developed set of policies in all four nations. All four have made a commitment to asset- and strengths-based approaches that seek to move away from deficit models of care assessment. However, the prevention agenda can struggle to sustain momentum when urgent pressures hit other parts of the system.

The difficulties of evidencing the effects of investment and the risk that savings accrue to a different part of the system continue to be disincentives to sustained commitment to prevention.

Integrate with health

Although integration between health and social care is widely considered vital if both systems are to be sustainable and effective, achieving this has been difficult in the four nations, with all experiencing persistent barriers to integration. The structural distinction between health and social care hampers coordination of assessment so long as social care remains means tested and the NHS is a universal service.

Northern Ireland, where systems have been formally integrated since the 1970s, has encountered many of the same problems as the other nations that have attempted to accelerate integration more recently (Pearson and Watson, 2018). In particular, the dominance of health has continued:

> Uniquely across the UK, Northern Ireland has a nominally fully integrated command structure for health and social care. The reality, as one individual with experience at a very senior level reflected, is that the latter has been 'the poor relation'. Another told us that integration could simply mean social care had its 'pocket picked' to support local health services, with cuts to domiciliary care one of the primary means to deliver savings. (Dayan and Heenan, 2019: 31)

The failings of the integrated approach in Northern Ireland were the focus of comments made by a civil service interviewee:

> 'The great prize of integrated care that people pursue is that you will avoid or delay: avoid unnecessary admissions into acute healthcare, or delay the progression of people's circumstances where there's a requirement for admission into acute healthcare. And that you will facilitate a smooth discharge from acute healthcare. The front door and the back door, people imagine work a lot better in an integrated system. That evidence is not there for us, on both the front and back door. ... [It is] lower middling when benchmarked against the rest of the UK. There are certainly worse places than us in the rest of the UK, but equally there are places that do not have the same integrated legislation funding or organisational structure, who seem to manage coordination of service better than we do.'

Another interviewee, from the third sector in Northern Ireland, explained:

'Social care is integrated, but on a lot of occasions it's almost in theory rather than in practice, I think. Also there is a real breakdown ... between things like health trusts and care home providers, for example, and that sort of side of social care stuff. ... Issues getting people out of hospital and into care homes over the weekend.'

Audit Scotland (2018) found that progress towards integration had been slow, particularly in relation to the sharing of information. Echoing the Northern Ireland findings, health was found to dominate in a 'hierarchical' partnership (Pearson and Watson, 2018: 402). Interviewees in our study expressed concern about the over-dominance of health priorities in integrated systems. An interviewee in a Scottish integration authority (which brings together health and care services) told us that the focus had been on NHS discharge because this was the metric on which they were measured, with the result that there was less emphasis on prevention or on other ways of using social care to help people attain wellbeing.

In 2021, the Scottish Government's consultation on plans for a National Care Service noted:

> The aim of integration was to improve people's experience of social care, and to focus on early intervention and preventative approaches, rather than only intervening when people reach a crisis. This has not worked as well as it should have done, particularly due to a lack of collaborative leadership in some areas. Financial planning is not always integrated, long-term, or focused on providing the best outcomes for people who need support. This limits the ability of integration authorities to improve the health and social care system. There is also a lack of strategic capacity and a high turnover of integration authority staff to support planning, commissioning, and delivery. Current commissioning and procurement processes are characterised by mistrust, conflict, and market forces. Procurement methodology and practices in community health and social care have increasingly driven and sometimes undermined commissioning decisions. (Scottish Government, 2021: 51)

These problems are also evident in the other UK nations. Problems of structural complexity and poor relationships become incorporated into integrated structures, rather than resolved by them. In England and in Wales, where public spending on care is lower than in Scotland, local authorities face intense pressures, with rising demand and shrinking capacity to respond. Workforce shortages are acute and providers are fragile. A fear of NHS dominance was a recurring theme in our interviews. As one Assembly

Member in Wales put it: "When you integrate health and social care, what that means, [is] that health takes everything over."

While different approaches have been taken to integration in the four nations, the problems are broadly similar. Social care sits within local government (except in Northern Ireland). It has a different assessment and funding process to the NHS. Health and care staff hold distinct professional identities and loyalties that can impede joint working. Many integration initiatives have foundered due to the domination of NHS priorities, such as hospital discharge targets (Allen et al, 2022). Yet attempts to integrate show no sign of slowing. It appears to be really hard to walk away from what the Barker Commission called 'the prize' of integration:

> This new path for health and social care, combined with the single ring-fenced budget and a single commissioner, and the provision of more equal support at the highest levels of need offers, we believe, a huge prize. Patients, users of care and support and their families would face a much simpler path through the current maze of cash benefits, health and social care. (Barker, 2014: 8)

Yet this prize – a path through the health and care maze – is one that still seems out of reach in all four nations. In a report on care systems under COVID-19, an interviewee observed: 'There's an old joke which is that integration of health and social care is five years away and always will be' (quoted in McHale and Noszlopy, 2021: 92). In our study, an interviewee questioned whether focusing so much on this prize is really helpful for social care:

> 'One of the dangers of some of the narrative around this, particularly politically, is that we see an equivalence between social care and health. And our concerns are that we have to recognise that there are fundamental differences between social care and health. One is about the fulfilment of citizenship and life. The other is about the attention to meet your [health] deficits and clinical needs.' (Scotland, provider representative)

Unforeseen side effects of aligning them too closely were also mentioned:

> 'We had a minister at the time, cabinet secretary, who because of integration, kind of flatly refused to get any legislation into Parliament that didn't say "health and social care". They tried to apply this to social care, safe staffing. Our members are [saying], like, "What, what are they doing, safe staffing?" We've got a narrative here, which is trying to reduce paid support; it's trying to move into more community stuff

120

and risk enablement and all of these exciting things, innovative things we've been talking about. Then we've got a bill that says, you need to apply this tool and you need to employ that many staff blah-blah-blah, it was just nonsense. It was all being driven out of a nursing and midwifery directorate.' (Scotland, third sector)

In a damning Nuffield Trust account of integration in all four nations, the authors concluded:

> Each of the UK's four countries has a long-standing goal to integrate health and social care services, which has been a principle of successive major reforms by each government since devolution. Despite this, we found there is limited evidence that policies in any of the UK countries have made a difference to patients, or to how well services are integrated. (Reed et al, 2021: 2)

The same report went on to note that policy makers were failing to learn the lessons of previous rounds of reform, and that there continued to be too much focus on structural change rather than culture, norms, systems and processes (Reed et al, 2021: 3).

Professionalise the workforce

As discussed in Chapter 4, improving the pay and conditions of care workers to enhance retention and quality is seen as a key reform mechanism in all four nations. Improving supply is also a concern, and has a high profile given the simultaneous pressures on staff numbers of Brexit and COVID-19 (Turnpenny and Hussein, 2022). The potential benefits of care worker registration, through improved retention and recognition for staff, as well as better quality and safer care have also been highlighted (Hayes et al, 2019). In our interviews, we found mixed attitudes towards registration. An interviewee from Social Care Wales, which oversees the Register of Social Care Workers, was supportive: "The regulations and the qualifications and the registration are really starting to impact, raise the profile, [and are] making sure we've got consistency. People are wanting to come and work in social care because it's a good place to work, because it's a growth industry."

Other interviewees raised a number of reservations about registration. These included the extent to which registration could exacerbate capacity issues in the sector:

> 'Now, we're nearly five years into post-registration for care homes and I think what we're seeing is serious work needing to be done to ensure and guarantee that we don't lose an experienced and skilled staffing

group, particularly in their late 50s and 60s, who simply don't either have the physical ability or the desire to go through a training process which is, to be blunt, at times not respectful of their experience or age.' (Scotland, provider representative)

A Welsh interviewee, a care provider, also expressed mixed feelings about care worker registration:

'I can understand the need to be registered, because then you are accountable for your own actions. But getting them through that process does put a lot of people off. Some of them, who may want to [work] part-time can't see what the need to do all this [is]. … It's not the cost of it, I think, it's more the work generated from it. To measure something which is quite vocational, isn't it, home care, rather than academic. There's value in vocation, I think, that we might be missing.'

Other Welsh respondents expressed similar concerns: "Some of what people say is that, well, actually it's just another – you've got to pay a fee, and you've got to jump through a lot of administrative hoops to do it, without actually being paid more, or getting any professional esteem" (Wales, Assembly Member).

Another reservation related to whether registration was likely to improve the quality of care: "One thing that the SSSC [Scottish Social Services Council] has never really been able to do is demonstrate that [registration] made any bloody difference to service users, actually. … There's an awful lot of assumed benefits [but] we have never seen any evidence that actually demonstrates it" (Scotland, third sector).

Another concern was about the additional bureaucracy of a compliance-oriented approach. The Feeley Report, on Scotland, noted, 'the workforce too often feel policed rather than supported as a consequence of current registration arrangements' (Feeley, 2021: 14). In Northern Ireland, a similar point was made in the *Power to people* report: 'Yet we surround care workers in a mire of paperwork, suspicion and when they get things wrong we pillory them' (Kelly and Kennedy, 2017: 53). We return in later chapters to questions of how far regulatory approaches to quality and safety are likely to be the most effective.

Another interviewee who was sceptical of the benefits of registration ('I think it's a solution looking for a problem, or a solution solving the wrong problem') nonetheless advocated a more interventionist workforce strategy:

'What [the government] has tended to do is kind of go, the public sector … isn't responsible for [social care] training, it's not responsible for workforce planning; and I think government is going to need to be more confidently in that space of actually thinking, this isn't the normal market, the public purchaser model has made this not a normal market, and therefore we've got to reach in more to shape the workforce.' (England, former civil servant)

Other mechanisms to improve the status of care workers, including better pay, have also been proposed (Hayes et al, 2019). In Scotland, the higher pay for care workers, discussed in Chapter 4, has been widely welcomed, despite some implementation issues:

'[The Scottish Living Wage] is the most progressive workforce policy I have ever seen in social care. It is also the most chaotically implemented. That makes a huge difference … a lot of social care in England is still minimum wage, and here you get paid [the Scottish Living Wage], including for sleepovers. The cost of that is astronomical, but ministers have invested in this. So that's huge, that's huge.' (Scotland, third sector)

However, in the absence of broader system change or investment, one interviewee recognised that this development had not eased the strain on the workforce. When asked if the introduction of the living wage for care workers had made any difference, a Scottish civil servant said, "I think it's made a difference to those people, but it's not generated any more capacity. It's actually reduced the capacity as well, because to be able to afford the living wage they've had to reduce the numbers of people that they employ". Steps to professionalise the workforce have, as we have shown, been taken in all four nations, with England's approach the least developed. Alongside registration, this has led to improved wages for care workers in Scotland, and in the other nations to a commitment to improve training and other forms of workforce support, although this has not addressed capacity issues in the sector.

Who's best?

One of McConnell's success criteria (discussed in Chapter 1) relates to benefits for target groups. This begs the question of whether a person using social care services, a carer or a care worker is better off living in one of the four nations rather than in the others. The limitations of these labels should be acknowledged: each refers to heterogeneous groups, many people are in two or more of these categories, and the labels can be highly reductive.

There are policy elements in each of the four nations that are likely to improve aspects of care. On balance, Scotland has most of these, with free personal care, registration and pay guarantees for care workers and more generous benefits for carers. Nonetheless, the implementation of SDS has been slow, and the proportion of people with direct payments is lower than in the other nations. This, and the ways in which free personal care may exacerbate rationing and encourage a functional time-based model of care commissioning, means that on average the experience of a person needing care and support services may be no better in Scotland than elsewhere.

Wales has a maximum charge for home care, a relatively generous means test, and a registered care workforce. However, implementation of carers' rights and the development of SDS are no more advanced in Wales than elsewhere. Northern Ireland has a registered workforce and *de facto* free personal care at home, but continues to have problems of care workforce supply, and delays in discharging people from hospital. England has made the least progress in most of these areas, and so may currently be the worst place to be a user of care services, a carer or a care worker. However, plans to reform care funding from 2025, and variability between England's 152 local authorities, makes generalisation about national experience particularly difficult in the largest of the four nations.

A key element to emphasise is that reform agendas do not necessarily deliver 'win-wins' for all these groups. Registering care workers may improve status – particularly if introduced as part of a broader package, with better training and pay – but may not enhance the quality of care. Choice and control for people using care services may require a higher tolerance of informality and risk than is currently seen in care systems, and may mean less, rather than more, regulation and consistency. Carers will benefit from greater rights, if these are implemented, and from more generous benefit payments, but a free personal care policy may not help much if it leads to tighter rationing of services that puts carers under even greater pressure. In Chapter 7 we suggest that there is a fault line between approaches that value formality, centralisation and standardisation (paradigm one) and those that prioritise informality, subsidiarity and diversity (paradigm two). We suggest that, to date, reforms have often tried to develop both at the same time, failing to acknowledge, let alone explore, the inherent tensions between them.

Social care institutions in the four nations are differently configured, following pursuit of different approaches over nearly 25 years. None has a sustainable care system. As set out in this chapter, there has been some change; the problem is not a lack of policy activity, but rather a failure to translate policy into a better experience of care for people who need support. An interesting feature of the four care systems is that 'macro' goals are so similar: the commitment to wellbeing, fairness, rights quality and sustainability (set out in Chapter 2), as are the mechanisms (Chapter 4) through which governments attempt change (redistribute the costs of care; personalise support; support unpaid carers; invest in prevention; integrate with health; and professionalise the workforce). However, funding has not been reformed to ensure there is sufficient money in the system to make it sustainable, in the short, medium or longer term. Integration either has not happened, or has not had the expected results. Quality and outcomes orientations have been very hard to operationalise. Despite legislative intentions, prevention has not been the focus of funding. Carers have become even more over-stretched, the workforce is still in crisis, and integration with health has had disappointing results.

In this context, there are questions to consider about how much legislation can achieve, and how long it takes for legislation to make a difference (Burn and Needham, 2021). Having rights has not guaranteed access to support or services for carers, even where there is a statutory duty for local authorities to provide these. In England, the revival of the care cap policy, seven years after it was passed into legislation in Section 18(3) of the Care Act 2014, could be an indication not to give up on implementation even after a long delay. Alternatively, now it has been postponed yet again, it may indicate a lack of fresh ideas and an over-optimism that the system frailties that derailed the proposals in 2017 will be any less severe this time. After 25 years of policy activity and debate on social care – evident in the documents we analysed for our study – it seems a more sustainable social care system remains elusive. Rationing of services has increased, making access harder for people with support needs, and pressures on local authorities, care providers, care workers and carers has intensified. In the 2010s, England bore the brunt of financial austerity policies, yet the strain is evident in all four nations.

Conclusion

In this chapter we have analysed what is known about how convergence and divergence in the practice and results of the policy developments set out in Chapter 4. We note the similar patterns in all four nations: funding reform is incomplete; personalisation and self-direction has stalled, at least in relation to individualised funding; carers' rights have not been implemented; integration has failed to deliver clear benefits; and registration and improved pay for care workers in some jurisdictions has been welcome, but may have intensified capacity issues, and does not assure quality work or quality care. In Chapters 6 and 7 we look at different explanatory factors to explore the patterns found in the four nations. In Chapter 6 we locate these in an analysis of distinctive features of four 'territorial policy communities' – London, Belfast, Edinburgh and Cardiff – focusing on the policy scale, style and scope in each nation. In Chapter 7, we shift the lens to look at implementation challenges and consider two social care paradigms – the 'standardised' and the 'differentiated' – that (often implicitly) coexist within the same systems. We argue that these need to be explored and disentangled if a more sustainable settlement is to be achieved.

6

Territorial policy communities: scale, style and scope

In the earlier chapters we set out patterns in the care contexts, policies (or mechanisms) and outcomes in the four nations of the UK, discussing convergence and divergence. This is the first of two chapters in which we explain the patterns that we found. Here the lens is on the 'territorial policy communities' (Keating et al, 2009) in the four nations, which we use to explain some of the similarities and differences in their care policy development. Earlier chapters have examined each nation's approach to social care policy-making over 25 years. At the end of Chapter 4 we summarised these approaches as, in the case of Scotland 'active', in Wales 'emergent', in England 'symbolic' and in Northern Ireland 'stalled'. This chapter considers the institutional design and approaches to policy-making in the territorial policy communities in the four nations. We look at how the *scale*, *style* and *scope* of policy has made it easier for Scotland to go furthest on care policy reform, making the most of a relatively consensual policy environment, with limited veto players. England has been hampered by its larger and more siloed institutions, influential veto players and an overloaded agenda. Wales and Northern Ireland have had constitutional factors to deal with throughout the period, which have delayed (Wales) or inhibited (Northern Ireland) their capacity to be active policy makers on social care. The chapter begins by setting out the concept of 'territorial policy communities', and then looks in turn at scale, style and scope.

Territorial policy communities

Keating et al (2009) propose the concept of 'territorial policy communities' to explore the 'rescaling' of policy that has accompanied devolution in many countries. They argue that the emergence of new policy communities is not an inevitable consequence of devolution: it will depend on the strength of devolution and the extent to which issues are part of the policy competencies of the new institutions. While their focus is particularly on interest group activity in devolved settings, Keating et al (2009) highlight how once a policy domain becomes the jurisdiction of a new institution, it is likely to gather momentum and legitimacy over time. In the case of social care, for example, this has been an area of competence for the newly created institutions in Scotland and Northern Ireland, and, to a more limited extent,

Wales, since 1998. However, it has taken time for each of them to develop new territorial policy communities, based on the terms of the devolution settlements and changes since then. Further, Keating et al differentiate between structural characteristics of policy communities and the 'cognitive frames' through which actors understand identity, shared norms, values and interests (2009: 53–4). Like broader work on discursive institutionalism, this draws attention to ideas and discourses as drivers of change within policy communities (Schmidt, 2008).

In all four nations of the UK, there is a path-dependence at work, with the situation before devolution being important in understanding how the policy communities have developed since 1998 (Keating and Wilson, 2014). As Sir Peter Housden puts it, reflecting on his experiences as Permanent Secretary within the Scottish Government, 'No Government of course writes on a blank slate. … But history does not present a uniform picture' (Housden, 2014: 65). Studying convergence means looking at how polities trace 'an uncertain trajectory through time' (Pollitt, 2002: 477). Keating et al similarly highlight the importance of the past, not only in shaping institutions but also in forming 'the national imaginary' (Keating et al, 2021).

Keating et al's (2009) interview-based research found that, prior to devolution, Scotland had a well-developed policy community and interest groups in most policy domains, but that this was more nascent in Northern Ireland and Wales. Northern Ireland's distinctive history of sectarianism and violence contributed to an underdeveloped and divided policy community, although before devolution – in the absence of political leadership on key issues – the voluntary sector played an important role in policy-making (Keating et al, 2009: 62). In Wales, there was little interest group activity prior to devolution, with most organisations focusing on Westminster due to the 'greater administrative integration of Wales with England, the lack of pre-union organizations, the weaker development of the Welsh Office and the cross-border flows of people and services' (Keating et al, 2009: 57).

This context contributed to the devolution readiness of the three nations in 1998. Scotland already had its own legal and educational system and a relatively autonomous civil service based in the Scottish Office in Edinburgh (Ferguson, 2019). Devolution offered Scotland its own Executive, with legislative power over issues not explicitly reserved. The devolution referendum in 1997 was passed by a convincing margin, and Scotland made relatively rapid progress in establishing its separateness from Westminster (Harvey, 2020). The Executive came to be called the Scottish Government after 2007, and since then new powers relating to taxation and social security have further extended the jurisdiction of the Scottish institutions. With the pro-independence Scottish National Party (SNP) in power since 2007, momentum has continued to gather towards greater separateness from policy at the UK level. The 2014 referendum on Scottish independence did not pass, but 44 per cent of voters supported independence. While the SNP remains in power, independence is likely to be high on the agenda, with implications for the other devolved nations and the Union itself.

In Wales, the 1997 referendum resulted in a very narrow margin in favour of devolution, highlighting ambivalence towards the move to self-government (Drakeford, 2005). The settlement delivered Wales an Assembly, with specific administrative competences but without executive power, a much weaker form of devolution than had been granted in Scotland (Harvey, 2020). Mark Drakeford, First Minister of Wales from 2018, and previously a social policy academic and adviser to the Welsh Government, noted that in 1998 'expectations of what the institution might provide were limited and without the sense of optimism and history making which surrounded the establishment of the Scottish Parliament' (2005: 498). Welsh institutions have been in almost permanent constitutional reform mode, gradually accruing powers on a par with those of Scotland and Northern Ireland. The Government of Wales Act 2006 created a separate Executive, formally confirming what had been emerging in practice since 2000. In 2011, following a referendum, Wales gained legislative competence over 20 policy domains (including health and social care) (Moon and Evans, 2017). Subsequently, through reform Acts in 2014 and 2017, the Welsh Assembly acquired jurisdiction over all matters not expressly reserved to Westminster, including over some taxation (Moon and Evans, 2017). In 2020, the Welsh Assembly was renamed the Senedd, in formal recognition of its role as a Parliament. This expansion in powers has been attributed to sustained policy entrepreneurship, with Wales also looking to other small nations for inspiration (Cole et al, 2015: 311).

In Northern Ireland, the 'Good Friday' (or Belfast) Agreement 1998, approved in referenda the same year, was freighted with the sectarianism and violence that preceded it. A 'power-sharing' Assembly and Executive were created, with ministerial positions shared by the two largest parties in the Assembly and competence in areas not reserved to Westminster. For most of the period since then, the unionists (predominantly the Democratic Unionist Party, the DUP) have held a majority, sharing power with the nationalists (predominantly Sinn Féin). This has been a punctuated process, with the Assembly suspended five times (including for five years between autumn 2002 and May 2007). The most recent suspension (2017–20) ended when the DUP and Sinn Féin agreed to work together in government. However, elections in 2022 which gave a majority to Sinn Féin, led to extensive delays in forming an Executive.

A public official from the Health and Social Care Board in Northern Ireland interviewed for our study commented on the impact of this 'stop-start' experience:

'After the Good Friday Agreement ... we got a devolved government. We got an Assembly. ... [W]hen the Assembly has then collapsed ... we've had a decision that the civil service will step into the space of the ministerial accountability and will make some decisions to keep the administration of government going. That, more so, blurs the lines as to what's political accountability. ... There's almost a bit about the system outpacing the politicians, which I think is unique to Northern Ireland because of the vacuum at the centre.'

The civil service has thus been able to assure continuity of policy in relation to social care, including sustaining high levels of spending relative to the rest of the UK, but new legislation does require political leadership.

English policy-making at Westminster, in terms of institutional formation and the size and shape of policy communities, has remained relatively stable during this 25-year period, in contrast to the experience in the other three nations. The 'radical asymmetry' of the devolution arrangements has left England without any form of separate representation (Keating et al, 2012: 289). This is not to say it has been a period of calm in Westminster politics. Since 2010 in particular, the traditions of single-party government have been disrupted by a Conservative-Liberal Democrat coalition (2010–15) and a minority Conservative government (2017–19, under Prime Minister Theresa May). Boris Johnson's replacement as Prime Minister by Liz Truss in summer 2022 and then Rishi Sunak in autumn 2022, without any electoral endorsement, has further challenged the legitimacy of government. These changes, alongside the paroxysms of Brexit, the murders of two sitting MPs (Labour's Jo Cox in 2016 and the Conservative MP Sir David Amess in 2021), and the COVID-19 pandemic, have created a sense of a democratic settlement under intense strain.

From a devolution perspective, the prospect of an English parliament seems as far away as ever, although the formation of combined authorities within some city regions since 2014 has restarted a regional agenda (Shutt and Liddle, 2019). In health and social care, Greater Manchester has developed a distinctive agenda, with pooled budgets and shared staffing, although reform there has been hampered by ongoing fiscal austerity (Walshe et al, 2016; Chang, 2022). As other combined authorities emerge, for example in the West Midlands and Tees Valley, without the history of joint local authority collaboration that characterises Greater Manchester (Shutt and Liddle, 2019), it is as yet unclear how far these will be engines for significant health and care reconfiguration.

Given the different starting points of the four nations in 1998, and how they have developed since then, we use the concepts of scale, style and scope to explain why Scotland has been the most active policy maker on social care, whereas the other nations have been more limited in their reforms.

Scale

One feature of the four nations that may explain their approach to social care is their size. Scale has implications for structure and identity and is important in understanding policy communities (Ansell and Torfing, 2015). Scotland, Wales and Northern Ireland have populations that are 10 times smaller than England's, and their legislative bodies are smaller too. Westminster has 650 Members of Parliament (MPs) compared with Scotland's 129 Members of the Scottish Parliament (MSPs), Wales' 60 Members of the Senedd (MS) (previously called Assembly Members, AMs) and Northern Ireland's 90 Members of the Legislative Assembly (MLAs).

It has been claimed that collaborative styles of government are easier in smaller polities; in larger systems, barriers include higher transaction costs, greater heterogeneity and a lack of trust-based social learning (Ansell and Torfing, 2015: 2). The role of personal contacts in small states, facilitating short lines of communication and helping overcome vetoes, has also been highlighted (Keating, 2015: 16). Small states are also considered to have relatively cohesive elites, particularly when there is a perceived sense of external threat, such as from a large neighbour (Katzenstein, 2016).

As has been argued earlier, since devolution, Scotland has gone furthest of the four UK nations in developing social care reform. It is pertinent to consider how far this may be due to its relatively small policy community. Small, cohesive policy communities can find it easier to reduce the impact of veto players who might otherwise block reform (Cairney et al, 2016; Rocco, 2017) Cairney et al (2016) argue that the limited policy capacity of Scotland's small Executive has led to reliance on external policy expertise, with strong professional and personal networks between interest groups and public bodies. Some of the Scottish interviewees linked specific policy approaches to Scotland's small population:

'[O]ne of the benefits of Scotland is we are quite a small country. Some of the co-production approach is probably a bit more straightforward than in other areas.' (Scotland, local government representative)

'[T]here is a sense in Scotland that because there's 5m rather than 55m (people), we can afford to be a bit more agile.' (Scotland, NHS)

External interviewees felt that they had access to policy makers in a way that they found helpful:

'The amount of influence and access we now have to Scottish Parliament, to ministers, they hear us very directly. We have no problem telling them what we think about stuff. They usually have no problem listening to it. It's kind of quite a collegiate atmosphere, they don't always listen, but sometimes they do. The [care] policy development has been quite collaborative in a way that I don't think it has [in England].' (Scotland, third sector)

Keating (2015: 16) emphasises that the strong links between policy makers and interest groups is a form of 'social concertation': 'Multiple venues for negotiation (rather than single peak bodies) which helps overcome veto points.' Others note that 'Scotland's emphasis on collaboration across different policy areas may mean that policy officials in Edinburgh require a slightly different mix of skills and training methods to their counterparts in Whitehall' (Paun and Munro, 2015: 24).

'Smallness' is even more pronounced in Wales. As Keating et al observe, if the folk identify of the Scottish policy community is a 'village', the Welsh equivalent is a 'family', with 'everyone round the table' (2009: 59). As in Scotland, the importance of smallness and accessibility were evident in the interviews:

'I think Welsh government has always very much been on that kind of open access, making sure we bring in a broad house of different organisations, voices, listening to them. Again, obviously there's always the political imperative and there are certain political cycles. I don't think anybody is naïve about that. Certainly the approach I've seen over in social services side is, yes, it's not just following the process, it is actually making sure we're listening to the voices, engaging with the stakeholders early on.' (Wales, civil servant)

This was echoed by a non-governmental interviewee from Social Care Wales, contrasting experience in Wales with that of peers in England:

'There is the advantage of being small. When I speak to my other UK colleagues and we'll have conversations about what we've been doing with the government or whatever, [they'll say] "What, really?" We are that close to the politicians as well as the civil servants. Sometimes you can see it as a pain, "Oh God, what do they want now?", but actually in the long run it's quite a good collaborative way of getting what needs to be done.'

A Welsh Local Government Association interviewee agreed:

'One of the biggest reasons is because of the size of Wales, and it's not a massive country, and actually if you want access to anybody then it's relatively easy. And I think that accessibility, both to lead Welsh Government officials, but it's also ministers as well, means that actually the third sector gets that accessibility and voice to the people that matter.'

Northern Ireland has the smallest population of the devolved nations, and the smallest legislative and executive institutions. As in the other jurisdictions, interviewees felt that this made a difference to the closeness of relationships and networks:

'I think we are a small society, so politicians, service users, social workers, policy makers, there's all sorts of networks of relationships and synergies, and people's paths may have crossed a number of times over the years in different roles, in different ways in society, because it is a small society. So, that probably helps to a degree.' (Northern Ireland, social work)

The perception of smallness in the other nations, and a feeling that this makes policy-making easier, was also noted by interviewees in England. An English care provider from the third sector commented:

'We've had the occasional meeting with the [Welsh] First Minister and he was personally saying he was going to offer to talk to a special adviser about staffing. You can't quite imagine the English Prime Minister … we've never managed to have that meeting, let alone that sort of personal engagement – and that is partly about that scale, as well as about somebody who just gets it.'

Scale is more than just a structural descriptor – and the interviewees' reflections on smallness may reflect national identities as well as policy systems. Cole and Stafford (2015) use Schmidt's (2008) 'discursive institutionalisation' lens to highlight the importance of the 'small country' narrative to the first decade of the Welsh Assembly. In the Foreword to the *Beyond Boundaries report*, the review chair Jeremy Beecham notes:

Wales has a marvellous opportunity, emanating in part from its traditions and in part from its scale, to lead the way in what we call 'small country governance', achieving for, but also with, its people excellent, responsive, accountable citizen-centred services in a way that its larger neighbours may find more difficult. (Beecham, 2006: 2)

Nicola Sturgeon, in her Foreword to a 2012 consultation paper on health and care integration (as Cabinet Member for Health), drew on a similar discursive claim in stating: 'Scotland is a small country, with a proud history of social co-operation' (Scottish Government, 2012: 3).

England's experience of institutional continuity at Westminster and lack of a self-conscious policy identity makes it harder to identify themes of scale in these ways. Some interviewees saw size and scale as factors in the relative complexity of adult social care reform in England, as stated here by a provider representative:

'I think the issue about England and these other countries in the UK is size and scale. If you look at what they can do in Scotland and Wales ... then you see the difference of how much easier it is to reconfigure the system in those particular areas, because of the scale of them. When you start talking about it in relation to the scale in England, it is much more difficult to do.'

A former civil servant in Westminster similarly drew attention to the way that different sizes shaped the policy context: "Certainly, the other three nations ... are in effect large local authorities in comparison to England, aren't they? Rather than England's scale with its multiple different regional markets." Just as the interviewees from smaller nations evoke smallness to emphasise the porosity of their policy communities, so, in England, its largeness is evoked here as evidence of its greater complexity and sophistication.

Looking across the four nations overall, then, we can see that Scotland was the nation most 'devolution-ready' in 1998 and appeared to benefit from having a relatively small policy community. The different starting points in Wales and Northern Ireland meant neither could capitalise on its small size to the same extent, although Welsh policy capacity has gathered momentum in the last decade. How far the foundational myths of 'smallness' can endure is perhaps a pertinent question. Writing about Scotland a decade after devolution, Keating et al noted that 'the village story about consensualism will no longer serve its purpose' (2009: 57). While Scotland has advanced care reform further than the other nations, this may be due not only to its size but also to the more incremental approach it has taken that minimises the target for veto players. As it designs its planned National Care Service, which has gone far beyond the Feeley Report in proposing changes to children's social work, community justice and GP contracts, it is harder to make claims about a consensual policy community. Responses to the consultation indicated intense opposition from a range of interest groups, including GPs, local government, children's services and parts of the third sector (Scottish Government, 2022b). COSLA (Convention of Scottish Local Authorities), which represents local government in Scotland, considered the proposals 'deeply concerning', a point we discuss later in this chapter (COSLA, 2021).

Style

The size of a policy community can also contribute to a distinctive policy-making *style*. Although not separate from issues of scale, a focus on styles draws attention to the *process* through which policy is made. As Howlett and Tosun define it, 'Although not inclusive of all aspects of a regime, the manner in which policy deliberations take place and the kinds of actors and ideas present combine to create a policy style' (2018: 16). It incorporates 'the interaction between (a) the government's approach to problem-solving and (b) the relationship between government and other actors in the policy process' (Richardson, 2013: 13). For example, it covers the extent to which governments proceed in a consensual manner or seek to enforce their will despite the resistance of organised groups. This is not just a matter of process, however; it also affects how policies and implemented: 'Styles affect the shape and character of policy outcomes in important ways and help determine aspects such as their effectiveness or content' (Howlett and Tosun, 2021: 2).

Much literature on policy styles has focused on national comparisons and classifications. In these, the UK was traditionally seen as adversarial and hierarchical, based on the Westminster model of strong government aimed at implementation of manifesto promises (Marsh, 2008). However, this is recognised to be overly simplistic (Richardson, 2018). Jordan and Richardson (1983) highlighted the *de facto* importance of policy communities at Westminster, rather than hierarchy and imposition. The 'strong government' thesis was further undermined by a growing academic focus on networks and governance rather than government (Rhodes, 1996). The majoritarianism that underpins the logic of the Westminster model has been further disrupted by a decade of coalitions and minority government from 2010 to 2019. However, Richardson argues that at Westminster the strong government thesis is now more plausible than when he was writing in 1979, with a succession of governments 'distributing costs and benefits in a top-down style, leaving interest groups in a reactive mode' (Richardson, 2018: 225). He continues: 'civil servants are now less able to strike a consensus with interest groups, as the civil servants often arrive at the table to more or less hand down decisions already made, rather than to engage in a process of mutual learning and exchange in order to generate policy solutions' (Richardson, 2018: 226).

The dominance of the Treasury and its role in policy innovation and imposition has been a key element in Westminster politics since Gordon Brown's decade as Chancellor of the Exchequer (1997–2007) (Andrews, 2022), and is seen as having played a particularly important role in relation to care reform due to the funding implications of change. This seems to have contributed to the abandonment of Care Act 2014 funding reforms in 2016. As one interviewee, a former civil servant from England, put it: "The Department of Health was happily engaging with the sector and building on many years' worth of development through the Law Commission work to come up with a long-term statutory framework, but the reality was the Treasury conversation about money was quite far detached from that."

A current civil servant at the Department of Health and Social Care noted:

'The Treasury has the … impossible task of squaring a circle financially on all these things. Basically what they do is they say, is there a legal requirement to provide this? Are we going to get sued if we don't provide this? Is there any credibly good evidence case that doing this actually saves the public sector money? You might be able to say "no, there isn't, it doesn't save the public sector money, but it really improves quality of life". And they're like, "Well, there's 15,000 of those arguments all over the place".'

The siloed nature of Whitehall was thought to block progress on care reform: "You get the Department of Health in battle with the DWP who are worried that your social care component is going to reduce people's savings for pension, and they're in battle with Treasury who are saying you're trying to mess around with inheritance tax" (England, former civil servant).

In Scotland, Wales and Northern Ireland, minority or coalition governments have been the norm, and indeed these institutions were designed to minimise the likelihood of developing a majoritarian and adversarial style of politics (St Denny, 2019). While partisan practices in the Scottish Parliament have increasingly come to resemble the adversarialism of Westminster (St Denny, 2019), Gallagher (2019: 250) notes a 'culture of consensus and avoiding hard choices' by the Scottish Government. The Scottish Government has articulated the 'Scottish approach' to policy and policy-making (Cairney et al, 2016). In relation to public services, it is most comprehensively expressed in the report of the Christie Commission and articulated through Scotland's National Performance Framework (NPF), discussed in Chapter 5. The approach is described as consultative and cooperative, based on principles of co-production; as asset-based and preventative; and as utilising improvement methodologies rather than narrow target setting (Housden, 2014; Cairney et al, 2016).

The Labour Party has held power in Wales since devolution, shifting between minority and coalition governments. Like the issue of scale, this has increased the accessibility of decision-makers. As Andrews notes: 'The minority nature of the National Assembly and the direct access of pressure groups to Assembly Members has given considerable opportunity for opposition parties to influence legislation, meaning that the role of government in policy networks is often circumscribed' (Andrews, 2022: 19).

Rhodri Morgan, Welsh First Minister from 2000 to 2009, noted the deliberate attempt in Wales to create institutions and procedures that differed from the Westminster approach: 'Well, we looked at how Parliament operated, and our usual guiding principle was to do the exact opposite!' (quoted in Andrews, 2022: 18).

An articulation of the discursive institutionalism that dominates in Wales can be found in the writings of current First Minister Mark Drakeford:

> Welsh policymaking relies on co-operation, rather than competition, as the route to better services; it prefers 'voice' rather than 'choice' as the best way of strengthening the influence of citizens (rather than consumers) in developing diverse and responsive services; it aims for a greater equality of outcome, rather than simply of opportunity. (Drakeford, 2005: 501)

Bradbury and Andrews note that Welsh Government documents are 'brimful of rhetoric promoting an inclusive sense of cultural and civic Welshness' (Bradbury and Andrews, 2010: 236). Cole et al similarly find that 'interviews with Welsh politicians and civil servants from 2001 to 2010 were replete with references to Team Wales, to cooperative modes of public service delivery, to policy innovation, to small country governance, to "genuinely joining up" policy' (Cole et al, 2015: 312).

Statements about the role of the market in social care provide a key source of differentiation between policy made by the devolved governments in Scotland and Wales and by the UK government for England. Although levels of outsourcing in the four countries are as much a product of history and ideology as of governing *style*, we can nonetheless note the extent to which a lack of enthusiasm for markets in Scotland and Wales is linked to a '*not-England*' rhetoric. While England continues to pursue market-based solutions to care (DHSC, 2021d), the other nations have sought to distance themselves from this. In relation to the crises of supply discussed in Chapter 3, we can see – particularly in Scotland and Wales – an aversion to addressing supply issues through the market, looking instead to community as the source of expansion.

Writing about Wales, Cole et al note: 'Defining the devolutionary project in terms of joined-up public service delivery and against market solutions (believed to prevail in England) was a constitutive article of faith for many policy makers in Wales' (2015: 312). A consumerist approach is explicitly seen as English; as one policy document put it: 'This has not found favour in Wales, on grounds of both principle and practicality' (Beecham, 2006: 5). According to the *Sustainable social services* White Paper: 'We look not for independence and separateness, but for interdependency with those around us. We also look outside our family to our web of wider friends and community for assistance' (Welsh Assembly Government, 2011: 9).

Rebalancing is a metaphor drawn on repeatedly by Drakeford and his government, and was used in the title of the Welsh Government's 2021 White Paper, *Rebalancing care and support*. This interviewee from Welsh local government highlights some ambiguity about what the term means:

'[T]he conversation in Wales was started under Mark Drakeford, the current First Minister, his manifesto to become First Minister talked about rebalancing. … I'm not sure we ever quite defined what we meant by rebalancing, but we've still got the term "rebalancing" floating around here. … I guess, the conversation we're having is more about that: how do we get an optimum, I suppose, mixed market?'

In Scotland, Hassan (2019) notes a similar lack of enthusiasm for choice and the market. One of the interviewees from Scotland, from the third sector, noted the reluctance to use the word 'market' in the self-directed support (SDS) legislation:

'We wanted the word "market" in there, and they wouldn't have it. They would not have the word "market" in Scottish legislation. People know that there's a market but they want to pretend that there isn't. My view is, you can't actually tackle it until you recognise what it is.'

This more pragmatic approach was endorsed in an interview with an MSP:

'But there's also a view that if it's run by the private sector it's terrible. And if it's run by the third sector, well, they're nice because they're the third sector and everybody likes their values, but actually there is poor practice across all of those. And it's, how do you drive everyone's practice up, so that you can actually squeeze out bad practice and poor practice out of the system altogether and actually lift everyone.'

The proposed National Care Service in Scotland does not propose nationalisation of services, despite scepticism about the market. The consultation documents states:

We have considered whether nationalisation – taking all of adult social care into public ownership and management – is desirable. The evidence suggests that nationalisation would not in and of itself improve outcomes for people using care. … We therefore think that the evidence does not support nationalisation into public ownership on the basis of improving the quality of care. (Scottish Government, 2021: 42)

Rather, the Scottish Government is attempting to fix perceived problems of commissioning and procurement, including 'short-termism' and a focus on low costs that make it difficult to attract and retain staff and provide quality care. It proposes a new 'National Commissioning and Procurement Structure of Standards and Processes for ethical commissioning and procurement of social care services and supports' (Scottish Government, 2021: 100).

Northern Ireland has found it more difficult to articulate a distinctive approach because of the challenges facing its power-sharing Executive in managing its politics. Party politics in Northern Ireland has continued to be dominated by sectarian tensions between the unionist and nationalist blocs. A Northern Irish interviewee from the NHS pointed to the lack of a political narrative to guide future policy compared to other parts of the UK: "If you look towards Scotland, they have very much got a social democratic view of the provision on welfare. The state will provide and meet the needs. ... England are much more laissez faire. ... We haven't had a narrative because we haven't had a Northern Ireland government."

Divisions between parties have not been primarily about different visions of social care. As one interviewee noted:

'I worked for a number of local ministers representing the Ulster Unionist Party and Democratic Unionist Party and Sinn Féin. What is striking is that they have very, very little manifesto-binding commitment to a particular direction in relation to social care. There is a very broad differentiation in that the DUP is probably more supportive of the private sector and Sinn Féin is more supportive of the public sector and would like to see more services provided by the public sector. Whereas the DUP are more accepting that there's a market economy. But in terms of having strong views, and this is the case about Northern Ireland politics in many areas. I mean even after the experience of a decade or two of devolution, the green and orange question still dominate the majority of their policy capacity.' (Northern Ireland, civil servant)

An aspect of the policy style in the three devolved nations has been to articulate a new relationship with their citizens, based on trust and co-production. In Wales, there has been a focus on building a new relationship of trust with citizens as a way of drawing a contrast with the Westminster government. As Drakeford describes this, 'One of the ways in which Welsh policymaking is distinctive and different lies in the efforts of the Assembly Government to create a high-trust, rather than a low-trust set of relationships between politicians and people' (Drakeford, 2005: 504). This aspiration was seen as particularly important given the narrow margin of victory for devolution in 1997, although generalised support for devolution in Wales is now higher (Scully and Wyn Jones, 2015).

In Northern Ireland, the relationship with state institutions has had to be 'detoxified' over several decades through the creation of institutions such as Health and Social Care Trusts (HSCTs). As one interviewee from the Health and Social Care Board put it,

> 'Our boards – and there are many of us within a public domain – are run by the departments, as in the government departments, who appoint non-executive directors to represent the public's interests on those boards. ... When there was a civil war going on, these were seen as kind of neutral places where you just go and get your services and support.'

The interviewee goes on:

> 'The concept of the state is really an interesting one in Northern Ireland. ... I think if I went out to people in certain communities and said, "The state will provide", I would be shown the door in no uncertain terms. ... It's, "Which state? No, no, no. The British state isn't going to do X, Y and Z." But if I go out to them and say, "The trust will do", which is the local provider, then they're grand.'

As in our discussion of scale, the articulation of distinctive policy styles has a performative quality, and distinctive elements may be harder to identify in practice. Andrews writes of 'The "foundation myths" of the establishment of a new Welsh democracy as a more inclusive, partnership-based form of governance' (Andrews, 2021: 2). Cairney et al note, in a Scottish context, 'the identification of distinctive policy styles can exaggerate the extent to which policy makers control the policy process, and the extent to which we can relate day-to-day decisions and outcomes to a coherent strategy produced by a single elected government' (Cairney et al, 2016: 335). Rummery and McAngus (2015) warn against taking too literally the claims of the Scottish Government. They suggest that Scotland's rhetoric of 'co-production' stands in contrast with a reality of 'path dependency and policy conservatism' (2015: 238).

Scope

The *scope* of policy-making is a third relevant variable affecting territorial policy communities. This relates to the policy areas over which the national governments in London, Edinburgh, Cardiff and Belfast have control.

There are three subaspects to this: first, their formal jurisdiction, as set out in the still evolving devolution settlements; second, their 'agenda capacity' to deal with a major issue like social care; and third, their relationship with local government and the extent to which powers regarding social care are localised. We look at these in turn, noting their interconnections with each other and with the issues about scale and style already discussed.

Jurisdictional powers

Following the 2017 changes to the settlement in Wales (Andrews, 2021: 512), Wales, Scotland and Northern Ireland now have reserved power arrangements, meaning that they have jurisdiction over all matters not reserved to Westminster. This gives each control over its health and care systems and related policy areas, such as housing and education. Since 2016, Scotland has had jurisdiction over aspects of social security, although in Wales and Northern Ireland, much of social security remains reserved to Westminster.

Andrews argues there are 'passive, activist, muscular and progressive' forms of unionism that coexist, shaping relationships between Westminster and the three devolved governments. In the realm of social care, it seems that passive unionism is at work – what Andrews calls 'devolve and forget' (2021: 516). However, the lack of control over social security policy and macro-economic planning remains a jurisdictional drag on social care reform. Two Welsh interviewees commented that care funding reforms plans were paused pending a UK-wide approach – according to a Welsh Assembly Member:

> 'At a Welsh Government level [it is] on their agenda, but it's still, at a UK level there has to be some changes as well, because just the amount of money that goes into the system and, obviously, there's only so much power that we have.'

And an interviewee from the third sector in Wales said:

> 'I think that Wales is different to Scotland, in that perhaps we haven't got that sort of independent streak through us, that we are very much used to being part of England.'

Other Welsh interviewees said they looked to Scotland for policy learning, one civil servant indicating: "Our Deputy Minister is going up to chat with various organisations in early September up in Scotland."

Scotland's 2016 independence referendum, and the likelihood of another, provides an incentive for the SNP government to emphasise its distinctiveness from England and Westminster (Harvey, 2020: 151). The Scottish Government has drawn explicitly on the 'Nordic' social investment model, with extensive references to Nordic states in the 2013 White Paper on independence (Harvey, 2020: 151). Awaiting a UK-wide approach was not mentioned in the Scottish interviews; by contrast, they discussed Scotland's desire to emphasise separateness: "I think Scotland likes to think they do things differently. I think there's a kind of, bit of self-mythologising about it, if you like" (Scotland, third sector). Interviewees were proud of the progress they felt Scotland had made, compared to elsewhere: "I am moaning about all the policy deficiencies in Scotland, but thank God I do not work in England and Wales, it would have driven me mad by now" (Scotland, third sector).

The sense of waiting for UK-wide or English reform has also diminished in Wales, with the Labour Party's governing alliance with Plaid Cymru involving a commitment to explore a National Care Service (Welsh Government, 2021a), although one of the interviewees, a civil servant, was sceptical about this as a clear vision for action:

> '[There] have been a bit, kind of, out there, throwaway lines, about a National Care Service – you know, perhaps we go to that. But that could mean anything, from everyone wears the same uniforms ... through to ... there's a national pay scale for social care, and it's a wholly owned subsidiary of the Welsh Government, administered locally by local authorities. There are no decisions about that.'

Given that Scotland is further advanced in its plans for an National Care Service, Wales may again look to Scotland for policy learning in designing its own reforms.

Agenda capacity

The scope each nation has to reform adult social care depends partly on its jurisdictional powers, but also on its capacity in the context of other demands. Interviewees in England, Northern Ireland and Wales mentioned pressures on agenda capacity. In England, the high turnover of Department of Health and Social Care (DHSC) staff and ministers in the past decade was seen as limiting capacity for sustained attention to social care. Regarding the decision to abandon parts of the Care Act, a civil servant noted:

> 'A lot of people left the DHSC. ... So, I think there was quite a lot of turnover in the people who were helping shape delivery who hadn't necessarily had the benefit of understanding how the model had evolved and what it was trying to achieve, and therefore who didn't always approach implementation in a way that was helpful for the model.'

At Westminster, the political focus on the Brexit negotiations was a major factor in pushing other issues off the policy agenda, with ramifications for Northern Ireland due to its land border with the Republic of Ireland (an EU member). One interviewee, a civil servant from Northern Ireland, explained: "The reality is that, because Westminster has been obsessed with Brexit, and also because of the complications of the DUP's role in supporting a minority government, we've not [had new social care legislation]."

In Wales, attention to institution-building since devolution was seen as a limiting factor in agenda capacity for care reform, as much of the past 20 years had been spent in expanding the devolution settlement:

'We're still in the very early phases of utilising our tax raising powers because there's only about three new taxes.' (Wales, Assembly Member)

'I think that we've really suffered from the fact that there's that inexperience, in terms of legislation and policy making.' (Wales, carers' organisation)

As in England, there were concerns in Wales about civil service capacity and expertise regarding social care:

'[T]hey're recycling staff in Welsh Government; there's very, very little external recruitment going on. And because of that you've got people coming into areas of work, such as carers. ... They're not people with a policy knowledge of this area. And as a result, it takes them a while to get up to speed. ... They haven't got the experience and the skills to be able to think about what are the policy requirements in this area, and what do we need to be doing.' (Wales, carers' organisation)

In Scotland there were again similar concerns about losing capacity in this case due to staff turnover: "Lots of people are really new because of Covid – the organisational memory has been lost in the Scottish Government. There are very few people working on [the National Care Service] that go back further than a year ago" (Scotland, provider representative).

Although the institutional pressures of COVID-19 may now be diminishing, the pressures it has placed on national health and care policy makers and systems (and the exchequer) will be much longer lasting (Pierson, 2021).

Multi-level governance

All four nations are nested in multi-level governance systems, within the UK and (for most of the period since devolution) the EU, as well as their own local and regional bodies. Leaving the EU (in December 2020) had major implications not only for supranational relationships, but also for the interplay between the UK and the devolved jurisdictions: 'The decision to leave the EU heralds a period of additional uncertainty and unpredictability as a complex system of multilevel governance forged over 47 years is dismantled and the UK Government wrestles with devolved governments for control over powers, functions and finances that are "repatriated" from the EU' (Elliott et al, 2022: 102).

Entwistle et al (2014) see this complex organisational configuration of multi-level governance as analogous to the features of a 'layer' cake and a 'marble' cake. The layer cake analogy (separate and autonomous spheres of government) is often seen as simplistic and 'zero sum', while the marble cake analogy (interconnected and overlapping jurisdictions) is more plausible. The 'marble cake' can be discerned within UK Government: 'Some Whitehall departments are, in effect, English departments, while others contain a mix of England, England-and-Wales, Great Britain, and UK responsibilities, which can be confusing, but the allocation of responsibility for service delivery is generally clear' (Keating et al, 2012: 290).

As we concluded our research, different parties were in power in the four nations (Conservatives at Westminster, the SNP in Scotland, Labour and Plaid Cymru in Wales and in Northern Ireland Sinn Féin had a majority – although no Executive had been formed). This marked a change from the period just after devolution, when the Labour Party was in power in all nations except Northern Ireland, providing some 'informal glue' in the system (Paun and Munro, 2015). This 'glue' meant less reliance on formal intergovernmental structures, such as the Joint Ministerial Committee (set up in 1999 to handle formal dialogue between the UK Government and the devolved nations). In a polycentric party context there has been a need for greater usage of formal channels (Paun and Munro, 2015; Andrews, 2021). These channels are currently going through a period of redesign following the Dunlop Review, which called for greater 'devolution awareness' by the UK Government (HM Government, 2019).

The recent flashpoints of tension between the four nations have been around Brexit and COVID-19 rather than social care (Andrews, 2021). Nonetheless, the partisan differences between the four nations' governments since 2010 has a bearing on social care because it inhibits the more informal learning that can go on within parties. Based on their interviews with policy makers in all four nations, Paun et al note:

[B]ecause the parties of government in Westminster, Scotland and Wales are in electoral competition, they may not trust each other to share information and have an open dialogue about policy. There may be particular reluctance to share information about unsuccessful policy experiments since this could easily become used as political ammunition. ... This all means ... that for a minister 'it's much easier to go and speak to your Swedish counterpart who you are not in competition with' than to have an open conversation with UK colleagues. (Paun et al, 2016: 15)

This more competitive approach between the nations may contribute to greater policy differences between them, although it is important to not to overstate closeness *within* the parties. Scotland's major break with UK care policy – the introduction of free personal care – came when Labour was in power in both London and Edinburgh. Hassan and Shaw (2020) suggest that this left a long-term legacy of bitterness between the English and Scottish Labour parties.

Centre-local relations

Relationships between the national governments and their local governments are particularly pertinent for care reform. In three of the nations, local authorities have jurisdiction over care services, and play a key role in assessing care need, commissioning services and managing markets. In Northern Ireland, this responsibility is instead held by local HSCTs.

Local powers and resources are often seen as 'gifted' or withdrawn by central governments, and this is true of recent decades in the UK (Hudson, 2021). However, the National Assistance Act 1948 gave local government the responsibility to find accommodation for those who required support due to 'age, infirmity or other circumstances' if it was not otherwise available to them (Hudson, 2021). The NHS and Community Care Act 1990 led to changes in care provision, although these were not evenly distributed across localities. As others note, 'even under a central policy spotlight, individual planning and care management developed in a variety of ways, based on ideologies, management and professional imperatives, operational expediency and wider demands from outside the service system' (Cambridge and Carnaby, 2005: 11). Local authorities were free to develop their own approach to needs assessment and, as costs rose, increasingly they rationed the available care, adjusting the needs threshold (Gingrich, 2011). Outsourcing of care services was pursued more vigorously in England than in Scotland and Wales, with the result that by the time of the devolution settlements in 1998, systems were already diverging (Gray and Birrell, 2013). Within England, outsourcing was undertaken more enthusiastically by Conservative than Labour-led local authorities (Hudson, 2021).

Since 1998, the legislative context described earlier in this book has further deepened differences between the countries. *Within*-country differences, driven by local socioeconomic context, politics and strategy also remain profound. Some authorities have retained in-house provision, or (more recently) taken services back in-house. In Northern Ireland, variance in the enthusiasm with which Trusts have pursed outsourcing is also evident, with a much higher proportion of care services outsourced in some areas than in others (Health and Social Care Board, 2015). As discussed in Chapter 3, this is affected in part by whether a local market offering services exists as well as to the strategy of the particular HSCT. There are also important demographic differences within countries. As Reed et al note, 'Healthy life expectancy at age 65 is twice as high in the most deprived as the least deprived areas in England and Wales, for men and women, and for women in Scotland. For men in Scotland it was three times higher in the most compared with the least deprived' (2021: 30).

Laffin (2004) refers to a 'regional centralism' logic within devolution that leads to a stripping away of local government's powers. Housden, as Permanent Secretary of the Scottish Government, set out his perspective on the Scottish approach to central-local relations in a journal article, arguing against the 'honeycombed and ramshackle' consequences of 'high localism' but in favour of local improvisation and 'bricolage' (Housden, 2014). This rather ambivalent account of the central-local balance in Scotland is also noted by others: McGarvey (2019) argues that the status of Scottish local government has diminished since 1999. Examples of centralisation include the creation of Police Scotland in 2013 (Elliott et al, 2022). Interviewees noted:

> 'Ministers feel they get blamed for everything, but they can't control it. They get frustrated with local agencies, so the change model is to pull things back into the centre.' (Scotland, third sector)

> 'If you have a polity that wants to hold the government responsible for everything that happens and a government that behaves as though it considers itself responsible for everything that happens, and one feeds off the other, inevitably you're going to have a more centralist approach.' (Scotland, NHS)

Scottish proposals for a new National Care Service, which would remove care commissioning from local government, have been driven primarily by a sense that the public expects the Scottish Government to take responsibility for social care particularly in the context of COVID-19. The Feeley Report explicitly uses this in its justification:

> The pandemic has demonstrated clearly that the Scottish public expect national accountability for adult social care support and look to Scottish Ministers to provide that accountability. Statutory responsibility for care homes sits with Local Authorities and individual providers. However, it was clear during the pandemic there was an expectation that Scottish

Ministers should be held to account, which makes sense from a public health perspective. We therefore recommend the establishment of a National Care Service – that brings together all adult social care support delivered in Scotland. (Feeley, 2021: 38)

Nicola Sturgeon, in setting up the Feeley inquiry, was full of optimism for what could be achieved through centralisation and national planning:

We won't achieve the potential of social care support in Scotland without a new delivery system. We need a National Care Service to achieve the consistency that people deserve, to drive national improvements where they are required, to ensure strategic integration with the National Health Service, to set national standards, terms and conditions, and to bring national oversight and accountability to a vital part of Scotland's social fabric. The National Care Service will bring together everyone with a role to play in planning and providing social care support to achieve a common purpose. (Quoted in Feeley, 2021: 5)

Unsurprisingly, Scotland's proposals have been resisted by local government. The representative body for Scottish local government (COSLA) was scathing about the proposal to centralise commissioning and move accountability for care to the Scottish care minister:

[I]t is an attack on localism and on the rights of local people to make decisions democratically for their Place. ... The lack of prior engagement with Local Government is not new – the partnership between the Scottish Government and Local Government which we have been seeking to build, continues to elude us in practice and it is the communities we serve who are losing out. (COSLA, 2021)

An MSP commented:

'There's going to have to be a negotiation, I think, between COSLA and Government on what the scope is. And then I think the political debate really becomes about, this has to be about culture, not about structural change. So already they're speaking in the debate, what we've heard, is a kind of the opposition parties lining up to essentially say, "Your big structural changes where you have drawn power into the centre have not worked, and so you need to really think about why are we doing this and what's the purpose?"'

There are clear challenges ahead as Scotland moves at pace towards establishing a National Care Service within this Parliament.

Within Wales, the Government's approach has been supportive of close links to local government (Laffin, 2004). Drakeford, like Housden in Scotland, is at pains to clarify what this is *not*: it is not 'the sort of government-distrusting new localism which seeks to clothe the managed decline of local government by substituting a version of participation for the substance of collective and electoral politics' (Drakeford, 2005: 502). As in Scotland, however, relations between central and local government have not been easy: 'Within a decade [of devolution] though, the "central-local partnership" in Wales came under strain due to pressures on funding, ministerial interventions in "failing" local authorities, and repeated calls to reduce the number of local authorities' (Elliott et al, 2022: 103).

Interviewees in the local Welsh site felt the Welsh Government was seeking to retain control:

'It feels as if Government are saying, "We want you to have a lot of autonomy. We want you to develop things locally. We want you to be innovative". But they're not 100% comfortable with it. So they released grants funding, for instance, and it's quite open-ended about what you can do with the grants funding. And you think, "Oh, this is great, we can develop something locally". And then every now and again it seems as if they want to kind of really zoom in and try and micro manage the way that you're spending the money, the way that you're measuring success. I don't think the Welsh Government is entirely comfortable around what it's trying to achieve.' (Wales, care commissioner)

Wales's *Rebalancing care and support* White Paper continued to express support for a strong role for local government in social care, but also expressed concern about a lack of consistency: 'The main issue identified with commissioning during the implementation of the [Social Services and Well-being (Wales)] Act was the lack of co-ordination between local authorities, leading to 22 distinct and different ways of doing things' (Welsh Government, 2021b: 19). There are clear resonances here with the Scotland debates, especially if Wales develops its own version of a National Care Service.

Northern Ireland has a distinct set of arrangements and processes for subnational tiers of government. Like other parts of the UK, these are in flux. Proposals to abolish the Health and Social Care Board were delayed due to the collapse of power sharing but are currently being implemented, with Board powers transferring to the Department of Health. One interviewee from the Health and Social Care Board gave a perspective on the over-complexity of institutional arrangements:

'We are over-administered and over-designed for the size of our population, I think for jolly good reasons, if you look at the history of our conflict. But for the size of a council area, we have a civil service, we have ministers, we have a local assembly, we have local authorities, we have boards ... quangos of public bodies who are in this space. ... You have half a dozen layers of decision making in the size of a council area. The art and science of negotiating through our complex bureaucracy and administration makes it slow to get things done. But it's there for good reason, if you think of the history of our Troubles.'

This highlights that complex arrangements can be part of securing the legitimacy of the state. The interviewee goes on:

'But it makes change difficult. ... Actually, I envy some of my colleagues in England where somebody in Whitehall says, "Thou shalt do" and they all go and do it! We're going, "Flip me". The last time I said, "Thou shalt do" I got cabbages thrown at me. So, the grass is always greener on the other side.'

In England, the scope for local government to develop its own approaches has been restated at key reform moments such as the NHS and Community Care Act 1990 or the Localism Act 2011 (Yeandle, 2016; Hudson, 2021). However, the response to ongoing concerns about care systems has been to further constrain local authorities' discretion in relation to care (Hudson, 2021). Yeandle notes that, 'In fact, the [Localism] Act gave increased local control only if services were "improved" or became "more competitive" and brought a complex mix of new centrally imposed controls and freedoms' (2016: 220). Hudson (2021) highlights the relative centralisation of the English system in which local government is starved of resources and autonomy compared to similar institutions outside the UK. In relation to care funding, a local Director of Adult Social Services interviewee in England said: "Everything I see makes me fearful for the future. Local government has been taking a hit now since 2008, and that isn't likely to change any time soon is what you'd have to say."

Across the decade of austerity, Needham et al's (2022) research on local care markets found that local authorities had lost internal commissioning skills and capacity, as well as having to cut direct care spend. This makes it difficult to implement the wide-range of mandates from the centre. England's regulator, the Care Quality Commission, has been given additional powers enabling it to inspect local authorities' commissioning of social care, rather than only inspecting health and care providers. Local authorities will also have a new duty to develop and publish 'fair costs of care' statements and 'market sustainability' plans (DHSC, 2021c). Working with providers to develop these is challenging for local authorities as they recover from the COVID-19 pandemic and the years of spending cuts that preceded it (CCN, 2022).

Conclusion

Having considered the issues of scale, style and scope, it is clear that these differ across the four polities of the UK in ways that are relevant to social care. In Scotland and Wales we found a commitment to more inclusive styles of policy-making. There are structural elements to this (for example, the institutional design that militates against majoritarianism in the three smaller nations), as well as a discursive and performative element. Scotland's more active policy-making over the period since devolution is due to the conducive institutional environment in which scale, style and scope have combined to facilitate a series of legislative interventions in adult social care. Wales passed a wide-ranging reform Act (the Social Services and Well-being [Wales] Act 2014), which has made significant changes to the costs of care for individuals, has enhanced rights for carers and has brought in a register of care workers. Northern Ireland has integrated health and social care and the registration of care workers, but has struggled to pass any reforms in the period, although it continues to propose many similar policies to the other nations. England passed the Care Act 2014 but had to abandon the care cap element of it, which has only recently been revived (and will continue to struggle in its implementation given that the issues that led to the earlier abandonment have not been resolved).

The distinctive styles of the four political communities also relate to how they frame the crises of supply that were discussed in Chapter 3. In Scotland and Wales there has been a discursive rejection of the market and consumerist approaches to care, with a preference for seeking to pursue care reform through community and co-production. In Northern Ireland, the crisis of the state has had a very distinctive hue, and some of the work of reforming social care has been about detoxifying the state. In England, the market continues to be discursively dominant – with the care market effectively being a synonym for the care system – although there is recognised to be a role for community in supporting people to stay out of formal care services.

In Chapter 7, we go on to look at the dynamics of policy change, recognising that – as set out in Chapter 5 – passing legislation does not equate to effective implementation. Policy makers in all four systems recognise social care reform as unfinished business, given the limits of what has been achieved to date despite the myriad of commissions, White Papers, and even formal legislative change over the 25 years since devolution. Scotland is on the brink of a new wave of reform with its proposed National Care Service (Feeley, 2021; Scottish Government, 2021). Wales is also in the early stages of exploring a National Care Service (Welsh Government, 2021a). As highlighted above, England plans to implement a care cap, although implementation has been delayed until 2025 (HM Treasury, 2022). Northern Ireland is consulting on the reforms proposed by the *Power to people* report

(Kelly and Kennedy, 2017); however, power sharing remains under strain from Brexit-related border issues (Cochrane, 2020).

In the next chapter we consider the tactics of policy change, and whether more incremental change is likely to be more effective than the 'big bang' of a National Care Service. We also consider the 'policy mix', highlighting that tensions between the policy mechanisms need to be addressed if future policies are to achieve their goals. We consider our findings through the lens of two paradigms of care (the standardised and the differentiated), and explore how far these can be reconciled.

7

The limits of social care reform

The previous chapter on scale, style and scope highlighted the extent to which the institutional context of the four nations shapes their approach to policy and their relationship with other institutions such as local government. This relates to structure but also to discursive patterns in framing and identity. Scotland and Wales have had a less complex, more consensual and inclusive policy-making style compared to England and Northern Ireland. This has included a focus on trust and co-production over competition and adversarialism, which is relevant to the process of policy-making but also to the types of policies that have been favoured. In this chapter we look at the challenges of social care reform, and why the four nations have not been able to achieve more change over the period despite the clear commitment across a series of policy documents to do so. We consider the patterns of divergence and convergence in relation to social care policy. We compare an incremental versus transformative approach to care reform, and highlight how both of these approaches must still resolve the challenges of implementation. We also explore the 'policy mix', highlighting tensions between different policies that make it hard to achieve all of them at once, even if implementation challenges could be avoided. We set out two paradigms of care policy – the standardised, centralised and formal versus the differentiated, local and informal – and suggest that policy makers must engage with the tensions between these rather than offering 'the best of both worlds'.

Divergence and convergence

Earlier chapters of this book highlighted the high degree of convergence between the four nations in relation to discursive framings of care (the key values underpinning it: wellbeing, fairness, rights, quality and sustainability) and aspirations about the decisions and practices that were required to reform it (redistribute costs of care; personalise support; support unpaid carers; invest in prevention; integrate with health; and professionalise the workforce). In achieving these policy reforms, the scale, style and scope of policy in Scotland has facilitated greater legislative activity than elsewhere. In Wales, devolution has been a more gradual process than in Scotland, and much time and policy capacity has been spent on institution building. Since 1998, the Welsh Government has been reviewing and renewing its constitutional settlement almost constantly, bringing it closer to the Scottish model over time. Primary legislative and tax-raising powers remain relatively new. The link to England and keeping in sync with its care reforms has been felt more strongly in Wales than in Scotland (Boyce, 2017). In Northern Ireland, the periodic and lengthy suspensions of the Executive have been a serious barrier to reform, although the integration with health has facilitated ongoing increases in care spending. In England, the prevalence of veto players, the partisan polarisation on reform proposals, a decade of austerity and the distractions of Brexit since 2016 have meant that care funding proposals have repeatedly been abandoned or delayed (Needham and Hall, 2022).

Despite this varying degree of activity on care policy reform, there is more convergence on results and outcomes across the four nations than might be expected. While formal outcomes measures do not exist across the four nations, we can see that none of them has fully reformed its care system, and (as Chapter 5 sets out) progress on outcomes is fairly similar. We have characterised Scotland as the most 'active' of the four nations, but, as Pearson et al (2018) observe, this may have contributed to policy overload that has hampered implementation. Uncertain outcomes and complexity remain key elements of care policy in all four nations. Scotland's free personal care has concentrated resources on a narrow and functional set of tasks. Improved rights for carers in Scotland, Wales and England have been symbolically important but have been inadequately implemented. Personalisation and self-directed support have lost momentum. Integration continues to have a disappointing record in relation to improving the experiences of people using services. Registration of the workforce in Scotland, Wales and Northern Ireland (along with improved pay in Scotland) has been broadly welcomed. However, workforce shortages remain severe in all four nations, intensified by COVID-19, and we remain some way off social care being a profession on a par with nursing. Prevention has been an important rhetorical commitment in all four nations, but evidence of investment in prevention and discernible benefits for people or communities remains scant.

In explaining why the aspirations of policy makers have yet to be translated into effective system change, we suggest that there is a need to be alert to the dynamics of change in the four nations. In the next section we look at the distinction between more radical and more incremental versions of change, and how these interact with implementation challenges. We then go on to focus on the interrelationships between the reforms (the policy mix), looking at the ways in which they draw on contending care paradigms, which makes reform inherently unstable.

Incremental versus transformative change

All six of the mechanisms set out in earlier chapters for reforming care (redistribute costs of care; personalise support; support unpaid carers; invest in prevention; integrate with health; and professionalise the workforce) are ambitious, wide-ranging and interrelated. Calls for a reformed care system are often framed as a 'new Beveridge', evoking the spirit of William Beveridge whose report was the foundation for welfare reform after the Second World War (see, for example, Demos, 2009; Glasby et al, 2011). New Labour's 2010 *Building the National Care Service* White Paper set out its agenda in terms that explicitly evoked the spirit of 1948:

> Our answer is bold, ambitious reform to create a system rooted firmly in the proudest traditions of our National Health Service. Its creation in 1948 wasn't just one of Britain's proudest moments; it was also a profound statement of what can be achieved through collective will in the face of adversity. (HM Government, 2010: 2)

The language of a National Care Service is an explicit attempt to mirror the language of the NHS. It suggests correcting the error of 1948 in which support for those who were 'dependent' was fragmented and means tested under the National Assistance Act, rather than universal and free at the point of use as in the NHS. The concept of a National Care Service was used by the New Labour government in 2010 (and has been revived by Labour in subsequent UK elections) and is also deployed in Scotland's current reforms (Feeley, 2021; Scottish Government, 2021). Plans are being developed for a National Care Service in Wales too, as part of the *Co-operation agreement* between Welsh Labour and Plaid Cymru (Welsh Government, 2021a).

Attempts to create a system-wide change analogous to the creation of the NHS take a transformative rather than incremental approach to social care reform. This is in line with the critique of 'piecemeal reform' offered by the Law Commission in its review of social care legislation in 2011:

> It is now well over 60 years since the passing of the National Assistance Act 1948 which remains to this day the bedrock of adult social care. Since then, adult social care law has been the subject of countless piecemeal reforms including new Acts of Parliament and a constant stream of regulations, circulars, directions, approvals and guidance. … Adult social care law, including how it relates to other legislation, has been described at various times by judges as 'piecemeal … numerous', 'exceptionally tortuous', [and] 'labyrinthine'. (The Law Commission, 2011: 1)

The Law Commission proposed instead 'a clear, modern and effective legal framework for the provision of adult social care' (2011: 2), which was the basis for the Care Act (2014) in England and the Social Services and Well-being (Wales) Act 2014.

Reforming social care through a 'big bang' – as the English and Welsh legislation attempted to do – offers a way to avoid the incoherence of a piecemeal and incoherent approach. It may also make it easier to build public and political support around a unified commitment to social care, evoking the post-war Beveridge spirit (Glasby et al, 2011). Reform of long-term care in non-UK systems has often been through a new 'national debate' about changing levels of need and entitlement. In Japan, for example, Peng (2016: 281) writes about how, to build public support for reform of older people's care, 'the government framed the country's demographic shifts as a national crisis, and communicated social care as a solution to the crisis.' In Australia, the National Disability Insurance Scheme (NDIS) for working-age disabled people followed on from a broad-based campaign – Every Australian Counts – that harnessed public and political support for reform (Needham and Dickinson, 2018).

There has been no equivalent 'national debate' in the UK on social care, and in the absence of that, we could argue that the 'big bang' approach is a poor tactic – maximising the target for veto players and leading to fatalism and 'review fatigue' (Bengoa, 2016) when implementation doesn't follow. Insistence on a 'once and for all' solution to care funding, as promised by Boris Johnson when he took office (Campbell, 2019), for example, may have contributed to the failure to make progress on care reform to date. In the old joke about how to eat an elephant, the answer ('one bite at a time') has resonance in social care. In a letter to *The Guardian*, critics noted: 'The search for the holy grail should be called off in favour of pragmatic reforms that would be feasible and fundable quickly, and would use the initiative of dedicated staff' (Bosanquet and Haldenby, 2020).

One of the interviewees, a civil servant from England, made a similar point about the effectiveness of incrementalism as a tactic, in relation to how the Treasury plans spending through annual Spending Reviews:

'We need to take the first steps; the thing to do is to embark on this journey. ... To try and say that ... the whole of reform, achieving the whole vision needs to be done in one SR [Spending Review] type period, is just asking for nothing to ever happen. I think to stretch it out across two or three SRs, and start on the journey is really good, for just beginning.'

New Labour suggested a staged approach in its 2010 proposals for reforming care funding. Its White Paper noted: 'To manage the impact on the public finances, and to ensure that it is affordable and sustainable, we need to build the National Care Service in stages' (DH, 2010: 8). The first phase was to be free personal care at home, followed by free care for anyone receiving more than two years of residential care. The Barker Report (2014) also suggested a staged approach, starting with free provision of support to people with critical care needs. While such changes lack the symbolic 'big bang' of a new Beveridge, they may be more tactically astute in spreading out the challenges and costs of implementation.

There is an extensive institutionalist literature on policy reform and the inertia that makes policy change difficult (for an overview, see Béland and Powell, 2016). Hacker (2004) points out that we need to recognise intermediate points in between no change and full reform. When change occurs it is often through incremental 'layering' or 'conversion' rather than full-scale reform. If the policy is mutable, then (drawing on the work of Thelen, 2003), Hacker (2004) suggests that we see *conversion* (in which policies are adapted over time rather than replaced or eliminated). If the institutional context allows new policies to emerge (but there are institutional barriers to changing older ones) we see *layering* (building on Schickler, 2001). If the policy doesn't change, despite declining effectiveness in achieving its goals, we can see a case of *drift* (Hacker, 2004; Béland et al, 2016; Needham and Hall, 2022).

We can see these elements of gradual change in the social care reforms of the four nations. Scotland has taken a *layering* approach, adding new social care legislation over time while continuing to work within the financial settlement determined by the UK government. In Northern Ireland we can see evidence of *conversion* – integration with health has given an 'automaticity' (Hacker, 2004) to care funding uplifts, which is not the case in the other nations, although formal legislative change has proved impossible. In Wales and England, their respective Acts in 2014 proposed full *reform*: 'the removal of existing rules and the introduction of new ones' (Mahoney and Thelen, 2010: 15). However, the ambition of the legislation has been not been achieved in either nation, with austerity and broader implementation challenges scaling back the planned reforms (Burn and Needham, 2021; Cheshire-Allen and Calder, 2022). In England in particular, the explicit abandonment of the funding cap element of the Care Act has led to *drift* as the means test has become more punitive over time (Watt and Varrow, 2018; Needham and Hall, 2022). In Wales, we can see *layering*: there has been some change – for example, in the residential means test threshold and weekly charge for home care. However, implementation of the elements of the Social Services and Well-being (Wales) Act relating to carers has been limited (Cooke et al, 2019; Cheshire-Allen and Calder, 2022).

Implementation problems are well known in public policy, as legislative aspirations interact with the complexity of organisational settings (Pressman and Wildavsky, 1973; Lipsky, 1980; Hupe and Hill, 2016). However, Béland et al (2016) argue that implementation has not been sufficiently explored in the policy change literature. They note how the passage of the Affordable Care Act in 2010 in the USA (following years of drift) was not in itself the marker of policy reform, as it has continued to be subject to amendment and reversal during its implementation in the states. In line with this, Carey et al (2019) argue that we need to pay more attention to the 'sticky layers' that inhibit implementation of policy reforms. The introduction of Australia's NDIS – the focus of Carey's study – offered a 'big bang' type of reform, with ambitious plans for the scale and timing of implementation. However, Carey et al (2019) found that even transformative changes have to deal with institutional stickiness as new initiatives are layered on top of existing systems and markets. In relation to social care, we have to be aware of the extent to which both gradual and more transformative reforms have had to address factors such as limited public funding, existing labour markets, the mixed economy of provision, and variable willingness and capacity in local government to introduce reform.

Policy makers themselves are aware of the challenges of implementation. The Care Act 2014 was accompanied by a designated Implementation Support Programme and a new regional infrastructure to support local transition (Hudson et al, 2019). Nonetheless, the implementation of the legislation has been disappointing, with ambiguity in the legislation itself intersecting with financial pressures on local authorities to inhibit change (Burn and Needham, 2021). These challenges of policy reform are part of the explanation of why, despite 25 years of reform, social care in England, Scotland, Wales and Northern Ireland remains unfinished business.

The policy mix

The implementation barriers facing large-scale system changes are an important part of understanding why care reform has been delayed or reversed in the four UK nations. There is a related element that needs to be considered in order to understand the challenges facing care reformers. This concerns the internal tensions between the reforms, and the failure of policy makers to articulate and resolve these tensions. Carey et al (2019: 494) draw attention to the 'policy mix' and the importance of ensuring that goals are coherent in the sense that they are 'related to the same overall policy aims and objectives and may be achieved simultaneously without requiring trade-offs, temporal sequencing, or value balancing'. They go on: 'This makes the composition of policy change important: these relations between different parts of policy over time are not simple additive ones; rather they are dynamic and complex, and typically have emergent, self-organizing properties' (Carey et al, 2019: 494).

The importance of understanding the relationships between parts of the 'policy mix' has been the focus of a number of studies (see, for example, Howlett and Rayner, 2007; Flanagan et al, 2011; Béland et al, 2020; Sewerin, 2020). Howlett and Rayner (2007) note that a policy mix often evolves over time: policies may be incoherent or counter-productive, leading to suboptimal outcomes. In considering the policy mix in social care reforms, we can explore how the six mechanisms (redistribute costs of care; personalise support; support unpaid carers; invest in prevention; integrate with health; and professionalise the workforce) come together as a policy mix. In particular, we draw attention to the rival paradigms at work here. Some of these reforms (particularly integration with health and professionalising the workforce) seek to promote more standardisation, centralisation and formality within the care system whereas others (particularly personalising provision and investing in prevention) encourage more differentiation, localism and informality.

Standardised versus differentiated approaches to social care

In 2021, Professor Nick Watson from the University of Glasgow gave evidence to the Scottish Parliament about the Feeley proposals for a National Care Service, saying:

> [O]ne problem that I see from reading the report ... is that it seems to present two different futures for social care. On the one hand, it suggests that good social care is the product of people power, the co-production of services and a diversity of approaches that are adapted to meet the needs of the locality and the needs of each service user. On the other hand, it calls for centralisation and standardisation, and institutional power, through a national care service. Those two approaches seem to be in tension with each other and, as I read through the report, I really struggled to see how they could be reconciled. (Scottish Parliament Health, Social Care and Sport Committee, 2021)

Watson's articulation of these two approaches – implicit and in tension – coheres with our analysis of two strands underpinning reform in the four nations since devolution. Across the policy documents all four indicate a clear commitment to self-direction and personalisation and to prevention, co-production and asset-based approaches to individuals and communities. Yet, there is also a centralising and standardising dynamic in all four nations, evident in the approach to regulation and registration and to structural integration with health.

One of the interviewees, reflecting on how the Social Services and Well-being (Wales) Act 2014 is working in practice, pointed to the tension between loosening and maintaining control:

> 'We're almost in a bit of a dichotomy aren't we? The Social Services and Well-being Act is all about power to the individual person. So, have

a direct payment, commission your own, employ your own, do what you want with that money. We've assessed your need, within limits, obviously, but you go ahead and you look after yourself. The counter argument is, regulation, regulation, we've got to keep everybody safe.' (Wales, social worker)

We see these as two paradigms that underpin reform initiatives in all of the four nations, but with insufficient attention to the tensions between them. They can be set out as ideal types in order to highlight the differences between them, and the problems that follow when reformers leave the tensions unacknowledged.

Paradigm 1: standardised care

This first paradigm is associated with strong state control of care, and with the provision of nationally standardised and regulated systems. Of our six mechanisms of care reform, this paradigm gives most attention to macro-level funding reform, integration and worker registration. It is least likely to prioritise self-directed support and prevention. A key characteristic of this paradigm is its emphasis on a professionalised and regulated workforce. This derives in part from concerns about safety. As this interviewee put it, raising concerns about unregistered care workers: "You wouldn't expect an electrician to come and do your house who wasn't qualified, yet we're saying it's okay for somebody to go in who is not qualified to do the most intimate things with individuals who are very vulnerable, not supervised, on their own" (Wales, regulatory/oversight body).

The rationale for the registration of care workers comes in part from a sense that policy has lagged behind the changes in care work, which now make it closer to nursing than to a 'home help', as discussed in Chapter 3. Given the focus on formalisation, this paradigm is also allied to the integration agenda, with the creation of the NHS seen as the model social care should move towards, as exemplified here by an Assembly Member from Wales:

'We have a mish-mash of public provision. Well-meaning charitable provision. Private provision. Somebody needs to have the courage to bring it all together into a standalone coherent service. Like Aneurin Bevan did for health. Somebody needs to do it for social care. And that's the challenge at the moment, because people say, "It's too difficult, it's going to be horrendously expensive". But that was all the arguments hurled at Aneurin Bevan, back in the day, which is why I am quite a fan, really.'

One rationale for staff registration is to make it easier for staff to move between social care and the NHS:

'Well, I'm a supporter of registration, but only if it's a properly backed system. ... The aim of registration should be about a proper skills and competency framework. It would be aligned to the NHS one, because we want staff who can move seamlessly between systems, just as citizens do.' (England, provider representative)

Personal assistants (PAs), who are not required to be registered in any part of the UK, can be seen as anomalous and problematic in this paradigm: "You think about personal assistants, are they not regulated because they're not dangerous? Because there's no risk there? I don't think that's the case. It's the 'too hard' pile, isn't it?" (England, regulatory/oversight body).

Some also see non-registered providers, such as PAs and micro-providers, as creating unfairness in the system, because they can work unregistered, while other providers must register their staff:

'From our point of view, if we, as a group of contracted, commissioned, service providers are legally obliged to register people, to have them qualified – for all the reasons that have been given – then what on earth is the justification for having a whole bunch of people who call themselves micro-providers, to exist entirely outside the regulatory framework? Who don't have to be scrutinised in any way at all. Who don't have to comply with any of these things, and furthermore who are outside the living wage policy of the Scottish Government.' (Scotland, third sector)

In Scotland, the proposed National Care Service, as set out in the Scottish Government's consultation document in 2021, is most closely aligned to the paradigm of standardised care. The problems of the care system are set out as being insufficient consistency and standardisation (Scottish Government, 2021). The language of personalisation and co-production is there, but the mechanisms of change – particularly a new national approach to commissioning – are standardising reforms. The Coalition of Care Providers Scotland (CCPS), representing 80 not-for-profit providers, expressed dismay that the consultation focused on structural change, not culture: 'As they are currently articulated, the changes proposed by the Scottish Government appear to rely on two key drivers – more control from the centre and greater enforcement of standards. However, the emphasis on structures and practices is not matched by an equally explicit focus on culture, relationships, and behaviours' (CCPS, 2021: 3).

Long-stay care institutions are part of this standardisation paradigm. This includes the 'Assessment and Treatment Centres' for people with learning disabilities, which have proved very difficult to close, despite media and political pressures to do so. Research on 'carceration' (Series, 2022) and 'new asylums' (Fox, 2018) finds that institutional models have been recreated or preserved, despite the elimination of long-stay hospitals. The COVID-19 pandemic highlighted that institutional settings can be high-risk environments (Knapp et al, 2021), and many relatives were distressed at the extent to which residential care settings remained closed institutions, even as broader COVID-19 restrictions eased (Tapper, 2021). Writing about 'the invisible asylum', Fox argues that even outside of formal institutions, norms of control can be present within social care in which notions of home, family and love have no currency: 'Most of the most obviously institutional buildings have gone, but the ideas behind that divide between those inside and those outside the community remain invisibly woven into our public services which provide long-term support' (Fox, 2018: 14).

The efficiency arguments around building large care institutions mean that they continue to be a part of care provision, despite quality concerns expressed by the English regulator (CQC, 2017). This efficiency logic is evident in claims from this interviewee that meeting future care needs is likely to require institutional solutions unless other ideas are forthcoming:

> 'You're not going to get good care and good carers to meet the ageing population across the UK, and particularly across parts of Northern Ireland. We're going to require them all to move to where we build big massive care homes. Or what arrangements are we going to put in place? And there is part of me that doesn't understand why that's too hard to plan for.' (Northern Ireland, regulatory/oversight body)

One interviewee, a social worker in Northern Ireland, felt that COVID-19 may have increased the tendency to favour large institutions:

> 'What we might do is actually take our large, big group care institutions and say, "Well, we have really high demographics, and actually these facilities are really good at discharging people from hospital quickly". And if we shore them up with better clinical care, they can feel a bit more like hospitals. We'll reduce the risks to people living in them, in terms of infection, and we'll reduce our risks as people running the system. We'll feel a bit happier that they feel a bit more like what we do in hospitals.'

There is a sense from these two interviewees that the crisis of demand and the pandemic experience may have strengthened the appetite for institutional care at scale.

Of the four types of supply discussed in Chapter 3 (state, market, family and community), the standardised paradigm is most closely connected to the legitimacy of the state. Restoring the state's role in designing, funding, commissioning, regulating, registering and potentially delivering care is a key priority. There may be roles for other points of the care diamond – the market, family and community – but in this paradigm each of these is considered too partial and unreliable to be trusted to provide consistent, high-quality care.

Paradigm 2: differentiated care

This paradigm starts with the person receiving support and what enhances their wellbeing. This might be a regulated care service, a non-regulated PA, or a range of family and community supports. Rather than keeping people safe through national standards there is more emphasis on local variance, co-design and co-delivery and involving people in informal networks. Safety is traded off with other goals through the lens of positive risk-taking rather than risk aversion (SCIE, 2010).

A commitment to this differentiated paradigm runs through many of the policy documents we analysed. It can be seen across the four nations – in *Putting people first* (HM Government), in England's Care Act 2014 and in the Social Services and Well-being (Wales) Act 2014, in Scotland's Feeley Report (2021) and in Northern Ireland's *Power to people* (Kelly and Kennedy, 2017). Support for this kind of approach comes in part from an awareness of the limits of what has been achieved through the standardised approaches of the first paradigm. This interviewee, for example, expressed reservations about relying on regulation to keep people safe:

> 'Like the rest of the UK, we've faced some fairly catastrophic failings in quality of provision. We've got some major adult safeguarding investigations going on, relating to managed care environments where the quality of the care certainly was neglectful and is sometimes abusive. I really don't think that we've cracked that, I also don't think inspection will crack it. ... I think there has to be something about how we commission that care that makes it inherently safer, rather than relying on inspection and regulators to catch it being unsafe. ... If you look at the failures of quality in provision, it's fairly classic, the two things that they require. If it's abuse, it is basically an unequal power relationship and if it's abuse and/or neglect, it's secretive and covered up. Now, the two tenets of co-produced services are that you share power, and that

they're totally transparent. I just think that people haven't connected co-production with avoiding those kinds of quality failures yet. But that's where you'll get to. I think that care that is co-produced, and care that has resulted from diffuse power and is transparent in its nature, it's just inherently safer.' (Northern Ireland, civil servant)

In the Feeley Report, the limits of inspection and regulation in assuring quality are acknowledged:

[W]holesale reliance on inspection is seldom appropriate, and is costly in both time and money. And most important, inspection cannot always catch problems that are inherent in the system itself. And yet, that is pretty much all we have in social care support a total reliance on external verification as a vehicle for improvement. It won't work. It distorts our sense of who is the 'customer' away from the person in need of care and support towards the inspector and it inhibits the sharing of learning and innovation. (Feeley, 2021: 58)

A local Welsh interviewee, a care commissioner, felt recent legislation had emphasised personalisation and flexibility, but that this was being lost in implementation:

'I think the Regulation and Inspection Act, 2016 has kind of missed the point with a couple of aspects. ... They start off really well, and in the main it's in line with the spirit of helping people live their lives like they want to live them, have good outcomes. But sometimes there's still that kind of aspect of ... micro-managing the providers creeping back in. And it's the same with the Social Services and Well-being Act. The values, the principles, are fantastic – but then once you delve into some aspects of the guidance, and some of the sections around the Act, you see, hmm, there's a little bit of tension here, between what you're saying as an overall vision you want to achieve, and what we have to do.'

An interviewee in Scotland, a civil servant, set out the limitations of the current model:

'We've trained [care workers] to be person-centred, and generally people going into those professions are genuinely wanting to do a good job. But actually ... we're training them to fill in the contractual obligations. So, you go in, and actually your top marks are to fill in that book to say "Joe's mood is low and we've given him his medication". Then, you've got five minutes to nuke the meal, but you've got another five minutes to write up what the meal was, and whether Joe ate it. But you're not sure if he ate it, because you've got to go next to Jessie. ... That's not good support. That's not good for the worker, for the person who's receiving it.'

The second paradigm – of differentiated support – aims to move care beyond a set of work tasks (Rummery and Fine, 2012). In relation to the care 'supply' crisis discussed in Chapter 3, this paradigm evokes family and community as having the most to offer. The state and the market are distrusted as too instrumental – treating care as a set of functional tasks. Families and communities, while they can be under immense strain, are seen as the most likely to offer love and reciprocity (Fox, 2018), as well as kindness (Unwin, 2018). This is evident in Northern Ireland's *Power to people* report, which states that 'Care and support involves supporting a human environment and culture that encourages relationships and kindness' (Kelly and Kennedy, 2017: 64).

Comparing the two paradigms

Having a preference for a standardised versus a differentiated paradigm has implications for the perspective taken on the social care values set out in Chapter 2. The first paradigm is suggestive of a care system that is highly formalised, standardised and regulated, with registration for care workers and a clear demarcation between what it means to be 'in' or 'out' of social care. It gives pre-eminence to making social care work for other systems connected to it – particularly the NHS. Attention is given to how to make the work of care more effective and efficient, foregrounding the perspectives of paid care workers. Policies include reasonable rates of pay and training for care workers, with good terms and conditions, and legislating for unpaid carers to have rights to support, including respite. Safeguarding is also important, as is regulating care systems so that care meets a quality standard and keeps people safe. The main problem that this paradigm seeks to tackle is a lack of consistency and inadequate protection for those who provide and receive care.

The second paradigm sets out a vision of care and support that is differentiated and less formal, with lower levels of regulation and greater variation between localities and between people. Social care here is not something you go 'into', in the way you might go into hospital; it is something that gives you support so that you can do the things that enhance your wellbeing (#socialcarefuture, 2019). Care here is approached through the perspective of the person who requires support and the focus is on what will give them choice and control so that they can flourish. Their preferences will be paramount, and formal systems will exist to facilitate these, while allowing maximum flexibility. So, for example, people may be able to choose a care worker from a regulated agency or use a non–registered PA. People can spend a direct payment on buying a traditional 'care package' or on a range of things that they feel will support their wellbeing.

We present our typology of the two paradigms in Table 7.1. Within the standardised paradigm, we can see the core values as being safety and consistency. A care system is effective if it is able to secure consistent care for all (as part of fairness) and ensure people are kept safe. The key reform mechanisms relate to integration with health (to improve service outcomes) and professionalisation of the workforce as the basis for safe and consistent care as well as making care work more consistent with other caring professions. Free personal care is an exemplar policy, in which everyone with an assessed need can have support in achieving an agreed list of Activities of Daily Living. In the differentiated paradigm, the focus is on prioritising choice and control for the individual,

Table 7.1: Two paradigms of social care

Features	Paradigm 1: standardised care	Paradigm 2: differentiated care
Core values	• Consistency • Safety	• Choice and control • Strength-/asset-based approaches
Exemplar funding reform	• Free personal care	• Direct payments
Exemplar mechanisms	• Integrate with health • Professionalise the workforce	• Personalise provision • Invest in prevention
Perception of wellbeing	• Wellbeing is a service outcome from efficient delivery of quality services to people with support needs	• Wellbeing emerges from a good life; social care facilitates people's pursuit of what matters to them
Rights	• Service users and service providers require clearly defined and enforceable rights and duties, to ensure safety and consistency	• Individual rights should be matched with recognition that people and communities have assets, and care is a mutual relationship
Quality	• Clear, enforceable quality standards • Powerful regulatory and inspection system	• Is negotiated between stakeholders • Emerges from good relationships • Requires positive risk-taking
System sustainability	• Achieved via a well-funded state that distributes services equitably to achieve well-defined outcomes	• Achieved by embedding people within caring communities supported by the state and the market
Key concerns	• Unsafe care • Inconsistent care across localities • Poor terms and conditions for staff	• Institutionalisation • Lack of personalisation and co-production • Lack of innovation • Stigmatisation

using direct payments as much as possible to enable people to purchase the services that they feel help support their preferred outcomes. Prevention is a key mechanism here, alongside personalisation and self-directed support, and recognition that people have strengths and assets rather than only 'needs'.

In relation to wellbeing, we can differentiate between wellbeing as something that the care system provides (in the standardised paradigm) and wellbeing as a broader life perspective (in the differentiated paradigm). Crowther captures that broader sense of wellbeing:

Figure 7.1: Neil Crowther tweet on wellbeing

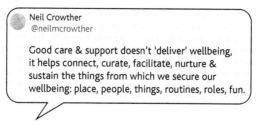

Source: Neil Crowther, Twitter, 28 October 2021

In the standardised paradigm, rights are a key focus for reformers, ensuring that people have protected rights to services and funding. In the differentiated paradigm, recognition of the difficulty of enforcing rights and duties means more attention is given to relationship building, trust and attributes such as kindness (Unwin, 2018). Quality in the standardised paradigm is about the match between the commissioned service and the service delivered, whereas in the differentiated paradigm, quality is defined by the people using the service. Two quotes from the interviews indicate this contrast. The first problematises the perspective of the person receiving care in not recognising the limits of what is being provided:

'I think it's very difficult, because what you hear at a personal level, and the personal experience, there's such a tension in that. There's nothing good about the care you're getting. "I know you think Edna's lovely, but there's nothing good about the care she's actually being paid to deliver".' (Northern Ireland, third sector)

In the second, the interviewee highlights the importance of what family carers value, which may not be covered by a service specification:

'My dad did agree to have the hairdresser come around to do mum's hair. Actually, she wasn't very good at hairdressing, but what he did, he paid her for an extra hour to do a bit of cleaning. She was a rubbish cleaner as well, not brilliant at hair or cleaning, but what she did was sat and talked to mum, so dad could go out into the garden and potter.' (England, third sector)

In the standardised paradigm in which services meet a specification, there is a clear failing here. In the differentiated paradigm, there is recognition that quality is developed in the relationships and can be defined by the people receiving support. This is not always straightforward, of course, and perhaps in this example, a good cleaner and a good hairdresser would have been more helpful. The point at issue is: who decides?

Key concerns for the two paradigms highlight the values and mechanisms that each prefer. The standardised paradigm gives priority to preventing exploitation of staff, unsafe care and inconsistency of provision. The differentiated paradigm has a different set of worries: deficit models that lead to institutionalisation of one kind or another, and to stigmatisation, service standards that are focused on functional tasks without scope for personalisation or innovation around what makes a good life. All of these are legitimate concerns: however, the two paradigms differ in what gets foregrounded in policy-making and implementation.

Universalism versus particularism

We present the two paradigms as ideal types rather than system descriptors. Nonetheless we argue that they do inform the 'policy cores' (Sabatier and Weible, 2019) or 'philosophies' (Schmidt, 2008) that sit behind specific policies and programmes. These paradigms align to a degree with the broader accounts of universalism versus particularism that underpin any welfare state (Taylor-Gooby, 1994; Thompson and Hoggett, 1996; Hoggett, 2006). In a care context they have been played out in the historical development of state care services that drew legitimacy from a narrative of universalism (or what we have called standardisation) in contrast to the particularism of market, family and community (Ouchi, 1980; Bartels, 2013). As the critique of institutionalisation gathered pace in the 1980s, the state was recognised to be just as particularistic in its treatment of people and its insensitivity to social diversity (Williams, 1989). Rather than a dysfunction to be designed out, some versions of particularism offered a way to move beyond the Fabian welfare model and provide more tailored forms for support (Thompson and Hoggett, 1996). Relational models of support came to be seen as essential to effective models of service delivery rather than a threat to bureaucratic impartiality (Bartels and Turnbull, 2020). People were understood to be co-producers and co-commissioners of their care (Needham and Carr, 2009), and communities to be a source of assets and wellbeing (#socialcarefuture, 2019).

In relation to social care, our two paradigms offer specific manifestations of these broader tensions within the welfare state. We distinguish between paradigms that seek to assure access to a standardised and regulated set of services versus those that seek to facilitate person-centred, relational forms of support, which may involve formal services but may also improve access to a range of informal activities. Hoggett argues that the tensions between universalism and particularism cannot be resolved, but they do generate 'value contradictions' for public officials (2006: 178). We suggest that it is these value contradictions that help to explain the lack of progress on many care issues that are being pursued simultaneously, particularly integration (universalism) and self-directed support (particularism), or free personal care (universalism) and prevention (particularism). Integration has often focused on how social care can help the NHS (for example, quicker hospital discharge packages) rather than on how people can have more choice and control. Free personal care has focused resources on a relatively narrow set of functional supports in the home, drawing attention and resources away from investing in the local assets and networks that keep people out of the formal care system.

By making explicit the two paradigms that run through care reform it is clear that care can contribute to narrow or broad understandings of wellbeing. In the differentiated paradigm, there is recognition that wellbeing cannot be *delivered* by services. Separating out these two paradigms has the advantage of helping to explain why systems that emphasise the importance of (say) integration with health appear to lose focus on personalisation or self-directed support (Pearson et al, 2018). It highlights the limits of claims that sustainability in social care is only about putting in more money, such as through capping care costs (DHSC, 2021d).

We can argue that the differentiated paradigm is the most appealing – with its emphasis on person-centredness and subjective wellbeing. However, it is important to also recognise its limits. This account has little to offer care staff in terms of routes into training, better pay or career progression commensurate with the kinds of work they do. Research on PAs highlights advantages of working in this way, but that there are disadvantages too (see, for example, Shakespeare et al, 2018; Manthorpe et al, 2020). Carers' right to breaks may be better protected in a system that gives primacy to standardisation and formalisation. The valorisation of love and family in the differentiated paradigm resonates with what many people would want from life, but family-based care is heavily gendered and can be inadequate (Tronto, 2013). It may be that standardised approaches fit certain contexts. For example, integration with health (which we suggest is part of the standardised paradigm) may be an effective way to offer short-term support, but be less suitable for longer term provision. As a former chair of England's Association of Directors of Adult Social Services, James Bullion, observed:

Figure 7.2: James Bullion tweet on integration

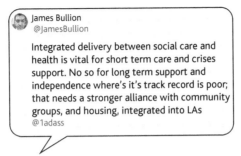

James Bullion
@JamesBullion

Integrated delivery between social care and health is vital for short term care and crises support. No so for long term support and independence where's it's track record is poor; that needs a stronger alliance with community groups, and housing, integrated into LAs
@1adass

Source: James Bullion, Twitter, 8 September 2021

Reconciling the two paradigms, and identifying how best to combine elements of them, requires being much more explicit about them. Responding to Watson's evidence to the Scottish Parliament, Derek Feeley acknowledged:

> [Nick Watson] is probably right that there is a tension between standardisation and personalisation. However, we need both of those: we need to enhance both standardisation and personalisation if we are to have the kind of social care support system that we want in Scotland. We are going to have to manage that tension in the best way we can. (Scottish Parliament Health, Social Care and Sport Committee, 2021)

While Feeley may be right that elements of both approaches are needed, many debates about social care feature a tendency either to ignore the tensions or to discredit the alternative. In the final chapter we set out ways to more explicitly debate the value tensions within social care.

Conclusion

This chapter has explored the patterns of convergence and divergence found in the book. It considered the distinction between transformational and incremental reforms, noting the tactical advantages of more incremental change as pursued in Scotland. Scotland's approach of 'layering' has avoided the risks of loading too much into a single transformational piece of legislation – as attempted in England and Wales – which may overwhelm implementing bodies. However, the implementation challenges of change have been a barrier in all four polities, and the dysfunctions of the care system remain such that all four nations are promising further large-scale reform in the future.

In understanding the barriers to policy change we also have to consider the 'policy mix'—in other words, how the proposed mechanisms of change fit together. In setting out two paradigms of care here, we have highlighted tensions in what care reformers are seeking to achieve. Approaches that seek to make care standardised and consistent, with a more professionalised workforce and a closer integration with health, offer one kind of care future. In contrast, approaches that seek to make care more local, more differentiated, more co-produced and more strengths-based are invoking a very different understanding of what constitutes good care and a good life. Failure to acknowledge these rival paradigms is part of the reason why care reforms have, to date, faltered, and will continue to be an issue as new sets of care reforms are tabled for the future. In developing care policy, the tensions between these two are either ignored altogether or are over-stated, to the extent that no accommodation is possible. In the next chapter we suggest ways in which it might be possible to develop more multi-vocal debates about care.

8

Conclusion: between care paradigms

In this book we have compared the adult social care systems of England, Scotland, Wales and Northern Ireland to understand convergence and divergence between them, in terms of discursive framings, decisions, practice and results (Pollitt, 2002; McConnell, 2010). We began by identifying a shared set of values across the policy reform documents of the four nations. Across the 25 years we can see a common articulation of the importance of wellbeing, rights, fairness, quality and sustainability within care systems. The importance of wellbeing in particular has grown over time, along with a commitment to asset-based approaches and person-centred care. All four nations highlighted the importance of fairness as an underpinning principle, particularly in relation to the reform of care funding. In Scotland, Wales and Northern Ireland rights remain an important underpinning principle of care reform, whereas in England this framing has been less evident under the Conservative-led governments in power since 2010.

In Chapter 3, we considered the supply and demand elements of care systems as part of understanding their contexts. In all four nations, demand for care is rising as a result of demographic pressures. Using the care diamond model, we looked at how care has tipped between the points of state, market, family and community, recognising that each of these has encountered a crisis in how it responds to care. In all four nations there is recognition that families and other unpaid carers need more support, particularly given the strains of the COVID-19 pandemic in which many formal services were withdrawn. The crisis of the state has been most evident in England where levels of funding have dropped well below the other nations, and where it is the market that is expected to respond to growing levels of demand. There is more optimism about the role of the state in Scotland and Wales, exemplified by their plans to develop a National Care Service to sit alongside the NHS and their diffidence about using the term 'market' in a care context. Northern Ireland has had to deal with the legacy of a contested state, in which care has been 'depoliticised' through being handed to Health and Social Care Trusts and integrated with health. In all four nations, there is optimism about the community as a site of care, which can relate to new forms of ownership, more co-production of services with people with lived experience, or more preventative investment to keep people out of formal services. While community is more than the 'fig leaf' that Pinker suggested in the minority Barclay Report (see Chapter 3), there may still be a tendency to over-invest in the concept of community without being clear about the conditions that enable communities to be inclusive sites of flourishing.

Convergence and divergence

In relation to care values and mechanisms there are clearly important areas of convergence across the four nations. Given their location within the UK, with all that this entails in relation to shared histories and path-dependence, this is perhaps to be expected. Nonetheless we suggest that over the past 25 years there has been significant divergence between their care reform policies, which, at the end of Chapter 4, we summarised as:

Active in Scotland: iterative, using targeted legislation for different issues, including free personal care, structural integration with health, self-directed support, worker registration and a home care contract to standardise fees.

Emergent in Wales, gathering more powers and momentum in the 25 years since devolution. Key reforms have included a maximum weekly charge for home care, raising the means test threshold for residential care and phasing in care worker registration.

England as *symbolic*, with the widely praised Care Act 2014 failing to deliver on key areas such as funding reforms and better support for carers. New legislation was passed in 2022 to revive the care cap (originally in the Care Act 2014) and then it was later delayed again.

Northern Ireland as *stalled*, with much-needed care reforms being blocked by the long suspensions of the Executive and the difficulties of passing legislation. Key legislative ambitions (carers' rights, funding reform) remain unaddressed.

As Chapter 5 highlighted, the extent to which Scotland's more active legislative agenda has led to a more sustainable care system should not be overstated. Indeed, some see Scotland's legislation on care as overactive, claiming its new policies detract from implementation of prior changes (Pearson et al, 2018). Harvey has pointed out that Scotland's 'Nordic' aspirations for social care have not been pursued with 'Nordic levels of taxation', and that such levels would be unlikely to find favour with the Scottish electorate (Harvey, 2020: 154). Scotland also lacks the tripartite bargaining model that underpins high pay in the Nordic states (Harvey, 2020: 161).

In explaining convergence and divergence and levels of success, we looked in Chapter 6 at the territorial policy communities of the four nations and how they compare in terms of scale, style and scope. We noted that, of the four, Scotland has had the combination most conducive to policy reform: a relatively small policy community; a policy style that minimised veto players; and policy scope sufficient to make reforms. In part, Scotland's success in making care policy may be due to tackling different elements of care sequentially, rather than with major 'set piece' legislation, as seen in England and in Wales. In relation to outcomes and results, however, many of the same issues are present in Scotland as elsewhere. The Scottish Government's proposals for a National Care Service, set out in 2021, are extremely wide-ranging and created a 'target' against which veto players (including GPs and local governments) have mobilised. It remains unclear whether this will mark a new, more adversarial, phase of care policy in Scotland.

In Chapter 7 we shifted the focus to on implementation challenges in all four nations and how the 'policy mix' has spanned two rival care paradigms, without sufficient acknowledgement of the tensions between them. These tensions need to be acknowledged and engaged with explicitly if progress is to be made towards more sustainable care systems. We believe that campaigners and policy makers alike will otherwise continue to be 'talking past' each other in debates and conversations about adult social care.

The evidence we have collected leads us to further caution against seeing these as four nations each pursuing care reform independently of one another. For most of the post-devolution period, crucial policy fields – welfare benefits, macro-economic policy (including taxation) – were matters reserved for the Westminster Parliament. These remain closely interlinked, with important implications for social care funding, and most money spent on care continues to come from the UK Government in block grants. Despite devolution, as Keating and Wilson note, 'the [UK] nation-state remains a powerful point of reference' (2014: 841).

The four nations also learn from and 'watch' each other, as they seek to tackle a common set of issues (Paun et al, 2016). In Wales and Northern Ireland there was a sense (for part of the period studied) that they were waiting for England to be the first mover on change. Over time, both nations seemed to be looking more to Scotland, around self-directed support (Northern Ireland) and the National Care Service (Wales). Both Scotland and Wales have been keen to articulate a more social democratic approach and differentiate themselves from the more marketised approach taken in England, a form of 'negative lesson drawing' (Rose, 1993). Indeed, according to some researchers, the devolved administrations 'have been engaged in a race to the top' that has put pressure on the UK Government to make equivalent reforms in England, while '(t)he UK government's response has been to try and insulate debate at the centre and to discredit innovations from the periphery' (Keating et al, 2021: 297).

Since 2020, COVID-19 has also shifted the balance between the four nations in ways likely to be long-lasting. As Andrews (2021: 64) puts it, 'The coronavirus crisis has shone a stronger UK spotlight on the devolved governments than anything since the tuition fee debates of 2010, and for a far more prolonged period'. The pandemic gave a new visibility and authority to the devolved leaders, especially in Wales and Scotland (Morphet, 2021). Magnified by COVID-19, the distinctiveness of the four nations' policy-making processes also has implications for the Union of the UK, with Scotland's First Minister promising a second referendum on Scottish independence (Brooks, 2021). Although beyond the scope of this book, further changes to constitutional arrangements in any of the four nations will have implications for how care and related social security benefits are funded and allocated.

Success for whom?

In evaluating policy outcomes, a key question to ask is, 'success for whom?' (McConnell et al, 2020). Throughout this book we have discussed how reforms can privilege certain groups over others, and the difficulty of pursuing a reform agenda that meets the needs of all. For example, reforms to (further) professionalise the paid care workforce and improve pay and conditions may clash with the interests of disabled people who may be concerned about power disparities (see the debate between Gerlich and Farquharson, 2020). Funding changes that introduce greater state subsidy may subsidise wealthy homeowners and fall hardest on those just above the means test threshold (Tallack and Sturrock, 2022).

Bottery (2020) separates out 12 different social care personas, all of whom have different perspectives on social care, and all of whom will have a different understanding of what constitutes success and failure:

1. The homeowner: "I shouldn't have to sell my house to pay for care."
2. The NHS defender: "What matters is the impact of social care on the NHS."
3. The radical transformer: "Only fundamental reform of care will do."
4. The family-firster: "Care is the responsibility of the family, not the state."
5. The nationaliser: "If Bevan was creating the NHS now, he'd have included social care within it."
6. The economic forecaster: "There's going to be a huge increase in demand for care, and we need to work out how to pay for it."
7. The personaliser: "I just want care that's centred on my needs, not determined by the services that are available."
8. The beleaguered provider: "I just want a decent rate for my services."
9. The overwhelmed carer: "I'm at my wit's end trying to provide care for my dad and husband."
10. The workforce campaigners: "It's all about paying careworkers more."

11. The needs-thresholder: "I just need that little bit of help to stay in my own home."
12. The local authority commissioner: "I just need more money."

All these perspectives are relevant to care reform as well as others (for example, the migrant care worker or the taxpayer). Making progress towards a more sustainable care system requires being alert to these personas and how they complement or compete with each other. Sensitivity to multiple perspectives can help ensure care reform is not discussed as if it only affects older people. Indeed, people often hold multiple identities in relation to care – and may articulate contradictory perspectives – which means we cannot treat the 'success for whom?' question as a matter of calculating costs and benefits.

An alternative to fracturing care into a kaleidoscope of different perspectives, we need to make more explicit the two rival paradigms that underpin care reform. By making these explicit, we expose key points of difference and why care reformers often speak 'past' each other because they are focused on different means and ends. The paradigms shape both specific mechanisms for reform and broader questions about what sustainability means in a context of care. These enable us to ask questions about wellbeing, fairness, quality, rights and sustainability in care.

Both of these paradigms underpin care reforms in all four nations. The failure to address the tensions between them and instead to opt for a 'best of both worlds' approach we see as contributing to the policy limitations set out in Chapter 5. Free personal care and investment in prevention are based on different understandings of what the state should do in relation to care. Similarly a commitment to integration with health can undermine the development of more self-directed approaches. We do not argue that these policies must be abandoned, but we do argue that policy makers need to move away from a blithe assumption that they can all be easily combined in practice.

The duality within care reforms could be dismissed as the same kind of bounded rationality that afflicts all policy-making, leading to failings to tackle crucial ambiguities and tensions. It might also be argued that there is a purposeful ambiguity here (Yanow, 1996), an effort to elide rather than to confront tensions in social care. In this view, the two paradigms may be part of a wider ambiguity within late modern societies that 'temporarily resolves conflicts and accommodates differences, allowing contending parties to legislate and move on to implementory actions' (Yanow, 1996: 228). Key developments in care legislation – the introduction of direct payments, England's Care Act 2014, and similar legislation in Scotland and Wales – could be at least partly due to the ability of contending interests to achieve consensus through ambiguity.

However, ambiguity has to be forced into clarity at the point where need is assessed and money is spent. Working pragmatically – and exploring, rather than ignoring, the tensions between the two paradigms – offers a way to engage with rather than ignore the dilemmas. This is consistent with the 'clumsy solutions' offered by Verweij and Thompson as an alternative to neat resolution in the context of divisive issues (2006). It highlights the importance of dialogue about the key trade-offs and compromises. Such debates – whether in policy arenas or interpersonal conversations – are, of course, not easy. From communication studies, Simons and Green's (2018) work on social threat suggests that some issues create such anxiety that we shy away from discussing them. They use examples such as affirmative action and drugs policy. We could also argue that the responsibility of the family versus the state for providing care might be similarly divisive and perceived as too threatening to broach, which then closes down opportunities to debate key issues. Hoggett argues that anxieties become not resolved by but held in the formal public service systems that we create: 'Central to this view is the idea that such institutions, besides performing their ostensible functions (health care, education, etc) also deal constantly with fundamental human anxieties. ... These anxieties ultimately express concerns about the survival of oneself, one's family or one's group' (Hoggett, 2006: 180, 176).

Building further on the role of anxiety, Hoggett (2006) and West (2013) offer psychoanalytic explanations of why it is difficult to talk about certain issues. In West's work this notion of anxiety is particularly invoked in relation to ageing. West and Needham (2017), writing about the lack of progress in implementing personalisation, draw on Gilleard and Higgs' (2010) account of the 'fourth age'. This, they suggest, is a 'feared imaginary', a contrast to the positive, consumer-driven discourse of the third age (West, 2013). In the fourth age, a key condition of eligibility for state support is a diagnosis of irreversible frailty, and this stage makes it hard to plan for or even talk about.

Such value conflicts and silences are not unusual in welfare systems, as Hoggett (2006: 175) argues. Rather than these tensions being resolved, he suggests that they must be 'lived out' at the front line: 'It is often at the level of "operations" that unresolved value conflicts are most sharply enacted, public officials and local representatives finding themselves "living out" rather than "acting upon" the contradictions of the complex and diverse society in which they live' (Hoggett, 2006: 179).

We cannot expect public services to resolve value conflicts in society. Given this, policy makers may take refuge in helpful ambiguity or in 'unseeing' other perspectives, in order to move a policy agenda forward. We might want them to be more explicit in surfacing and debating the tensions but we also need to confront our own ambivalence and discomfort about the issues at stake. Hoggett calls for a more pragmatic engagement with the limits of policy, giving up on excellence in favour of systems of welfare that are 'good enough' (Hoggett, 2006: 187). Like Verweij and Thompson's 2006 account of 'clumsy solutions', the notion of being 'good enough' steers away from the idea of a 'once-and-for-all' fix of social care. Instead it suggests greater humility in experimenting and learning. Smaller, more iterative, local approaches may be a better approach for some issues, particularly relating to outcomes and wellbeing. National mandates have a role – for example, in relation to human rights and funding – but these are about creating the conditions for better support, not a way to 'deliver' care or wellbeing.

Making progress on care reform requires recognition of the enormous trust problems between stakeholders in the care system. Lack of trust between providers and commissioners was a key finding from Needham et al's (2022) market shaping research. From the provider perspective, a key barrier to trust was the high turnover of local authority commissioners, care managers and social workers, which inhibits communication, continuity and a coherent organisational long-term strategy. Broader attitudes among citizens and towards the state are relevant here too, for example on the place of kindness in public policy (Unwin, 2018). There is also the understandable wariness of disabled people towards the state given continued issues of control and neglect, which COVID-19 has intensified (Flynn et al, 2021; Series, 2022).

For policy makers, a multi-vocal conversation requires recognising the tensions between standardisation and differentiation within localities and engaging with their tensions rather than cycling between contesting paradigms. This may require working differently with partners, making a joint commitment to some policies as overarching goals, rather than only one of several contending priorities. For example, if self-directed support were to be given primacy over health and care integration, it is likely that the structural approaches to integration that have been favoured to date would be reconsidered in favour of those that facilitate cultural shifts towards choice and control.

Conclusion

We have offered here an account of almost 25 years of policy-making on care in England, Scotland, Wales and Northern Ireland. We have focused on the contexts, mechanisms and outcomes in their care systems. We have highlighted points of discursive convergence around the values of care, convergence on the care mechanisms that are required, but divergence in effectiveness in making policy to address these mechanisms. In relation to results and outcomes, we again found much convergence, with all of the nations struggling to achieve their goals, and all looking to new waves of reform to solve ongoing issues. We have highlighted key institutional factors in the policy communities of the four nations – scale, style and scope – and argued that Scotland has had the most conducive environment in which to address care issues. Nonetheless, Scotland, like the other nations, has struggled with implementation due to a failure to acknowledge and debate the tensions within the 'policy mix'. The two rival paradigms at work in care reform require attention, without which an excessive focus on the standardised and formalised – which we see in all four systems – stifles the local, the personalised and the co-productive.

There are future research agendas here, particularly around exploring different local care regimes within the nations. We have discussed issues of what Pettigrew et al (1988) call 'outer context' (care funding, the market and the workforce). It is also clear that some localities perform better than might be expected on care, despite having similar funding to other areas, suggesting that issues of 'inner context', such as leadership and culture, may have a part to play (Humphries and Timmins, 2021). Future studies can helpfully build on existing approaches that compare localities, such as the market shaping typology (Needham et al, 2022) and the cultural and behavioural factors of inner context (Pettigrew et al, 1988). The analysis we have developed in this book can also inform studies of care systems within other federal or quasi-federal systems, in which component parts experiment and learn from each other in competitive and collaborative modes (Benz, 2012; Benz and Fürst, 2002; Needham and Hall, 2022).

Care systems do not stand still. Scotland is on the brink of major reform, with Wales likely to follow. Proposals published so far in Scotland suggest it will favour the standardisation paradigm, despite expressing discursive commitment to differentiation, self-directed support and co-production. We hope our work will contribute to an understanding of the limits of this, and to encouraging a more explicit engagement with the standardisation paradigm and its interface with the differentiated model. Free personal care, nationalised commissioning, more regulation, integrated care systems and a register of care workers will not deliver wellbeing; it may not even create the conditions for it. If care is commissioned in chunks of time, with no dialogue with the people and families being supported, and no opportunities to build and sustain relationships, it will not contribute to wellbeing. If levels of unmet need increase, and pressure on carers continues to build, systems will not achieve the expressed aims of reform. There is, of course, a money question here – support is heavily rationed in part because demand is growing and social care remains underfunded. Bringing more money into the system is vital, but it is only a starting point. It does not resolve the question of what a care system should be and do.

What underpins wellbeing for us all is not that different at a basic level. The social movement #socialcarefuture campaigns on the statement, 'We all want to live in the place we call home with the people and things that we love, in communities where we look out for one another, doing the things that matter to us'. It is an easy statement to agree with, but it involves committing to the primacy of the differentiated paradigm. It means requiring that reforms falling within the standardisation paradigm (like the much-needed improvement in the pay and conditions of care workers) must be done in ways that do not compromise differentiation and self-direction. This can lead to distinctive conversations in Cardiff, London, Edinburgh and Belfast – and indeed in Powys, Derbyshire, Fife and Antrim. It might lead to nervousness about a National Care Service if that looks too much like a National Health Service for care, offering structural solutions for issues that are cultural and relational. Care can never be reduced to what is or isn't done by the state, but across all four nations of the UK, the national and the local state can have new and better conversations about a sustainable social care system, with wellbeing at its heart.

References

Age UK (2019) *Estimating need in older people: Findings for England*, London, www.ageuk.org.uk/globalassets/age-uk/documents/reports-and-publi cations/reports-and-briefings/active-communities/id204303-estimating- needs-report.pdf [Accessed 24 March 2022].

Abrams, F. (1978) *Neighbourhood care and social policy: A research perspective*, Berkhamstead: The Volunteer Centre.

Alarilla, A., Grimm, F. and Stafford, M. (2021) 'What happened to unpaid caring during the COVID-19 pandemic?', UK Data Service, Data Impact blog, 8 June, https://blog.ukdataservice.ac.uk/unpaid-caring-during-covi d19 [Accessed 9 February 2022].

Alberti, A., Forde, C., Graham, G., Bessa, I., Cutter, J., Ciupijus, Z. et al (2022) *From a health crisis to a labour crisis: Omicron, Brexit and labour shortages*, Centre for Employment Relations, Innovation and Change blog, 13 January, https://cericleeds.wordpress.com/2022/01/13/from-a-health- crisis-to-a-labour-crisis-omicron-brexit-and-labour-shortages [Accessed 19 January 2022].

Allan, G., Hawker, S. and Crow, G. (2001) 'Family diversity and change in Britain and Western Europe', *Journal of Family Issues*, 22(7): 819–37.

Allen, K. and Glasby, J. (2013) ' "The billion dollar question": Embedding prevention in older people's services – Ten 'high-impact' changes', *British Journal of Social Work*, 43(5): 904–24.

Allen, K., Burn, E., Hall, K., Mangan, C. and Needham, C. (2023) '"They made an excellent start … but after a while, it started to die out": Tensions in combining personalisation and integration in English adult social care', *Social Policy and Society*, 22(1): 172–86.

APPG (All Party Parliamentary Group) on Adult Social Care (2019) *Elevation, registration and standardisation: The professionalisation of social care workers*, London: APPG on Adult Social Care, www.gmb.org.uk/sites/default/ files/APPG_SOCIALCARE_REPORT.pdf [Accessed 27 October 2021].

Alliance Scotland (2018) *Adult social care reform in Scotland: A discussion paper*, https://www.alliance-scotland.org.uk/wp-content/uploads/2018/10/ ALLIANCE-response-Discussion-paper-on-Adult-social-care-reform- for-Scotland.pdf [Accessed 18 February 2022].

Andrews, L. (2021) 'The forward march of devolution halted – and the limits of progressive unionism', *The Political Quarterly*, 92(3): 512–21.

Andrews, L. (2022) 'Performing Welsh Government 1999–2016: How insider narratives illuminate the hidden wiring and emergent cultural practices', *Contemporary British History*, 36(1): 124–56.

Ansell, C. and Torfing, J. (2015) 'How does collaborative governance scale?', *Policy & Politics*, 43(3): 315–29.

Archer, M.S. (2012) *The reflexive imperative in late modernity*, Cambridge: Cambridge University Press.

Arnott, M. (2019) 'The Scottish Government', in G. Hassan (ed) *The story of the Scottish Parliament: The first two decades explained*, Edinburgh: Edinburgh University Press, pp 52–63.

Asthana, A. (2017) 'Take care of your elderly mothers and fathers says Tory minister', *The Guardian*, 3 January, www.theguardian.com/society/2017/jan/31/take-care-of-your-elderly-mothers-and-fathers-says-tory-minister [Accessed 26 November 2020].

Atkins, G., Dalton, G., Phillips, A. and Stojanovic, A. (2021) *Devolved public services: The NHS, schools and social care in the four nations*, London: Institute for Government, www.instituteforgovernment.org.uk/sites/default/files/publications/devolved-public-services.pdf [Accessed 14 November 2021].

Audit Scotland (2018) *Health and social care integration: Update on progress*, Health and social care series, Edinburgh, www.audit-scotland.gov.uk/uploads/docs/report/2018/nr_181115_health_socialcare_update.pdf [Accessed 12 July 2020].

Audit Wales (2020) *So, what's different? Findings from the Auditor General's sustainable development principle examinations*, Cardiff, www.wao.gov.uk/sites/default/files/Well-being-of-Future-Generations-report-eng_11.pdf [Accessed 2 March 2022].

Austin, A. (2020) *A universal declaration of human well-being*, London: Springer International Publishing.

Bache, I. and Reardon, L. (2013) 'An Idea whose time has come? Explaining the rise of well-being in British politics', *Political Studies*, 61(4), https://doi.org/10.1111/1467-9248.12001.

Ballard, C., Orrell, M., Moniz-Cook, E., Woods, R., Whitaker, R., Corbett, A. et al (2020) *Improving mental health and reducing antipsychotic use in people with dementia in care homes: The WHELD research programme including two RCTs*, Programme Grants Application, Res 2020, 8(6), https://evidence.nihr.ac.uk/alert/wheld-dementia-care-homes-person-centred-care [Accessed 21 February 2021].

Barclay, P. (1982) *Social workers: Their role and tasks* (Barclay Report), London: Bedford Square Press.

Barker, K. (2014) *A new settlement for health and social care* (Barker Report), London: The King's Fund.

Bartels, K.P. (2013) 'Public encounters: The history and future of face-to-face contact between public professionals and citizens', *Public Administration*, 91(2): 469–83.

Bartels, K. and Turnbull, N. (2020) 'Relational public administration: A synthesis and heuristic classification of relational approaches', *Public Management Review*, 22(9): 1324–46.

BBC News (2017) 'General Election: Theresa May denies social care U-turn', 22 May, www.bbc.co.uk/news/election-2017-40001221 [Accessed 30 October 2020].

Beecham, J. (2006) *Beyond boundaries: Citizen centred local services for Wales* (Beecham Review), Cardiff: Welsh Assembly Government.

Béland, D. and Powell, M. (2016) 'Continuity and change in social policy', *Social Policy & Administration*, 50(2): 129–47.

Béland, D., Rocco, P. and Waddan, A. (2016) 'Reassessing policy drift: Social policy change in the United States', *Social Policy & Administration*, 50(2): 201–18.

Béland, D., Howlett, M., Rocco, P. and Waddan, A. (2020) 'Designing policy resilience: Lessons from the Affordable Care Act', *Policy Sciences*, 53(2): 269–89.

Bell, D. (1973) *The coming of post-industrial society*, New York: Basic Books.

Bell, D. (2018) *Free personal care: What the Scottish approach to social care would cost in England*, London: The Health Foundation, www.health.org.uk/newsletter-feature/free-personal-care-what-the-scottish-approach-to-soc ial-care-would-cost-in [Accessed 26 November 2020].

Bell, D. and Rutherford, A. (2013) 'Individual and geographic factors in the formation of care networks in the UK', *Population, Place and Space*, 19(6): 727–37.

Bengoa, R. (2016) *Systems not structures: Changing health and social care* (Bengoa Report), Belfast: Expert Advisory Panel.

Bengtson, V.L. and Martin, P. (2001) 'Families and intergenerational relationships in aging societies: Comparing the United States with German-speaking countries', *Zeitschrift für Gerontologie und Geriatrie*, 34(3): 207–17.

Benz, A. (2012) 'Yardstick competition and policy learning in multi-level systems', *Regional and Federal Studies*, 22(3): 251–67.

Benz, A. and Fürst, D. (2002) 'Policy learning in regional networks', *European Urban and Regional Studies*, 9(1): 21–35.

Beresford, B.A., Mann, R.C., Parker, G.M., Kanaan, M., Faria, R., Rabiee, P. et al (2019) 'Reablement services for people at risk of needing social care: The MoRe mixed-methods evaluation', *Health Services and Delivery Research*, 1–254, doi:10.3310/hsdr07160.

Bergene, A. (2007) 'Towards a critical realist comparative methodology: Context-sensitive theoretical comparison', *Journal of Critical Realism*, 6(1): 5–27.

Berrington, A. (2017) 'Childlessness in the UK', in M. Kreyenfeld and D. Konietzka (eds) *Childlessness in Europe: Contexts, causes, and consequences*, Cham: Springer International Publishing, pp 57–76.

Bertin, G. and Carradore, M. (2016) 'Differentiation of welfare regimes: The case of Italy', *International Journal of Social Welfare*, 25(2): 149–60.

Bevan, A. (1952) *In place of fear*, London: Quartet.

Bigby, C. (2020) 'Dedifferentiation and people with intellectual disabilities in the Australian National Disability Insurance Scheme: Bringing research, politics and policy together', *Journal of Intellectual and Development Disability*, 45(4): 309–19.

Birrell, D. and Gray, A.M. (2018) 'Outcomes-based approaches and the devolved administrations', *Social Policy Review* 30, Bristol: Policy Press, pp 67–86.

Bolton, J. (2015) *Emerging practice in outcome-based commissioning for social care*, Discussion Paper, April, Oxford: Institute for Public Care, https://ipc.broo kes.ac.uk/files/publications/John_Bolton_Outcome_Based_Commissioni ng_Paper_April_2015.pdf [Accessed 12 May 2020].

Bosanquet, N. and Haldenby, A. (2020) 'There is no magic fix for our social care crisis', *The Guardian*, 30 July, www.theguardian.com/society/ 2020/jul/30/there-is-no-magic-fix-for-our-social-care-crisis [Accessed 31 July 2021].

Bottery, S. (2020) 'Twelve social care personas: Which one(s) are you?', The King's Fund blog, 23 November, www.kingsfund.org.uk/blog/2020/11/ twelve-social-care-personas [Accessed 26 March 2022].

Bovaird, T. (2014) 'Attributing outcomes to social policy interventions – "gold standard" or "fool's gold" in public policy and management?', *Social Policy & Administration*, 48(1): 1–23.

Boyce, S. (2017) *Paying for social care*, Cardiff: National Assembly for Wales.

Bradbury, J. and Andrews, R. (2010) 'State devolution and national identity: Continuity and change in the politics of Welshness and Britishness in Wales', *Parliamentary Affairs*, 63(2): 229–49.

Brindle, D. (2009) 'Taking the long view: Social care reform', *The Guardian*, 25 February, www.theguardian.com/society/2009/feb/25/interview-stew art-sutherland [Accessed 20 March 2022].

Brooks, L. (2021) 'Sturgeon says second independence vote "a matter of when, not if"', *The Guardian*, 9 May, www.theguardian.com/politics/ 2021/may/09/scottish-indyref2-battle-distraction-covid-michael-gove [Accessed 18 September 2021].

Brown, T. (2021) *Social care provision in the UK and the role of carers*, London: House of Lords Library.

Bulmer, M. (1987) *The social basis of community care*, London: Routledge.

Burke, S. (2021) 'Post-pandemic challenges for all ages in an ageing society', *Quality Ageing for Adults*, 22(3/4): 172–7.

Burn, E. and Needham, C. (2014) Implementing the Care Act, 2014 – a synthesis of project reports on the Care Act commissioned by the National Institute for Health Research, Birmingham: University of Birmingham, https://www.birmingham.ac.uk/documents/college-social-sciences/soc ial-policy/publications/implementing-the-care-act-2014.pdf [Accessed 13 March 2022].

Burns, D., Rees Jones, I., Earle, J., Froud, J., Williams, K., Cowie, L. et al (2016) *Where does the money go? Financialised chains and the crisis in residential care*, CRESC Public Interest Report, Manchester: Centre for Research on Socio-Cultural Change (CRESC), University of Manchester.

Caiels, J., Forder, J., Malley, J., Netten, A. and Windle, K. (2010) *Measuring the outcomes of low-level services*, Discussion Paper 2699, Canterbury: University of Kent.

Caiels, J., Milne, A. and Beadle-Brown, J. (2021) 'Strengths-based approaches in social work and social care: Reviewing the evidence', *Journal of Long-Term Care*, 401–22, https://journal.ilpnetwork.org/articles/10.31389/jltc.102 [Accessed 1 March 2023].

Cairney, P., Russell, S. and St Denny, E. (2016) 'The "Scottish approach" to policy and policymaking: What issues are territorial and what are universal?', *Policy & Politics*, 44(3): 333–50.

Cambridge, P. and Carnaby, S. (2005) *Person centred planning and care management with people with learning disabilities*, London: Jessica Kingsley Publishers.

Campbell, D. (2019) 'Pledges to fix social care could cost Boris Johnson dearly', *The Guardian*, 1 August, www.theguardian.com/uk-news/2019/aug/01/promising-to-fix-social-care-could-cost-boris-johnson-dearly [Accessed 16 September 2020].

Carers UK (2020) *Caring behind closed doors: Six months on*, London, www.carersuk.org/images/News_and_campaigns/Behind_Closed_Doors_2020/Caring_behind_closed_doors_Oct20.pdf [Accessed 2 February 2021].

Carey, G., Kay, A. and Nevile, A. (2019) 'Institutional legacies and "sticky layers": What happens in cases of transformative policy change?', *Administration & Society*, 51(3): 491–509.

Carey, G., Dickinson, H., Malbon, E. and Reeders, D. (2018) 'The vexed question of market stewardship in the public sector: Examining equity and the social contract through the Australian National Disability Insurance Scheme', *Social Policy & Administration*, 52(1): 387–407.

Cascio, M.A., Lee, E., Vaudrin, N. and Freedman, D. (2019) 'A team-based approach to open coding: Considerations for creating intercoder consensus', *Field Methods*, 31(2): 116–30.

CCN (County Councils Network) (2022) 'New analysis warns government has "seriously underestimated" the costs of adult social care charging reforms', CNN News, 18 March, www.countycouncilsnetwork.org.uk/new-analysis-warns-government-has-seriously-underestimated-the-costs-of-adult-social-care-charging-reforms [Accessed 12 July 2022].

CCPS (Coalition of Care and Support Providers Scotland) (2021) 'A National Care Service for Scotland, CCPS Consultation Response', Edinburgh, www.cosgrovecare.org.uk/wp-content/uploads/2022/01/anationalcareserviceforscotland-ccpsconsultationresponse.pdf [Accessed 12 December 2021].

Chapman, A. (2018) 'Playing catch-up? Adult social care in Northern Ireland', *Journal of the Institute of Public Administration of Ireland*, 66(3): 99–115.

Chaney, P.J. (2022) 'Exploring the politicisation and territorialisation of adult social care in the United Kingdom: Electoral discourse analysis of state-wide and meso elections 1998–2019', *Global Social Policy*, 22(1): 141–71.

Chang, M.-F. (2022) 'Challenges and chances for local health and social care integration: Lessons from Greater Manchester, England', *Journal of Integrated Care*, 30(2): 146–59.

Cheshire-Allen, M. and Calder, G. (2022) '"No one was clapping for us": Care, social justice and family carer wellbeing during the COVID-19 pandemic in Wales', *International Journal of Care and Caring*, 6(1–2): 49–66.

Cheung, A. (2020) *The Barnett formula*, London: Institute for Government, www.instituteforgovernment.org.uk/explainers/barnett-formula [Accessed 4 November 2022].

Christie, M. (2011) *Christie Commission on the future delivery of public services*, Edinburgh: Scottish Government, www.gov.scot/publications/ commission-future-delivery-public-services/documents [Accessed 26 November 2020].

Clarke, J., Newman, J., Smith, N., Vidler, E. and Westmarland, L. (2007) *Creating citizen-consumers: Changing publics and changing public services*, London: SAGE.

CMA (Competition and Markets Authority) (2017) *Care homes market study: Final report*, London, https://assets.publishing.service.gov.uk/media/ 5a1fdf30e5274a750b82533a/care-homes-market-study-final-report.pdf [Accessed 7 November 2022].

Cochrane, F. (2020) *Breaking peace: Brexit and Northern Ireland*, Manchester: Manchester University Press.

Cole, A. and Stafford, I. (2015) *Devolution and governance: Wales between capacity and constraint*, Basingstoke: Palgrave Pivot.

Cole, A., Harguindéguy, J.-B., Stafford, I., Pasquier, R. and de Visscher, C. (2015) 'States of convergence in territorial governance', *Publius: The Journal of Federalism*, 45(2): 297–321.

Collie, F. (2019) *State of caring in Scotland 2019*, Edinburgh: Carers Scotland, www.carersuk.org/scotland/policy/policy-library/state-of-caring-in-scotl and-2019 [Accessed 16 January 2021].

Cominetti, N., Gardiner, L. and Kelly, G. (2020) *What happens after the clapping finishes? The pay, terms and conditions we choose for our care workers*, London: Resolution Foundation.

Common Weal Care Reform Group and Smith, M. (2021) *Common Weal's manifesto for a social care service*, Common Weal, https://discovery.dundee. ac.uk/ws/portalfiles/portal/56146500/Manifesto_for_a_National_C are_Service.pdf [Accessed 7 November 2022].

The Conservative and Unionist Party (2019) *Forward, together: Our plan for a stronger Britain and a prosperous future*, Manifesto, London, https://ucrel.lancs.ac.uk/wmatrix/ukmanifestos2017/localpdf/Conservatives.pdf [Accessed 25 November 2020].

Cooke, K., Iredale, R., Williams, R. and Wooding, N. (2019) *Measuring the mountain: What really matters in social care to individuals in Wales*, Pontypridd: University of South Wales.

COPNI (Commissioner for Older People for Northern Ireland) (2015) *Prepared to care: Modernising adult social care in Northern Ireland*, Belfast.

COSLA (Convention of Scottish Local Authorities) (2021) 'COSLA response to consultation on national care service', News, www.cosla.gov.uk/news/2021/cosla-response-to-consultation-on-national-care-service [Accessed 3 September 2022].

Courtin, E. and Knapp, M. (2017) 'Social isolation, loneliness and health in old age: A scoping review', *Health and Social Care in the Community*, 25(3): 799–812.

CQC (Care Quality Commission) (2017) *The state of health care and adult social care in England*, London: CQC, https://www.cqc.org.uk/sites/default/files/20171123_stateofcare1617_report.pdf [Accessed 16 February 2019].

Crowther, N. (2018) 'Don't panic! Why the social care crisis will not be solved by making a crisis out of social care', #socialcarefuture Blog, 14 March, https://socialcarefuture.blog/2018/03/14/dont-panic-why-the-social-care-crisis-will-not-be-solved-by-making-a-crisis-out-of-social-care [Accessed 9 August 2020].

Curry, N. and Oung, C. (2021) *Fractured and forgotten? The social care provider market in England*, London: Nuffield Trust, www.nuffieldtrust.org.uk/research/fractured-and-forgotten-the-social-care-provider-market-in-england [Accessed 6 December 2021].

Curtice, J. Scholes, A., Ratti, V., Cant, J., Bennett, M., Hinchcliffe, S. et al (2022) *British Social Attitudes Survey 39*, London: NatCen, https://natcen.ac.uk/our-research/research/british-social-attitudes/ [Accessed 2 December 2022].

Dahl, H.M. (2021) 'The "care crisis": Its scientific framing and silences', in L.L. Hansen and H.M. Dahl (eds) *A care crisis in the Nordic welfare states? Care work, gender equality and welfare state sustainability*, Bristol: Policy Press, pp 20–38.

Daly, M. (2020) 'COVID-19 and care homes in England: What happened and why?', *Social Policy & Administration*, 54(7): 985–98.

Daly, M. and Lewis, J. (2000) 'The concept of social care and the analysis of contemporary welfare states', *The British Journal of Sociology*, 51(2): 281–98.

Danermark, B., Ekström, M. and Karlsson, J.C. (2019) *Explaining society: Critical realism in the social sciences*, London: Routledge.

Dayan, M. and Heenan, D. (2019) *Change or collapse: Lessons from the drive to reform health and social care in Northern Ireland*, London: Nuffield Trust, www.nuffieldtrust.org.uk/research/change-or-collapse-lessons-from-the-drive-to-reform-health-and-social-care-in-northern-ireland [Accessed 18 June 2020].

Dayrell, C., Semino, E., Kinloch, K. and Baker, P. (2020) *Social care in UK public discourse*, Lancaster: University of Lancaster.

Demos (2009) *A constitution for social care*, London.

DH (Department of Health) (2009) *Shaping the future of care together*, London.

DH (2010) *A vision for adult social care: Capable communities and active citizens*, London.

DH (2012) *Transforming care: A national response to Winterbourne View Hospital*, London, https://assets.publishing.service.gov.uk/government/uploads/system/uploads/attachment_data/file/213215/final-report.pdf [Accessed 22 July 2021].

DH (2018) *Domiciliary care workforce review: Northern Ireland 2016–2021*, Belfast, www.health-ni.gov.uk/sites/default/files/publications/health/Workforce%20Plan%20Domiciliary%20Care%202016%20-%202021.pdf [Accessed 2 June 2021].

DH (2022a) *Consultation on Power to people*, Belfast, www.health-ni.gov.uk/articles/power-people [Accessed 7 November 2022].

DH (2022b) *Quarterly direct payment statistics, December 2021*, Belfast, www.health-ni.gov.uk/publications/quarterly-direct-payments-statistics-december-2021 [Accessed 2 June 2021].

Department of Health and Social Services (1990) *People first: Community care in Northern Ireland in the 1990s*, Belfast: HMSO.

DHSC (Department of Health and Social Care) (2018) *Carers action plan: 2018–2020*, London, www.gov.uk/government/publications/carers-action-plan-2018-to-2020 [Accessed 7 November 2022].

DHSC (2021a) *Integration and innovation: Working together to improve health and social care for all*, London: The Stationery Office, www.gov.uk/government/publications/working-together-to-improve-health-and-social-care-for-all/integration-and-innovation-working-together-to-improve-health-and-social-care-for-all-html-version [Accessed 3 March 2022].

DHSC (2021b) *People at the heart of care: Adult social care reform*, White Paper, London: The Stationery Office, https://assets.publishing.service.gov.uk/government/uploads/system/uploads/attachment_data/file/1061870/people-at-the-heart-of-care-asc-reform-accessible-with-correction-slip.pdf [Accessed 3 March 2022].

DHSC (2021c) *Market sustainability and fair cost of care fund: Purpose and conditions 2022 to 2023*, London, www.gov.uk/government/publications/market-sustainability-and-fair-cost-of-care-fund-2022-to-2023/market-sustainability-and-fair-cost-of-care-fund-purpose-and-conditions-2022-to-2023 [Accessed 3 March 2022].

DHSC (2022) *Adult social care charging reform: Further details*, London, www.gov.uk/government/publications/build-back-better-our-plan-for-hea lth-and-social-care/adult-social-care-charging-reform-further-details [Accessed 3 March 2022].

Dilnot, A. (2011) *Fairer care funding: The Report of the Commission on Funding of Care and Support* (Dilnot Report), London: The Stationery Office.

Drakeford, M. (2005) 'Wales and a third term of New Labour: Devolution and the development of difference', *Critical Social Policy*, 25(4): 497–506.

Dromey, J. and Hochlaf, D. (2018) *Fair care: A workforce strategy for social care*, Newcastle: IPPR North, www.ippr.org/research/publications/fair-care [Accessed 30 November 2020].

Elliott, I.C., Bottom, K.A., Carmichael, P., Liddle, J., Martin, S. and Pyper, R. (2022) 'The fragmentation of public administration: Differentiated and decentered governance in the (dis) United Kingdom', *Public Administration*, 100(1): 98–115.

Entwistle, T., Downe, J., Guarneros-Meza, V. and Martin, S. (2014) 'The multi-level governance of Wales: Layer cake or marble cake?', *British Journal of Politics and International Relations*, 16(2): 310–25.

Esping-Andersen, G. (1990) *The three worlds of welfare capitalism*, Cambridge: Polity Press.

Ettelt, S., Damant, J., Perkins, M., Williams, L. and Wittenberg, R. (2020) *Personalisation in care homes for older people: Final report*, London: Policy Innovation and Evaluation Research Unit, https://piru.ac.uk/assets/files/Personalisation_ in_care_homes-Final-report.pdf [Accessed 22 February 2022].

Etzioni, A. (2012) 'A communitarian critique of human rights', in T. Cushman (ed) *Handbook of human rights*, London: Routledge, pp 153–8.

Fair Work Convention (2016) *Fair work framework 2016*, Edinburgh, www.fairworkconvention.scot/wp-content/uploads/2018/12/Fair-Work-Con vention-Framework-PDF-Full-Version.pdf [Accessed 19 May 2022].

Feeley, D. (2021) *Independent review of adult social care in Scotland* (Feeley Report), Edinburgh: Scottish Government.

Ferguson, I. (2007) 'Increasing user choice or privatizing risk? The antinomies of personalization', *British Journal of Social Work*, 37(3): 387–403.

Ferguson, Z. (2019) 'The Scottish Civil Service', in G. Hassan (ed) *The story of the Scottish Parliament: The first two decades explained*, Edinburgh: Edinburgh University Press, pp 64–72.

Ferrant, G., Pesando, L.M. and Nowacka, K. (2014) *Unpaid care work: The missing link in the analysis of gender gaps in labour outcomes*, Boulogne-Billancourt: OECD Development Centre.

Fine, M.D. (2007) *A caring society? Care and the dilemmas of human service in the twenty-first century*, Basingstoke: Palgrave.

Flanagan, K., Uyarra, E. and Laranja, M. (2011) 'Reconceptualising the "policy mix" for innovation', *Research Policy*, 40(5): 702–13.

Flynn, S., Caton, S., Gillooly, A., Bradshaw, J., Hastings, R.P., Hatton, C. et al (2021) 'The experiences of adults with learning disabilities in the UK during the COVID-19 pandemic: Qualitative results from Wave 1 of the Coronavirus and people with learning disabilities study', *Tizard Learning Disability Review*, 26(4): 224–29.

Folbre, N. (2006) 'Measuring care: Gender, empowerment, and the care economy', *Journal of Human Development*, 7(2): 183–99.

Foster, D. (2021) *Reform of adult social care funding: Developments since July 2019 (England)*, London: House of Commons Library, https://commonslibrary.parliament.uk/research-briefings/cbp-8001 [Accessed 4 April 2022].

Foster, D. (2022) *Adult social care funding (England)*, London: House of Commons Library, https://researchbriefings.files.parliament.uk/docume nts/CBP-7903/CBP-7903.pdf [Accessed 3 September 2022].

Fox, A. (2018) *A new health and care system: Escaping the invisible asylum*, Bristol: Policy Press.

Fraser, G. (2019) 'Why won't Remainers talk about family', UnHerd, 22 February, https://unherd.com/2019/02/why-wont-remainers-talk-about-family [Accessed 12 May 2020].

Friedman, M. (2005) *Trying hard is not good enough: How to produce measurable improvements for customers and communities*, Victoria, BC: Trafford Publishing.

Future Care Capital (2018) *Facilitating care insight to develop caring economies*, London, https://futurecarecapital.org.uk/wp-content/uploads/2020/03/Full-Report-%E2%80%93-Facilitating-Care-Insight-to-Develop-Caring-Economies.pdf [Accessed 5 January 2022].

Gallagher, J. (2019) 'Devolution: An assessment', in G. Hassan (ed) *The story of the Scottish Parliament: The first two decades explained*, Edinburgh: Edinburgh University Press, pp 242–51.

Gerlich, K. and Farquharson, C. (2020) 'Experts debate: Registering care workers', *The Guardian*, 27 February, www.theguardian.com/soci ety/2020/feb/27/experts-debate-registering-care-workers [Accessed 19 March 2022].

Giddens, A. (1990) *The consequences of modernity*, Chichester: John Wiley & Sons.

Giddens, A. and Pierson, C. (1998) *Conversations with Anthony Giddens: Making sense of modernity*, Stanford, CA: Stanford University Press.

Gilleard, C. and Higgs, P. (2010) 'Aging without agency: Theorizing the fourth age', *Aging and Mental Health*, 14(2): 121–8.

Gingrich, J.R. (2011) *Making markets in the welfare state: The politics of varying market reforms*, Cambridge: Cambridge University Press.

Glasby, J. (2007) *Understanding Health and Social Care*, Bristol: Policy Press.

Glasby, J. and Littlechild, R. (2016) *Direct payments and personal budgets: Putting personalisation into practice*, Bristol: Policy Press.

Glasby, J., Duffy, S. and Needham, C. (2011) 'Debate: A Beveridge report for the 21st century? The implications of self-directed support for future welfare reform', *Policy & Politics*, 39(4): 613–17.

Glasby, J., Zhang, Y.N., Bennett, M.R. and Hall, P. (2021) 'A lost decade? A renewed case for adult social care reform in England', *Journal of Social Policy*, 50(2): 406–37.

Gori, C., Fernandez, J. and Wittenberg, R. (2016) 'Conclusion: Looking ahead in long-term care policies', in C. Gori, J. Fernandez and R. Wittenberg (eds) *Long-term care reforms in OECD countries*, Bristol: Policy Press, pp 293–306.

Gorski, P.S. (2013) 'What is critical realism? And why should you care?', *Contemporary Sociology*, 42(5): 658–70.

Gray, A.M. and Birrell, D. (2013) *Transforming adult social care: Contemporary policy and practice*, Bristol: Policy Press.

Greenhalgh, T. (2002) 'Understanding family values', *Young Consumers*, 4(1): 13–20.

Gregory, A. (2022) 'Number of adults with dementia to exceed 150m by 2050, study finds', *The Guardian*, 6 January, www.theguardian.com/soci ety/2022/jan/06/number-adults-with-dementia-exceed-150-million-2050-study?utm_term=AutofeedandCMP=twt_b-gdnnewsandutm_med ium=Socialandutm_source=Twitter [Accessed 7 January 2022].

Hacker, J.S. (2004) 'Privatizing risk without privatizing the welfare state: The hidden politics of social policy retrenchment in the United States', *American Political Science Review*, 98(2): 243–60.

Hamblin, K. (2019) *Adult social care and wellbeing policy in the four nations of the UK*, Sheffield: University of Sheffield, http://circle.group.shef. ac.uk/wp-content/uploads/2019/12/WPO_final-v2.pdf [Accessed 1 December 2021].

Hamblin, K. (2020) *Care system sustainability: What role for technology? An evidence review*, Sustainable Care Paper 3, Sheffield: University of Sheffield.

Hanssen, J.I., Pettersen, P.A. and Tveit Sandvin, J. (2001) 'Welfare municipalities: Economic resources or party politics? Norwegian local government social programs of the 1920s', *International Journal of Social Welfare*, 10(1): 27–44.

Harvey, M. (2020) 'Devolution', in M. Keating (ed) *The Oxford handbook of Scottish politics*, Oxford: Oxford University Press, pp 371–85.

Hassan, G. (2019) *The story of the Scottish Parliament: The first two decades explained*, Edinburgh: Edinburgh University Press.

Hassan, G. and Shaw, E. (2020) 'The Scottish Labour Party', in M. Keating (ed) *The Oxford handbook of Scottish politics*, Oxford: Oxford University Press, pp 255–77.

Hastings, A. (1997) *The construction of nationhood: Ethnicity, religion and nationalism*, Cambridge: Cambridge University Press.

Hayes, L., Johnson, E. and Tarrant, A. (2019) *Professionalisation at work in adult social care*, London: GMB, www.gmb.org.uk/sites/default/files/Professionalisation_at_Work_0309.pdf [Accessed 12 February 2022].

Heald, D. (2020) 'The politics of Scotland's public finances', in M. Keating (ed) *The Oxford handbook of Scottish politics*, Oxford: Oxford University Press, pp 512–42.

Health and Social Care and Housing, Communities and Local Government Committees (2018) *Long-term funding of adult social care*, London: The Stationery Office, https://publications.parliament.uk/pa/cm201719/cmselect/cmcomloc/768/768.pdf [Accessed 22 May 2019].

Health and Social Care Board (2015) *A managed change: An agenda for creating a sustainable basis for domiciliary care in Northern Ireland*, Belfast.

Health and Social Care Board (2016) *eHealth and care strategy for Northern Ireland*, Belfast.

Health and Social Care Northern Ireland (2011) *Transforming your care: A review of health and social care in Northern Ireland*, Belfast: Northern Ireland Executive.

Health Foundation, The (2021) *Social care funding gap*, London, www.health.org.uk/news-and-comment/charts-and-infographics/REAL-social-care-funding-gap [Accessed 8 June 2022].

Heenan, D. and Birrell, D. (2018) *The integration of health and social care in the UK*, London: Macmillan.

Heitmueller, A. (2007) 'The chicken or the egg? Endogeneity in labour market participation of informal carers in England', *Journal of Health Economics*, 26(3): 536–59.

HM Government (2007) *Putting people first: A shared vision and commitment to the transformation of adult social care*, London: The Stationery Office.

HM Government (2009) *Shaping the future of care together*, London: The Stationery Office.

HM Government (2010) *Building the National Care Service*, London: The Stationery Office.

HM Government (2012) *Caring for our future: Reforming care and support*, London: The Stationery Office.

HM Government (2019) *Review of UK government union capability* (Dunlop Review), London, https://assets.publishing.service.gov.uk/government/uploads/system/uploads/attachment_data/file/972987/Lord_Dunlop_s_review_into_UK_Government_Union_Capability.pdf [Accessed 20 March 2022].

HM Government (2021) *Build back better: Our plan for health and social care*, London: Department of Health and Social Care.

HM Government (2022) Health and Care Act, London: The Stationery Office.

HM Treasury (2016) 'Country and regional analysis', www.gov.uk/government/collections/country-and-regional-analysis [Accessed 13 November 2021].

HM Treasury (2017) 'Public expenditure Statistical analyses 2017', London: HMSO, https://assets.publishing.service.gov.uk/government/uploads/system/uploads/attachment_data/file/630570/60243_PESA_Accessible.pdf

HM Treasury (2022) *Autumn Statement*, London: HM Treasury, https://www.gov.uk/government/publications/autumn-statement-2022-documents/autumn-statement-2022-html#:~:text=The%20Autumn%20Statement%20sets%20out%20a%20package%20of%20targeted%20support,bill%20increases%20following%20the%20revaluation. [Accessed 24 November 2022].

Hochschild, A.R. (2015) 'Global care chains and emotional surplus value', in D. Engster and T. Metz (eds) *Justice, politics, and the family*, London: Routledge, pp 249–61.

Hoggett, P. (2006) 'Conflict, ambivalence, and the contested purpose of public organizations', *Human Relations*, 59(2): 175–94.

Holmes, J. (2021) *Brexit and the end of the transition period: what does it mean for the health and care system?* London: King's Fund, https://www.kingsfund.org.uk/publications/articles/brexit-end-of-transition-period-impact-health-care-system [Accessed 23 November 2022].

Holthman, G. (2018) *Paying for social care: An independent report commissioned by the Welsh Government*, Cardiff: Welsh Government.

Housden, P. (2014) 'This is us: A perspective on public services in Scotland', *Public Policy & Administration*, 29(1): 64–74.

Howlett, M. and Rayner, J. (2007) 'Design principles for policy mixes: Cohesion and coherence in "new governance arrangements"', *Policy and Society*, 26(4): 1–18.

Howlett, M. and Tosun, J. (eds) (2018) *Policy styles and policy-making: Exploring the linkages*, London: Routledge.

Howlett, M. and Tosun, J. (eds) (2021) *The Routledge handbook of policy styles*, London: Routledge.

Hudson, B. (2011) 'Big society: A concept in pursuit of a definition', *Journal of Integrated Care*, 19(5): 17–24.

Hudson, B. (2021) *Clients, consumers or citizens? The privatisation of adult social care in England*, Bristol: Policy Press.

Hudson, B., Hunter, D. and Peckham, S. (2019) 'Policy failure and the policy-implementation gap: Can policy support programs help?', *Policy Design and Practice*, 2(1): 1–14.

Humpherson, E. (2021) 'Glimmers of light for social care statistics', Office for Statistics Regulation, 8 July, https://osr.statisticsauthority.gov.uk/glimmers-of-light-for-adult-social-care-statistics [Accessed 4 January 2022].

Humphries, R. and Timmins, N. (2021) *Stories from social care leadership: Progress and pestilence and penury*, London: The King's Fund, www.kingsfund.org.uk/publications/social-care-leadership [Accessed 30 January 2022].

Hupe, P. and Hill, M. (2016) '"And the rest is implementation": Comparing approaches to what happens in policy processes beyond Great Expectations', *Public Policy & Administration*, 31(2): 103–21.

IFS (Institute for Fiscal Studies) (2017) *Public spending on adult social care in England*, London.

Independent Age (2015) *Moved to care: The impact of migration on the adult social care workforce*, London.

Independent Commission on Social Services in Wales (2010) *From vision to action: The report of the Independent Commission on Social Services in Wales*, Cardiff: Welsh Assembly Government.

ISER (Institute for Social and Economic Research) (2022) *Understanding society: Waves 1–11, 2009–2020 and harmonised BHPS: Waves 1–18, 1991-2009* [data collection], 16th edn, UK Data Service, University of Essex, SN: 6614, doi:10.5255/UKDA-SN-6614-17.

Jenson, J. (2015) 'Social innovation: redesigning the welfare diamond', in A. Nicholls, J. Simon and M. Gabriel (eds) *New frontiers in social innovation research*, Basingstoke: Palgrave Macmillan, pp 89–106.

Jenson, J. and Saint-Martin, D. (2003) 'New routes to social cohesion? Citizenship and the social investment state', *Canadian Journal of Sociology/Cahiers canadiens de sociologie*, 28(1): 77–99.

Jones, R. and Lewis, H. (2019) 'Wales and the Welsh language: Setting the context', in R. Jones and H. Lewis (eds) *New geographies of language*, London: Springer, pp 95–145.

Jordan, A.G. and Richardson, J.J. (1983) 'Policy communities: The British and European policy style', *Policy Studies Journal*, 11(4): 603–15.

Joseph, J. and McGregor, J.A. (2019) *Wellbeing, resilience and sustainability: The new trinity of governance*, Cham: Springer Nature Switzerland AG.

Karlsberg Schaffer, S. (2015) 'The effect of free personal care for the elderly on informal caregiving', *Health Economics*, 24: 104–17.

Katzenstein, P.J. (2016) *Small states in world markets: Industrial policy in Europe*, New York: Cornell University Press.

Keating, M. (2015) 'The political economy of small states in Europe', in M. Keating (ed) *Small states in the modern world*, Cheltenham: Edward Elgar, pp 3–20.

Keating, M. and Wilson, A. (2014) 'Regions with regionalism? The rescaling of interest groups in six European states', *European Journal of Political Research*, 53(4): 840–57.

Keating, M., Cairney, P. and Hepburn, E. (2009) 'Territorial policy communities and devolution in the UK', *Cambridge Journal of Regions, Economy and Society*, 2(1): 51–66.

Keating, M., Cairney, P. and Hepburn, E. (2012) 'Policy convergence, transfer and learning in the UK under devolution', *Regional and Federal Studies*, 22(3): 289–307.

Keating, N., McGregor, J.A. and Yeandle, S. (2021) 'Sustainable care: Theorising the wellbeing of caregivers to older persons', *International Journal of Care and Caring*, 5(4): 611–30.

Kelly, D. and Kennedy, J. (2017) *Power to people: Proposals to reboot adult care and support in NI*, Belfast: Department of Health, www.health-ni.gov.uk/sites/default/files/publications/health/power-to-people-full-report.PDF [Accessed 4 November 2022].

King's Fund, The (2021) *Social Care 360*, London, www.kingsfund.org.uk/sites/default/files/2021-05/social-care-360-2021_0.pdf [Accessed 20 February 2022].

Kingston, A., Comas-Herrera, A. and Jagger, C. J. (2018) 'Forecasting the care needs of the older population in England over the next 20 years: Estimates from the Population Ageing and Care Simulation (PACSim) modelling study', *The Lancet Public Health*, 3(9): e447–e455.

Kirkegaard, S. and Andersen, D. (2018) 'Co-production in community mental health services: Blurred boundaries or a game of pretend?', *Sociology of Health and Illness*, 40(5): 828–42.

Kittay, E.F. (2013) *Love's labor: Essays on women, equality and dependency*, Abingdon: Routledge.

Knapp, M., Hardy, B. and Forder, J. (2001) 'Commissioning for quality: Ten years of social care markets in England', *Journal of Social Policy*, 30(2): 283–306.

Knapp, M., Cyhlarova, E., Comas-Herrera, A. and Lorenz-Dant, K. (2021) *Crystallising the case for deinstitutionalisation: COVID-19 and the experiences of persons with disabilities*, London: Care Policy and Evaluation Centre, www.lse.ac.uk/cpec/assets/documents/CPEC-Covid-Desinstitutionalisation.pdf [Accessed 18 April 2022].

Knijn, T. and Ungerson, G. (1997) 'Introduction: Care work and gender in welfare regimes', *Social Politics*, 4(3): 323–7.

Kotecha, V. (2020) 'The hidden profits behind collapsing care homes', Centre for Health and the Public Interest blog, 28 May, https://chpi.org.uk/blog/the-hidden-profits-behind-collapsing-care-homes [Accessed 2 June 2021].

Kröger, T. (2011) 'Retuning the Nordic welfare municipality: Central regulation of social care under change in Finland', *International Journal of Sociology and Social Policy*, 31(3/4): 148–59.

Laffin, M. (2004) 'Is regional centralism inevitable? The case of the Welsh Assembly', *Regional Studies*, 38(2): 213–23.

Laing Buisson (2022a) *Care homes for older people: UK market report*, London.

Laing Buisson (2022b) *Impact assessment of the implementation of Section 18(3) of the Care Act 2014 and Fair Cost of Care*, London.

Laslett, B. and Brenner, J. (1989) 'Gender and social reproduction: Historical perspectives', *Annual Review of Sociology*, 15(1): 381–404.

Law Commission, The (2011) *Adult social care*, London: The Stationery Office, https://s3-eu-west-2.amazonaws.com/lawcom-prod-storage-11jsxou24uy7q/uploads/2015/03/lc326_adult_social_care.pdf [Accessed 8 November 2021].

Lee, T. and Stoye, G. (2017) *UK health and social care spending*, London: Institute for Fiscal Studies.

Leece, J. (2010) 'Paying the piper and calling the tune: Power and the direct payment relationship', *British Journal of Social Work*, 40(1): 188–206.

Lemmon, E. (2020) 'Utilisation of personal care services in Scotland: The influence of unpaid carers', *Journal of Long-Term Care*, 54–69, doi: http://doi.org/10.31389/jltc.23.

Lemmon, E. and Bell, D. (2019) *Variations in domiciliary free personal care across Scottish local authorities*, Working Paper 91, Centre for Population Change, January, www.cpc.ac.uk/docs/2019_WP91_Variations_in_domiciliary_free_personal_care_across_Scottish_Local_Authorities_Bell.pdf [Accessed 19 September 2021].

LE Wales (2020) *Use of additional funding for social care*, Cardiff: Welsh Government, https://gov.wales/sites/default/files/publications/2021-04/use-of-additional-funding-for-social-care-final-report.pdf [Accessed 7 November 2022].

Lewis, J. (1992) 'Gender and the development of welfare regimes', *Journal of European Social Policy*, 2(3): 159–73.

Lewis, J. and Glennerster, H. (1996) *Implementing the new community care*, Buckingham: Open University Press.

Lipsky, M. (1980) *Street-level bureaucracy: Dilemmas of the individual in public services*, New York: Russell Sage Foundation.

Llewellyn, M., Verity, F. and Wallace, S. (eds) (2020) Evaluation of the Social Services and Well-being (Wales) Act 2014: Literature review, Cardiff. Welsh Government, GSR report number 60/2020, https://gov.wales/evaluation-social-services-and-well-being-wales-act-2014-literature-review [Accessed 12 February 2021].

Lowndes, V. and Lemprière, M. (2018) 'Understanding variation in processes of institutional formation', *Political Studies*, 66(1): 226–44.

Macmillan, R. and Paine, A.E. (2021) 'The third sector in a strategically selective landscape: The case of commissioning public services', *Journal of Social Policy*, 50(3): 606–26.

Mahoney, J. and Thelen, K. (2010) 'A theory of gradual institutional change: Explaining institutional change', *Ambiguity, Agency, and Power*, 1: 1–37.

Malone, S. and Hayes, M. (2017) 'Integrated care partnerships Northern Ireland - leading integration: Delivering better outcomes', *International Journal of Integrated Care*, 17(5): 1-8.

Mansell, J. and Beadle-Brown, J. (2004) 'Person centred planning or person-centred action? Policy and practice in intellectual disability services', *Journal of Applied Research in Intellectual Disabilities*, 17(1): 23–6.

Manthorpe, J., Woolham, J., Norrie, C. and Samsi, K. (2020) 'Family matters: Personal assistants' experiences of engaging and working with their employers' families', *International Journal of Care and Caring*, 4(4): 497–511.

Marczak, J., Fernandez, J.L., Manthorpe, J., Brimblecombe, N., Moriarty, J., Knapp, M. et al (2022) 'How have the Care Act 2014 ambitions to support carers translated into local practice? Findings from a process evaluation study of local stakeholders' perceptions of Care Act implementation', *Health and Social Care in the Community*, 30(5): e1711–e1720.

Marsh, D. (2008) 'Understanding British government: Analysing competing models', *The British Journal of Politics and International Relations*, 10(2): 251–68.

McConnell, A. (2010) *Understanding policy success: Rethinking public policy*, Basingstoke: Macmillan International Higher Education.

McConnell, A., Grealy, L. and Lea, T. (2020) 'Policy success for whom? A framework for analysis', *Policy Sciences*, 53(4): 589–608.

McCormick, J., McDowell, E. and Harris, A. (2009) *Policies for peace of mind? Devolution and older age in the UK*, London: Institute for Public Policy Research, www.ippr.org/publications/policies-for-peace-of-mind-devolut ion-and-older-age-in-the-uk [Accessed 17 June 2019].

McGarvey, N. (2019) 'British political tradition and Scottish local government', in G. Hassan (ed) *The story of the Scottish Parliament: The first two decades explained*, Edinburgh: Edinburgh University Press, pp 116–22.

McHale, J. and Noszlopy, L. (2021) *Adult social care provision under pressure: Lessons from the pandemic*, Birmingham: University of Birmingham, www.birmingham.ac.uk/documents/college-artslaw/law/research/adult-social-care-provision-under-pressure-lessons-from-the-pandemic-novem ber-2021.pdf [Accessed 20 January 2022].

Miller, R., Brown, H. and Mangan, C. (2016) *Integrated care in action: A practical guide for health, social care and housing support*, London: Jessica Kingsley Publishers.

Miller, R., Glasby, J. and Dickinson, H. (2021) 'Integrated health and social care in England: Ten years on', *International Journal of Integrated Care*, 21(4): 6, 1–9.

Miller, R., Williams, I., Allen, K. and Glasby, J. (2013) 'Evidence, insight, or intuition? Investment decisions in the commissioning of prevention services for older people', *Journal of Care Services Management*, 7(4): 119–27.

Ministry of Housing and Local Government (1968) *Report of the Interdepartmental Committee on Local Authorities and Allied Personal Social Services* (Seebohm Report), London: The Stationery Office.

Morris, J. (1993) *Independent lives: Community care and disabled people*, Basingstoke: Macmillan.

Moon, D.S. and Evans, T. (2017) 'Welsh devolution and the problem of legislative competence', *British Politics*, 12(3): 335–60.

Morel, N. (2007) 'Providing coverage against new social risks in Bismarckian welfare states: The case of long-term care', in K. Armingeon and G. Bonoli (eds) *The politics of post-industrial welfare states*, London: Routledge, pp 245–65.

Morphet, J. (2021) *The impact of COVID-19 on devolution: Recentralising the British state beyond Brexit?*, Bristol: Policy Press.

Moussa, M.M. (2019) 'The relationship between elder care-giving and labour force participation in the context of policies addressing population ageing: A review of empirical studies published between 2006 and 2016', *Ageing & Society*, 39(6): 1281–310.

Mulhall, S. and Swift, A. (1992) Liberals and communitarians, Oxford: Blackwell Oxford.

NAO (National Audit Office) (2021) *The adult social care market in England*, London, www.nao.org.uk/report/adult-social-care-markets [Accessed 20 January 2022].

Needham, C. (2007) *The reform of public services under New Labour: Narratives of consumerism*, Basingstoke: Palgrave.

Needham, C. (2011) *Personalising public services: Understanding the personalisation narrative*, Bristol: Policy Press.

Needham, C. and Carr, S. (2009) *Co-production: An emerging evidence base for adult social care transformation*, London: Social Care Institute for Excellence.

Needham, C. and Dickinson, H. (2018) '"Any one of us could be among that number": Comparing the policy narratives for individualized disability funding in Australia and England', *Social Policy & Administration*, 52(3): 731–49.

Needham, C. and Hall, P. (2022) 'Dealing with drift: Comparing social care reform in the four nations of the UK', *Social Policy & Administration*, https://doi.org/10.1111/spol.12858.

Needham, C., Allen, K., Burn, E., Hall, K., Mangan, C., Al-Janabi, H. et al (2022) 'How do you shape a market? Explaining local state practices in adult social care', *Journal of Social Policy*, 1–21, doi:10.1017/S0047279421000805.

Nesom, S. and MacKillop, E. (2021) 'What matters in the implementation of sustainable development policies? Findings from the Well-Being of Future Generations (Wales) Act, 2015', *Journal of Environmental Policy and Planning*, 23(4): 432–45.

NIHR (National Institute of Health Research) (2021) *Improving the quality of care homes, What does the evidence tell us?*, London.

Noddings, N. (2013) *Caring: A relational approach to ethics and moral education*, Berkeley, CA: University of California Press.

Northern Ireland Executive (2020) *New decade, new approach*, Belfast: Northern Ireland Executive, https://assets.publishing.service.gov.uk/government/uploads/system/uploads/attachment_data/file/856998/2020-01-08_a_new_decade__a_new_approach.pdf [Accessed 30 October 2021].

Nuffield Trust (2020) 'How much social care does each country fund?', Nuffield Trust, 28 March, https://www.nuffieldtrust.org.uk/news-item/how-much-social-care-does-each-country-fund

O'Dowd, A. (2016) 'NHS is pushed to the limit as adult social care system reaches "tipping point", warns regulator', *British Medical Journal*, 355: i5553.

O'Neil, M., Gerstein Pineau, M., Kendall-Taylor, J., Volmert, D. and Stevens, A. (2017) *Finding a better frame: How to create more effective messages on homelessness in the United Kingdom*, London: Crisis.

ONS (Office for National Statistics) (2015) 'Internal migration, England and Wales: Year ending June 2015', www.ons.gov.uk/peoplepopulationandcommunity/populationandmigration/migrationwithintheuk/bulletins/internalmigrationbylocalauthoritiesinenglandandwales/yearendingjune2015 [Accessed 14 May 2021].

ONS (2016) '2011 Census analysis: Internal and international migration of older residents (aged 65 and over) in England and Wales in the year prior to the 2011 Census', http://www.ons.gov.uk/ons/rel/census/2011-census-analysis/internal-and-international-migration-of-older-residents--aged-65-and-over--in-england-and-wales-in-the-year-prior-to-the-2011-census/story-on-internal-and-international-migration.html [Accessed 14 May 2021].

ONS (2020) 'Care homes and estimating the self-funding population, England: 2019 to 2020', www.ons.gov.uk/peoplepopulationandcommunity/healthandsocialcare/socialcare/articles/carehomesandestimatingtheselffundingpopulationengland/2019to2020 [Accessed 14 May 2021].

ONS (2021a) 'Mid-year population estimates (2020), by Welsh local authorities, English regions and UK countries, by single year of age and sex', https://www.ons.gov.uk/peoplepopulationandcommunity/populationandmigration/populationestimates/bulletins/annualmidyearpopulationestimates/mid2020 [Accessed 28 February 2022].

ONS (2021b) 'Estimates of the population for the UK, England and Wales, Scotland and Northern Ireland', www.ons.gov.uk/peoplepopulationandcommunity/populationandmigration/populationestimates/datasets/populationestimatesforukenglandandwalessco tlandandnorthernireland [Accessed 18 February 2022].

ONS (2022) 'GDP – Data tables', www.ons.gov.uk/economy/grossdomesticproductgdp/datasets/uksecondestimateofgdpdatatables [Accessed 2 December 2022].

Orloff, A.S. (1993) 'Gender and the social rights of citizenship: The comparative analysis of gender relations and welfare states', *American Sociological Review*, 58(3): 303–28.

Ouchi, W.G. (1980) 'Markets, bureaucracies and clans', *Administrative Science*, 25(1): 129–41.

Oung, C., Schlepper, L. and Curry, N. (2020) *Adult social care in the four countries of the UK*, Explainer Series, London: Nuffield Trust.

Paun, A. and Munro, J. (2015) *Governing in an ever looser union: How the four governments of the UK co-operate, negotiate and compete*, London: Institute for Government, www.instituteforgovernment.org.uk/sites/default/files/publications/Governing%20in%20an%20ever%20looser%20union%20-%20final.pdf [Accessed 18 December 2021].

Paun, A., Rutter, J. and Nicholl, A. (2016) *Devolution as a policy laboratory: Evidence sharing and learning between the UK's four governments*, London: Institute for Government, Alliance for Useful Evidence and Carnegie UK Trust, www.instituteforgovernment.org.uk/sites/default/files/publications/Alliance%20Policy%20Laboratory%20paper%20v3.pdf [Accessed 18 December 2021].

Pearson, C. (2000) 'Money talks? Competing discourses in the implementation of direct payments', *Critical Social Policy*, 20(4): 459–77.

Pearson, C. (2004) 'Keeping the cash under control: What's the problem with direct payments in Scotland?', *Disability & Society*, 19(1): 3–14.

Pearson, C. and Ridley, J. (2017) 'Is personalization the right plan at the wrong time? Re-thinking cash-for-care in an age of austerity', *Social Policy & Administration*, 51(7): 1042–59.

Pearson, C. and Watson, N. (2018) 'Implementing health and social care integration in Scotland: Renegotiating new partnerships in changing cultures of care', *Health and Social Care in the Community*, 26(3): e396–e403.

Pearson, C., Watson, N. and Manji, K. (2018) 'Changing the culture of social care in Scotland: Has a shift to personalization brought about transformative change?', *Social Policy & Administration*, 52(3): 662–76.

Pearson, C., Brunner, R., Porter, T. and Watson, N. (2020) 'Personalisation and the promise of independent living: Where now for cash, care and control for disability organisations across the UK?', *Scandinavian Journal of Disability Research*, 22(1): 285–95.

Peng, I. (2016) 'Testing the limits of welfare state changes: The slow-moving immigration policy reform in Japan', *Social Policy & Administration*, 50(2): 278–95.

Pettigrew, A., McKee, L. and Ferlie, E. (1988) 'Understanding change in the NHS', *Public Administration*, 66(3): 297–317.

Phillips, A. and Morgan, G. (2014) 'Co-production within health and social care – The implications for Wales?', *Quality in Ageing and Older Adults*, 15(1): 10–20.

Pierson, C. (2021) *The next welfare state? UK welfare after COVID-19*, Bristol: Policy Press.

Plant, R., Lesser, H. and Taylor-Gooby, P. (1980) *Political philosophy and social welfare: Essays on the normative basis of welfare provision*, London: Routledge & Keegan Paul.

Pollitt, C. (2002) 'Clarifying convergence. Striking similarities and durable differences in public management reform', *Public Management Review*, 3(4): 471–92.

Pressman, J.L. and Wildavsky, A.B. (1973) *Implementation: How great expectations in Washington are dashed in Oakland*, Berkeley, CA: University of California Press.

Prior, L. (2003) *Using documents in social research*, London: SAGE.

Public Health Scotland (2021) *Care home census for adults in Scotland*, Edinburgh, https://publichealthscotland.scot/publications/care-home-cen sus-for-adults-in-scotland/care-home-census-for-adults-in-scotland-statist ics-for-2011-to-2021-part-1 [Accessed 25 January 2022].

Razavi, S. (2007) The political and social economy of care in a development context: Conceptual issues, research questions and policy options, Geneva: UN Research Institute for Social Development.

Razavi, S. (2011) 'Rethinking care in a development context: An introduction', *Development and Change*, 42(4): 873–903.

Razavi, S. and Staab, S. (2012) *Global variations in the political and social economy of care: Worlds apart*, London: Routledge.

Reed, S., Oung, C., Davies, J., Dayan, M. and Scobie, S. (2021) *Integrating health and social care: A comparison of policy and progress across the four countries of the UK*, London: Nuffield Trust, https://www.nuffieldtrust.org.uk/ files/2021-12/integrated-care-web.pdf [Accessed 28 February 2022].

Rennie, J. (2022) 'Northumbria NHS Trust to be first in England to provide home care services to community', homecare.co.uk, 13 January, www. homecare.co.uk/news/article.cfm/id/1663284/northumbria-nhs-trust-home-care [Accessed 14 January 2022].

Rhodes, R.A.W. (1996) 'The new governance: Governing without government', *Political Studies*, 44(4): 652–67.

Richardson, J. (2013) *Policy styles in Western Europe*, London: Routledge.

Richardson, J. (2018) 'The changing British policy style: From governance to government?', *British Politics*, 13(2): 215–33.

Roantree, B. and Vira, K. (2018) *The rise and rise of women's employment in the UK*, London: Institute for Fiscal Studies, https://ifs.org.uk/ publications/rise-and-rise-womens-employment-uk [Accessed 19 March 2022].

Roberts, J. (2020) 'The leadership of place and people in the new English combined authorities', *Local Government Studies*, 46(6): 995–1014.

Robertson, R., Appleby, J., Evans, H. and Hemmings, N. (2019) *Public satisfaction with the NHS and social care in 2018: Results from the British Social Attitudes Survey*, London: The King's Fund and Nuffield Trust.

Robson, C.M.K. (2016) *Real world research: A resource for users of social research methods in applied settings*, Chichester: John Wiley & Sons.

Rocco, P. (2017) 'Informal caregiving and the politics of policy drift in the United States', *Journal of Aging and Social Policy*, 29(5): 413–32.

Rodríguez-Pose, A. and Gill, N. (2003) 'The global trend towards devolution and its implications', *Environment and Planning C: Government and Policy*, 21(3): 333–51.

Rose, R. (1993) *Lesson-drawing in public policy: A guide to learning across time and space*, Chatham: Chatham House Publishers.

Rummery, K. and Fine, M. (2012) 'Care: A critical review of theory, policy and practice', *Social Policy & Administration*, 46(3): 321–43.

Rummery, K. and McAngus, C. (2015) 'The future of social policy in Scotland: Will further devolved powers lead to better social policies for disabled people?', *Political Quarterly*, 86(2): 234–9.

Sabatier, P.A. and Weible, C.M. (2019) 'The advocacy coalition framework: Innovations and clarifications', in Sabatier, P.A. (ed) *Theories of the policy process*, London: Routledge, pp 189–220.

Sayer, A. (1992) *Method in social science: A realist approach*, London: Psychology Press.

Sayer, A. (1999) *Realism and social science*, London: SAGE.

SCIE (Social Care Institute for Excellence) (2010) *At a Glance 31: Enabling risk, ensuring safety: Self-directed support and personal budgets*, London, www.scie.org.uk/publications/ataglance/ataglance31.asp [Accessed 20 June 2021].

Schickler, E. (2001) *Disjointed pluralism: Institutional innovation in the US Congress*, Princeton, NJ: Princeton University Press.

Schmidt, V.A. (2008) 'Discursive institutionalism: The explanatory power of ideas and discourse', *Annual Review of Political Science*, 11: 303–26.

Scottish Executive (2001) *Fair care for older people*, Edinburgh.

Scottish Executive (2006a) *Care 21: The future of unpaid care in Scotland*, Edinburgh.

Scottish Executive (2006b) *Changing lives: Report of the 21st Century Social Work Review*, Edinburgh, www.gov.scot/publications/changing-lives-report-21st-century-social-work-review [Accessed 13 February 2022].

Scottish Government (2010a) *Caring together: The carers strategy for Scotland 2010–2015*, Edinburgh.

Scottish Government (2010b) *Reshaping care for older people: A programme for change 2011–2021*, Edinburgh.

Scottish Government (2010c) *Self-directed support: A national strategy for Scotland*, Edinburgh.

Scottish Government (2012) *Integration of adult health and social care in Scotland: Consultation on proposals*, Edinburgh.

Scottish Government (2013) *Free personal and nursing care, Scotland, 2011–12*, https://www.gov.scot/publications/free-personal-nursing-care-scotland-2011-2012/pages/12/ [Accessed 28 February 2022].

Scottish Government (2016) *Health and social care delivery plan*, Edinburgh, www.gov.scot/binaries/content/documents/govscot/publications/strategy-plan/2016/12/health-social-care-delivery-plan/documents/00511950-pdf/00511950-pdf/govscot%3Adocument/00511950.pdf [Accessed 13 February 2022].

Scottish Government (2021) *A National Care Service for Scotland: Consultation*, Edinburgh.

Scottish Government (2022) *Free personal and nursing care, Scotland, 2020–21*, https://www.gov.scot/publications/free-personal-nursing-care-scotland-2020-21/documents/ [Accessed 28 February 2022].

Scottish Government (2022) 'National Care Service consultation responses published', Edinburgh, www.gov.scot/news/national-care-service-consultation-responses-published [Accessed 18 February 2022].

Scottish Government and COSLA (Convention of Scottish Local Authorities) (2021) *Enabling, connecting and empowering: Care in the digital age*, Edinburgh: Scottish Government.

Scottish Parliament Health, Social Care and Sport Committee (2021) *Official report*, 28 September, www.parliament.scot/api/sitecore/CustomMedia/OfficialReport?meetingId=13339 [Accessed 7 November 2022].

Scully, R. and Wyn Jones, R. (2015) 'The public legitimacy of the National Assembly for Wales', *Journal of Legislative Studies*, 21(4): 515–33.

Self Directed Support Scotland (2020) *My support my choice: People's experiences of self-directed support and social care in Scotland*, Edinburgh, www.sdsscotland.org.uk/wp-content/uploads/2020/10/MSMC-Scotland-Report-2020.pdf [Accessed 1 March 2022].

Series, L. (2019a) 'Disability and human rights', in N. Watson and S. Vehmas (eds) *Routledge handbook of disability studies*, London: Routledge, pp 72–88.

Series, L. (2019b) 'On detaining 300,000 people: The liberty protection safeguards', *International Journal of Mental Health and Capacity Law*, 25: 82–123.

Series, L. (2022) *Deprivation of liberty in the shadow of the institution*, Bristol: Bristol University Press.

Sewerin, S. (2020) 'Understanding complex policy mixes: Conceptual and empirical challenges', in G. Capano and M. Howlett (eds) *A modern guide to public policy*, Cheltenham: Edward Elgar, pp 191–201.

Shakespeare, T., Stöckl, A. and Porter, T. (2018) 'Metaphors to work by: The meaning of personal assistance in England', *International Journal of Care and Caring*, 2(2): 165–79.

Shutt, J. and Liddle, J. (2019) 'Are combined authorities in England strategic and fit for purpose?', *Local Economy*, 34(2): 196–207.

Simonazzi, A. (2009) 'Care regimes and national employment models', *Cambridge Journal of Economics*, 33(2): 211–32.

Simons, J.J. and Green, M.C. (2018) 'Divisive topics as social threats', *Communication Research*, 45(2): 165–87.

Skills for Care (2021) *The state of the adult social care sector and workforce in England, 2021*, London: Skills for Care, www.skillsforcare.org.uk/adult-soc ial-care-workforce-data-old/Workforce-intelligence/documents/State-of-the-adult-social-care-sector/The-State-of-the-Adult-Social-Care-Sec tor-and-Workforce-2021.pdf [Accessed 9 January 2022].

Sloan, B. (2021) '"Easing" duties and making dignity difficult: COVID-19 and the Care Act 2014', *Public Law*, 1: 37–46.

Smith, M. (2021) 'What is care?', Common Weal blog, 4 November, https://commonweal.scot/what-is-care [Accessed 7 November 2022].

#socialcarefuture (2019) *Talking about a brighter social care future*, www.camph illvillagetrust.org.uk/wp-content/uploads/2019/10/iC-SCF-report-2019-d-1.pdf [Accessed 18 November 2021].

Spencer-Lane, T. (2011) 'The Law Commission's final recommendations for a new adult social care statute', *Social Care and Neurodisability*, 2(4): 226–33.

St Denny, E. (2019) 'The Scottish Parliament and "new politics" at twenty', in G. Hassan (ed) *The story of the Scottish Parliament: The first two decades explained*, Edinburgh: Edinburgh University Press, pp 73–83.

Sussex, J., Burge, P., Lu, H., Exley, J., King, S. and RAND Europe (2019) *Public acceptability of health and social care funding options: Funding options for the NHS and social care in the UK*, London: The Health Foundation, www.health.org.uk/sites/default/files/upload/publications/2019/Public%20ac ceptability%20of%20health%20and%20social%20care%20funding%20op tions_0.pdf [Accessed 4 May 2020].

Sutherland, S. (1999) *With respect to old age – Report of the Royal Commission on Long-Term Care* (Sutherland Report), London: The Stationery Office.

Sutherland, S. (2008) 'Free personal and nursing care in Scotland', *European View*, 7(2): 297–302.

Talbot, C. (2010) *Theories of performance: Organizational and service improvement in the public domain*, Oxford: Oxford University Press.

Tallack, C. and Sturrock, D. (2022) *Does the cap fit? Analysing the government's proposed amendment to the English social care charging system*, London: The Health Foundation and Insitute for Fiscal Studies, www.health.org.uk/publications/reports/does-the-cap-fit-analysing-the-proposed-amendm ent [Accessed 18 September 2022].

Tapper, J. (2021) '"This is an attack on human rights": UK care homes still denying family visits to residents', *The Guardian*, 20 November, www.theguardian.com/society/2021/nov/20/uk-care-homes-deny-family-vis its-human-rights [Accessed 15 March 2022].

Taylor-Gooby, P. (1994) 'Postmodernism and social policy: A great leap backwards?', *Journal of Social Policy*, 23(3): 385–404.

Tew, J., Duggal, S., Carr, S., Ercolani, M., Glasby, J., Kinghorn, P. et al (2019) *Implementing the Care Act (2014): Building social resources to prevent, reduce or delay needs for care and support in adult social care in England*, Birmingham: University of Birmingham.

Thelen, K. (2003) 'How institutions evolve: Insights from comparative-historical analysis', in J. Mahoney and D. Rueschemeyer (eds) *Comparative historical analysis in the social sciences*, Cambridge: Cambridge University Press, pp 208–40.

Theobald, H. and Luppi, M. (2018) 'Elderly care in changing societies: Concurrences in divergent care regimes – a comparison of Germany, Sweden and Italy', *Current Sociology*, 66(4): 629–42.

Thompson, S. and Hoggett, P. (1996) 'Universalism, selectivism and particularism: Towards a postmodern social policy', *Critical Social Policy*, 16(46): 21–42.

Tinker, A. (2002) 'The social implications of an ageing population', *Mechanisms of Ageing and Development*, 123(7): 729–35.

TLAP (Think Local, Act Personal) (2019) 'Payment cards as a means of managing a personal budget', London, www.thinklocalactpersonal.org. uk/_assets/Resources/SDS/TLAP-PaymentCardsFinal.pdf [Accessed 17 June 2020].

Triggle, N. (2019) 'Whorlton Hall: Hospital "abused" vulnerable adults', BBC News, 22 May.

Tronto, J.C. (1993) *Moral boundaries: A political argument for an ethic of care*, London: Routledge.

Tronto, J.C. (2013) *Caring democracy: Markets, equality, and justice*, New York: New York University Press.

TUC (Trades Union Congress) (2021) *A new deal for social care: A new deal for the workforce*, London, www.tuc.org.uk/sites/default/files/2021-09/ Social%20care%20report%20KB%20comments%20and%20additions.pdf [Accessed 3 March 2022].

Turbett, C. (2021) 'National care service – Opportunity or setback?', Common Weal blog, 14 October, https://commonweal.scot/national-care-service-opportunity-or-setback [Accessed 7 November 2022].

Turnpenny, A. and Hussein, S. (2022) 'Migrant home care workers in the UK: A scoping review of outcomes and sustainability and implications in the context of Brexit', *Journal of International Migration and Integration*, 23: 23–42.

Ungerson, C. and Yeandle, S. (eds) (2007) *Cash for care in developed welfare states*, Basingstoke: Palgrave.

Unwin, J. (2018) *Kindness, emotions and human relationships*, Dunfermline: Carnegie UK Trust.

Verweij, M. and Thompson, M. (eds) (2006) *Clumsy solutions for a complex world: Governance, politics and plural perceptions*, London: Springer.

Vlachantoni, A. (2019) 'Unmet need for social care among older people', *Ageing & Society*, 39(4): 657–84.

Walshe, K., Coleman, A., McDonald, R., Lorne, C. and Munford, L.J.B. (2016) 'Health and social care devolution: The Greater Manchester experiment', *British Medical Journal*, 352, i1495.

Wanless, D. (2006) *Securing good care for older people* (Wanless Report), London: The King's Fund.

Watt, T. and Varrow, M. (2018) 'The "do nothing" option: How public spending on social care in England fell by 13% in 5 years', The Health Foundation blog, 29 May, www.health.org.uk/blogs/the-%E2%80%98do-nothing%E2%80%99-option-how-public-spending-on-social-care-in-engl and-fell-by-13-in-five-years [Accessed 9 January 2022].

Welsh Assembly Government (2003) *The review of health and social care in Wales*, Cardiff.

Welsh Assembly Government (2011) *Sustainable social services for Wales: A framework for action*, Cardiff.

Welsh Assembly Government (2020) *Connected communities*, Cardiff.

Wales Fiscal Analysis (2020) *The cost of free personal care: Lessons from Scotland*, Cardiff, www.cardiff.ac.uk/__data/assets/pdf_file/0003/2470152/fpnc_br iefing_21102020.pdf [Accessed 18 February 2022].

Welsh Government (2003) *Review of health and social care in Wales*, Cardiff.

Welsh Government (2015a) *Well-being of Future Generations (Wales) Act 2015: Guidance*, Cardiff, https://gov.wales/well-being-future-generati ons-wales-act-2015-guidance [Accessed 18 January 2022].

Welsh Government (2015b) *Informed health and care: A digital health and social care strategy for Wales*, Cardiff.

Welsh Government (2019) *Social services: The national outcomes framework for people who need care and support and carers who need support*, Cardiff, https://gov.wales/sites/default/files/publications/2019-05/the-national-outco mes-framework-for-people-who-need-care-and-support-and-carers-who-need-support.pdf [Accessed 7 November 2022].

Welsh Government (2021a) *The co-operation agreement: 2021*, Cardiff.

Welsh Government (2021b) *Rebalancing care and support*, White Paper, Cardiff.

West, K. (2013) 'The grip of personalization in adult social care: Between managerial domination and fantasy', *Critical Social Policy*, 33(4): 638–57.

West, K. and Needham, C. (2017) 'Making it real or sustaining a fantasy? Personal budgets for older people', *International Journal of Sociology and Social Policy*, 37(11/12): 683–95.

White, C., Wray, J. and Whitfield, C. (2020) '"A fifty mile round trip to change a lightbulb": An exploratory study of carers' experiences of providing help, care and support to families and friends from a distance', *Health and Social Care in the Community*, 28(5): 1632–42.

Williams, F. (1989) *Social policy, a critical introduction: Issues of class, race and gender*, Oxford: Blackwell.

Wittenberg, R. (2016) 'Demand for care and support for older people', in C. Gori, J. Fernandez and R. Wittenberg (eds) *Long-term care reforms in OECD countries*, Bristol: Policy Press, pp 9–24.

Wright, J. (2020) *Technology in social care: A review of the UK policy landscape*, Sheffield: University of Sheffield.

Wright, J. (2021) 'The Alexafication of adult social care: Virtual assistants and the changing role of local government in England', *International Journal of Environmental Research and Public Health*, 18(2): 812.

Yanow, D. (1996) *How does a policy mean? Interpreting policy and organizational actions*, Washington, DC: Georgetown University Press.

Yanow, D. (2007) 'Interpretation in policy analysis: On methods and practice', *Critical Policy Analysis*, 1(1): 110–22.

Yeandle, S. (2016) 'From provider to enabler of care? Reconfiguring local authority support for older people and carers in Leeds, 2008 to 2013', *Journal of Social Service Research*, 42(2): 218–32.

Yeandle, S., Kröger, T. and Cass, B. (2012) 'Voice and choice for users and carers? Developments in patterns of care for older people in Australia, England and Finland', *Journal of European Social* Policy, 22(4): 432–45.

Yeates, N.J (2009) 'Women's migration, social reproduction and care', in S. Razavi (ed) *The gendered impacts of liberalization*, London: Taylor & Francis, pp 219–43.

Zarb, G. and Nadash, P. (1994) *Cashing in on independence: Comparing the costs and benefits of cash and services*, London: British Council of Organisations of Disabled People.

Zhang, Y. and Bennett, M. (2019) 'The likelihood of being a carer in adult life', in Carers UK, *Will I care? The likelihood of being a carer in adult life*, London: Carers UK, www.carersuk.org/images/News__campaigns/Care rsRightsDay_Nov19_FINAL.pdf [Accessed 7 November 2022].

Index